YEARS OF GLORY

✴ WORLDING THE MIDDLE EAST

YEARS OF GLORY

NELLY BENATAR AND
THE PURSUIT OF JUSTICE IN
WARTIME NORTH AFRICA

Susan Gilson Miller

STANFORD UNIVERSITY PRESS
Stanford, California

STANFORD UNIVERSITY PRESS
Stanford, California

This book has been partially underwritten by the Susan Groag Bell Publication Fund in Women's History. For more information on the fund, please see www.sup.org/bellfund.

Printed in the United States of America on acid-free, archival-quality paper

ISBN-13: 978-1-503-62845-8 (cloth)

ISBN-13: 978-1-503-62969-1 (e-book)

Library of Congress Control Number: 2021942714

Cover images: Above: Nelly Benatar greeting new arrivals, Casablanca, 1940. Courtesy of the United States Holocaust Memorial Museum. Below: Passengers aboard the S/S Monte Viso, 1941. © The Estate of Erwin Blumenfeld.

Cover and text design: Kevin Barrett Kane

Typeset at Stanford University Press in 11/14 Arno Pro

to David

צֶ֫דֶק צֶ֫דֶק תִּרְדֹּף

Justice, justice shalt thou pursue.

Deuteronomy 16:20

Contents

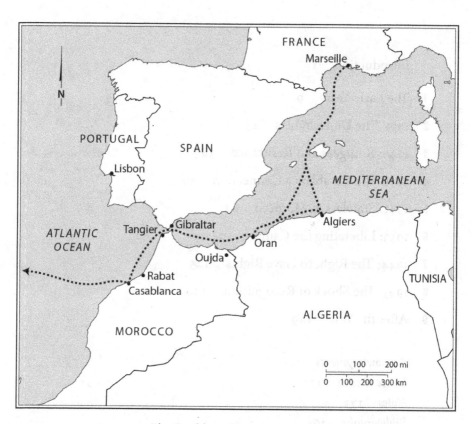

The Casablanca Route, 1941–1942.

YEARS OF GLORY

INTRODUCTION

IMAGINE A HUSHED MOVIE THEATER in Middle America at the height of World War II, the audience enveloped in dark intimacy. Another cinematic adventure is about to begin. The red velvet curtains part, revealing the familiar Warner Brothers logo, accompanied by a few stirring bars of "La Marseillaise," the French national anthem. A title flashes across the screen, pinpointing a geography that is exotically distant, yet lately much in the news. A map appears—a slowly spinning globe animated by tiny humanlike forms that flow into a surging stream, crossing the face of Europe and converging at a single point on the African coast.

The deep, authoritative voice of the narrator takes over: "Refugees streaming from all corners of Europe towards the freedom of the New World. All eyes turned toward Lisbon, the great embarkation point. But not everybody could get to Lisbon directly, so a Refugee Trail sprang up—Paris to Marseille—across the Mediterranean to Oran—then by train, or auto, or foot across the rim of Africa to Casablanca in French Morocco. Here the fortunate ones through money, or influence, or luck, obtain exit visas and scurry to Lisbon, and from Lisbon to the Americas. But the others wait in Casablanca, and wait, and wait."[1]

The Hollywood blockbuster *Casablanca* was released at the end of November 1942, just two weeks after the launching of Operation Torch, the Allied landings on the coast of North Africa that marked the first step in the

1

retaking of Fortress Europe. In bold strokes, the movie told a tale of a love lost, regained, and lost again, instantly capturing the hearts of Americans dispirited by the grinding monotony of war.

More than a simple love story, the film also touched on a subject of political concern; the tide of European refugees knocking on the doors to the West. The message was clear. North Africa was awash with people fleeing Hitler's Reich, with nowhere to go. It was a human wave of such force, energy, and chaotic power that whole cities—in this case, Casablanca in French Morocco—had been engulfed by it.

The movie *Casablanca* spoke directly to the American people, and eventually to audiences around the world. It brought home to Americans the anxieties of the refugee experience, the obstacles that individual refugees faced, the precariousness of their situation. The conjuncture of cinematic fantasy and the quotidian gave *Casablanca* an emotional intensity that went far beyond the bounds of script or casting. The movie turned nameless and faceless forms into real people facing genuine dilemmas.

Refugee lives frame our story. Between the years 1939 and 1945, many thousands of people fleeing fascism found a temporary haven in North Africa, then under French dominion. How they got there, what they did once they arrived, who helped them, and how they dispersed so completely at the end of the war is our theme in this book. The subject is not a new one. Bits of it were stolen by Hollywood, and serious historians have had their turn, focusing mainly on the military aspects. Yet the topic of refugees in North Africa during the war has never been the subject of a study of its own, with its own cast of characters and its own inner logic.

The topic of refugees fleeing from Nazism has recently come into its own. Under the rubric of "the last million," scholars have explored the enormity of the wartime refugee crisis by unraveling its bearing on postwar politics— and especially on its entanglement with two mega-themes: the incubation of the Cold War and the growth of an international movement for human rights.[2] Yet North Africa has been strikingly absent from these discussions, even though some of the most important decisions during the war about how to treat refugees, including concerns about refugee rights, took place in the region. Independent aid organizations like the American Joint Jewish Distribution Committee and giant government-led efforts like the United Nations

Relief and Rehabilitation Administration (UNRRA) got their start in wartime refugee relief on Maghribi soil, at camps such as Fedala in Morocco and Philippeville in Algeria. North Africa provided a proving ground for even more ambitious experiments that unfolded in Europe after 1945, when refugee resettlement became a topic of global concern. In this book, we explore those early efforts and the people who made them happen, and how they helped lay the groundwork for the postwar treatment of Europe's multitudes of displaced persons.

In the first two years of war, our subject is humanitarian relief in Morocco, the politics of "rescuing" homeless people—many of them stripped of their citizenship—and the mechanisms in place for sending them on to safe havens in the West. In 1942, we turn to the dark secret of the forced-labor camps in the pre-Sahara region and the relentless war on Jews and other ostracized groups waged by Vichy, the collaborationist regime led by Maréchal Philippe Pétain that governed France and its colonies during most of the war years. In 1943, 1944, and 1945, the subject is the liberation of the North African prison camps, and the massive effort directed toward rebuilding broken lives on the basis of democratic values. The tissue that connects these distinct yet related phases of the conflict is provided by a Moroccan Jewish lawyer who dedicated herself to helping those people set adrift by the excesses of war.

Hélène Cazes Benatar is the pivotal figure in our account. Between the years 1939 and 1945, her life offers a vantage point on the full spectrum of events relating to the war in North Africa, including the fall of France in 1940, the turmoil of the Vichy years, the post-1942 period of liberation, and the fate of Morocco's Jews after the war. Her background and education, her values and outlook, her strengths and vulnerabilities, are the inflection points of our narrative. Yet for all her virtues, it is curious that Nelly Benatar, as she was known to all, left such a small footprint on historical memory. No street in Casablanca is named for her; no forest in the Holy Land bears her name; no monuments stand in her honor. Hers is an example of what Virginia Woolf called the "infinitely obscure lives [that] remain to be re-corded."[3] For years, Benatar tried to win recognition from the French government for her wartime exploits, but without success. Yet she stood at the confluence of major events, thanks to her extraordinary charisma and her sense of how to make use of the ebbs and flows of history.

In the course of the war, Benatar faced down Gestapo operatives, pro-Vichy thugs, and obstinate bureaucrats, refusing to retreat. She built entire structures of humanitarian relief almost single-handedly from materials at hand: her social connections, her legal expertise, and most all, her friendships with people in power, such as General Charles Noguès, the head of the French Protectorate in Morocco between 1936 and 1943. A complex personality whose motives were not always transparent, Benatar was a study in contrasts: both rescuer and collaborator, fervidly Francophile but wary of French parochialism, secular by temperament yet intensely Jewish in feeling. After Paris was overrun in June 1940, her preoccupation was refugees—feeding, protecting, and caring for them, and whenever possible, moving them on, for Morocco was a point of transit, never a permanent home. In November 1942, following the Allied landings in North Africa, she took on new causes: repatriating prisoners, restoring broken families, working to rebuild a Moroccan Jewish community upended by the war. After the war, she staked out a position of activism that inevitably led to her separation from her homeland. She tried to stay on, but when she realized that Morocco was no longer a suitable stage for her ambitions, she left, as did many thousands of others.

Benatar was not a theorist, dedicated to the lofty goal of remodeling the postwar world to prevent a recurrence of the errors of the past. She was a practitioner who understood that concrete questions of individual rights, embedded in reality, were at the heart of the refugee problem. Helping her clients rebuild their lives with dignity was the purpose of her work. She must have felt she had succeeded, because she called the period 1939–1945 *les années glorieuses*—her "years of glory." Why glory when everything else around her was permeated with loss? The paradox implicit in this small phrase—given the immense human tragedy on which it rests—is one of the mysteries we will try to resolve in the course of our narrative.

The organization of this book is chronological. Each chapter concerns a single year between the years 1939 and 1945—seven chapters in all, bookended at one end by a sketch of the prewar context, and concluding with a chapter on the postwar. Each chapter brings together multiple layers of action: the *longue durée*, consisting of the overarching events of the wider war; the actual situation on the ground in Morocco and North Africa; and finally, at the microhistorical level, Benatar's entanglement with refugee politics and refugee lives.

Each layer of action marches in step with the others to create an interrelated whole. In the first few months of the war, stranded refugees were a local problem, bedeviling French officials in Morocco with an unwanted responsibility. Transients stranded on their way to the New World depended on the help of people of good conscience like Nelly Benatar. But as the number of refugees grew, and as the opportunities to move on diminished, the refugee situation became increasingly internationalized. In 1942, when news of deportations to the Nazi death camps leaked out, the clamor for Allied intervention became deafening.[4] By mid-1943, the picture had changed completely, from indifference to refugees to extreme concern for those who may have survived. The Allied governments hastily founded UNRRA in November 1943, specifically to "[provide] for the relief of victims of war in any area under the control of any of the United Nations." Spearheaded by UNRRA, a massive program of refugee relief grew up practically overnight. Throughout these transitions, Nelly Benatar was on the scene, playing a leading role in transforming refugees from inert objects of pity to individuals with legally defined rights.

My own pursuit of Nelly Benatar began by chance but quickly became an obsession. While carrying out research in the Moroccan National Archives, I was startled to find letters from a Moroccan woman lawyer addressed to high French colonial officials about refugee affairs. Her epistolary voice was so strong that I was curious to learn more about her. With the help of the internet, I discovered that she never wrote her memoirs or was the subject of intensive research. I also learned that she left behind a large personal archive—eighteen thousand pages in all—letters, documents, directives, requests, memos, reports, lists, and intelligence briefings from the period 1939–1945—tracing, in their ensemble, the arc of her wartime activities.[5]

Her personal archive is the main source for this book, and it is complemented by material found in other collections in France, Morocco, the United Kingdom, Israel, and the United States. The documents reveal aspects of Benatar's private and public life during the war with a richness of detail that a memoir could never provide. Stored in her apartment in Casablanca, her papers eventually made their way to Paris, and from there to Geneva, before finally coming to rest at the Central Archives for the History of the Jewish People in Jerusalem.[6] Along the way, the original order was disrupted, and papers went missing. Research on some aspects of her wartime work were published, but an in-depth consideration of her place within larger themes of the modern history of North Africa and its Jews was lacking.[7] This aspect, dormant in her papers, was waiting to be addressed. As the French historian Arlette Fargue has written, archives resonate with something deep inside us; they are "small lives that have become ashes" revealed in just a few sentences.[8] Among my reasons for writing this book, recovering Nelly Benatar and relocating her to a meaningful place within the broader framework of her times, takes precedence.

My own historical studies of modern North Africa have focused, in one way or another, on Muslim-Jewish relations and on the *convivencia* that existed between the two groups that was gradually lost over the first half of the twentieth century. Like many others, I have always been perplexed by the suddenness and finality with which Jews abandoned their Moroccan homeland in the 1950s and 1960s, never to return, and I never fully understood why. It seemed to me that the standard explanations (pro-Zionism, religious fervor, economic fears, collapse of empire, anti-Semitism, pan-Arabism) were too pat, too diffuse, to explain the epic break that dispersed such precious human material and left Morocco a poorer place. I hoped that by studying the critical period of World War II through the life of a compelling personality like Nelly Benatar, I would discover connections among refugee lives, the end of empire, and the Jewish problem. I was not disappointed; in the course of writing this story, I learned that the three topics converge in surprising ways.

In Benatar's archive, I looked for the nuances that defined her personality, treating her as an exemplary subject as well as a deeply human one. I tried to identify the critical turning points in her self-perception as a Moroccan Jew, beginning with her response to the stigmatization of European Jews before the war, passing though her personal connections to the trauma of the Holocaust, and culminating in the demise of Casablanca's Jewish community after the war—each turning point loosening the emotional bonds that kept her in place. I wanted to imagine what she thought and why she made certain decisions, often with little to go on other than the barest of facts and her own intuitions. The convergences among the long list of her interests—rescue and humanitarian work, refugee rights, justice and equality for all—offered, at the very least, a framework for observing a considered life.

The reader will notice that when I write, I often use conditional signifiers usually banished from the historian's quiver of words—"perhaps," "it may be," "it seems that"—phrases that nakedly expose the fragility of some of my own arguments. I reach conclusions that may convince some, but that others may find tendentious. It is possible that I have become too familiar with my subject, assumed too much, omitted too much, and overstepped my bounds as a historian. But I leave that to the reader to judge.

Susan Gilson Miller
Davis, California
January 2021

CHAPTER 1

THE EARLY YEARS

RACHEL HÉLÈNE CAZES was born in Tangier on October 27, 1898, the first daughter and the second of five children of Amram and Myriam Cazes. The Cazeses were a Jewish family whose roots were in the "lost paradise" of Sepharad, the Hebrew name for the Iberian Peninsula in the late Middle Ages. After the expulsion of Jews from southern Spain in 1492, the Cazes clan dispersed like leaves in the wind around the Mediterranean basin, arriving in Morocco sometime in the eighteenth century. They settled first in Tetuan and later moved to Tangier, a town coming into its own as a hub of Mediterranean commerce.[1]

Spanish-speaking Jews like the Cazes family were different from other Moroccans, certainly from Muslims but also from the Arabic- and Berber-speaking Jews of the south. They brought from Spain their own liturgy, codes of behavior, styles of dress, and culinary traditions. Imbued with a sense of aristocratic privilege, they clung to their clannish behaviors, worshipped in their own synagogues, married their own kind, and chose one another as business partners.[2]

Amram Cazes, Nelly's father, was an enterprising businessman who spoke French, Italian, Spanish, English, and Arabic.[3] The international trading company he inherited from his father was not his only business. When offered the post of consul of Italy in the 1880s, he readily accepted. Soon thereafter, he added the title of vice-consul of Brazil to his diplomatic portfolio. Amram's collection of passports grew even fatter after 1912, when Morocco became a French Protectorate and he acquired French citizenship. Amram promptly naturalized his entire family. This privilege came his way through his services as chief arms supplier to the French colonial army, which was engaged in a protracted war against a determined Berber resistance in the Middle Atlas Mountains.[4]

Following the French occupation, the precolonial state was divided into two regions, a French Protectorate in the south and a Spanish-held zone in the north. The sultan of Morocco retained formal sovereignty over the entirety and kept his traditional role as head of the Muslim religious community, but in reality, he was reduced to a symbolic figurehead with no real political power. Meanwhile, behind the scenes in the French zone, another authority rose up—the colonial Residency, the administrative heart of the Protectorate that set the course for a modern state in the making.[5] Amram's circle of contacts embraced men of influence in the new regime: General Louis Hubert Gonzalve Lyautey, the Protectorate's first resident-general, and his right-hand man, Charles Noguès, were among his acquaintances.

Don Amram, as he was known, was generous and civic minded. With his business interests in mind, he bought property in the neighborhood known as the Fuente Nueva, or "New Fountain," the most ancient part of the old town, with the intention of building a shop. Excavations for the cellar revealed a perfectly intact Roman mosaic floor. He immediately changed his building plan so that the municipal treasure would remain intact.[6] A dapper, likable fellow, Amram bequeathed to his daughter his business acumen and his finely tuned air of noblesse oblige. A photo taken of him around 1900 shows a sportingly dressed gentleman in white spats and a jaunty panama hat, carrying a furled umbrella on a bright summer day. In the background is a likeness of the Jungfrau, suggesting a studio photograph taken far from alpine snows.

Nelly's mother, Myriam Nahon, did not share the incandescence of her husband. Modest and serene, she came from an old Gibraltarian family with a Sephardic pedigree equal to that of the Cazes. A favorite of Nelly's was her maternal uncle, Isaac Nahon, a London lawyer with the title of "king's counsel" who died at an early age, bequeathing to the family his barrister's wig. The wig was one of the totems of the household in which Nelly grew up, where she was surrounded by rituals of her class: piano lessons, afternoon teas, excursions to the beach, large family gatherings conducted in a swirl of languages. Serge

FIGURE 1.1 Amram Cazes, studio photograph, sometime before World War I.

Lapidus, the family's biographer, wrote that "under the watchful eye of her father, [Nelly] began to take on his qualities, developing an aura of charisma and authority that would serve her well in the years to come."[7]

Sephardic culture was the glue that held Tangier's Jewish society together, with language as the chosen medium for fashioning character and a sense of self. From a very young age, Nelly spoke proper Spanish as well as *haketiya*, the local Jewish dialect of Spanish mixed with Arabic and Hebrew, rich in endearments, admonitions, and curses, which flavored the intimacy of family life.[8] At home in this variable cultural matrix, Tangier's Jews moved effortlessly between worldly temporalities and ritual time. Sabbath gatherings were the occasion for indulging in delicacies that evoked tradition, served up with female pride—*pastelitos, tortitas, galletas*—made according to recipes passed from one generation to another. A manner of speaking and eating were not the only distinctive qualities of this community. There was also a certain social style for the men, gallantry and good humor, and for the women, "discretion, modesty, sobriety, a preference for fewer words rather than long vacuous speeches." And for both sexes, rigor and self-restraint, along with a disdain for sentimentality (*bobería*) and verbal excess.[9]

Nelly's parents chose to send her to the primary school of the Alliance Israélite Universelle (AIU), a Paris-based Jewish philanthropic and educational organization that followed closely on the heels of France's imperial expansion. The mission of the AIU schools was to offer a modern education propagating French culture and republican values to all social classes.[10] Nelly's primary education, begun in 1904 and completed eight years later, was as eclectic as her companions in class: language and literature from Molière to Balzac; French history from a universalist and secular point of view; a smattering of math, geography, and science. Also on the curriculum was a mix of Jewish topics, such as Jewish history, Hebrew language, and the Hebrew Bible. These lessons connected Nelly to two elemental sources: her Jewish heritage and the legacy of the French Enlightenment. Born in a Muslim country, impregnated with Judeo-Spanish customs and mores, Moroccan in sensibility, Western in intellect and outlook, French by citizenship and taste, Nelly Benatar had an upbringing that was a diverse mix of beliefs, loyalties, cultures, and histories.[11]

The city of Tangier also played a role in her education as a special school for life. The old city, the medina, pulsated with the purely local—country women from the nearby Rif mountains, Moroccan men in white robes, and

Jews—over a third of a town of thirty thousand people—some in modern dress, others clad in black caftans and skullcaps. Turn-of-the-century postcards show Jews everywhere in the urban setting. The American visitor Mark Twain wrote that the Jews of Tangier looked like the "Hebrew prophets" and "phantoms of past ages."[12] Winter watering hole for European aristocrats and wealthy Americans, the town was a compact yet cosmopolitan node. Despite its small size, it pulsated with the rhythms of the *fin de siècle*: prosperity, energy, and innovation. Tangier was a delight to the senses, a candid mix of old and new, a microcosm of the modernizing world.

Amram Cazes was a restless seeker, and his family often accompanied him on his excursions abroad. In 1910, he was sent by the French military on a mission to Turin, a center for arms manufacturing, where Nelly and her older brother were enrolled in an Italian school. Nelly learned Italian, adding it to the French and Spanish in which she was already fluent. When the Great War broke out in 1914, the family moved to Seville, where Nelly demonstrated enthusiasm for the Allied cause, volunteering at the French consulate to prepare packages to be sent to the Western Front. The gravity of the Great War completely enveloped the Cazes household.

In 1916, when Nelly was eighteen, the family moved to Casablanca, into the newly built Villa Riviera, located in a neighborhood settled mainly by Tangier Jews. Rabat was established as the administrative center of the Protectorate, while Casablanca, with its expanding port facilities, was designated by French planners as its future commercial hub. To Nelly, Casablanca must have felt like an outpost on the edge of civilization. Not ten years earlier, in 1907, rebellious tribesmen from the surrounding countryside had invaded the mellah, the poor Jewish quarter of Casablanca, leaving its dank alleyways littered with corpses.[13] Brought fully under French control, Casablanca was a more peaceful place, but it retained the aura of a frontier town, with muddy streets, unfinished storefronts, and crowded outdoor markets.

Nelly's life in Casablanca acquired a regularity based on school, family, and social obligations. Well-traveled and multilingual, she chose the women's Collège Mers Sultan as the next step in her education, receiving the *baccalauréat* in 1917, a rare achievement for a Moroccan woman in that day. At the age of nineteen, she was fully formed intellectually. Her family loyalties and her education had instilled in her a sense of patriotism and a love of French culture, along with a fierce idealism based on an abhorrence of injustice in all its forms.

FIGURE 1.2 Nelly Cazes, high school graduate, Casablanca, 1917.

In 1920, at the age of twenty-two, Nelly married Moyses Benatar, for whom she had held a passionate attachment for years. Moyses was born in Brazil, where his father, Marcos James (Haim) Benatar, had migrated as a youth to profit from the rubber trade.[14] In 1904, while visiting Tangier with his family, Marcos died suddenly, leaving behind a penniless widow and several young children. Moyses's childhood, like Nelly's, was spent in Tangier. At age fifteen, Moyses left the AIU boys' school in Tangier to help support his family. Bright and dreamy, his passion was stamp collecting, which he learned as an aide to the fourth Marquess of Bute, a Scottish lord who wintered in Tangier, where he owned considerable property. Later in life, philately became Moyses's main source of livelihood.[15]

Following her marriage, Nelly settled into the comfortably upholstered life of a Jewish matron. A daughter, Myriam, was born in 1925, and a son, Marc, in 1930. In 1930, the Benatars moved into a spacious apartment at 85, rue Gallieni, in central Casablanca, overlooking two icons of colonial architecture—the main post office and the Banque du Maroc.[16] The sweeping expanse of Place Lyautey and its towering equestrian statue of General Lyautey were also in view, as well as the Palais de Justice and the central law courts, where Nelly would eventually practice her craft. The rue Gallieni apartment would be Nelly Benatar's home until her last days in Morocco in 1962.

Nelly and Moyses's social set was composed of AIU school alumni who gathered at the club of the AIU Graduates' Association on rue Lacépède in the center of Jewish Casablanca. The Benatars' inner circle included a small coterie of Ashkenazi Jews who had settled in Casablanca in the 1920s. An outstanding acquaintance was the Algerian Jewish lawyer Léon René Sultan (1905–1945), who won public attention for his silver tongue and his organizing skills. Founder of and chief contributor to *Clarté*, the first genuinely leftist journal in Morocco, Sultan was an outspoken advocate for political reform and social justice. In 1936, he headed a group of activists who supported the socialist Léon Blum's Popular Front in France by organizing rowdy street demonstrations in Casablanca that drew enthusiastic crowds from the left of the political spectrum. Opponents on the Right scorned him for creating a "Judeo-Bolshevik-Popular Front conspiracy," but Sultan was undeterred. A brilliant strategist with a doctorate in law, his politics were far more colorful than the Benatars', yet they shared a warm friendship. During the war, when Nelly Benatar and Léon René Sultan were both disbarred by

FIGURE 1.3 Nelly and Moyses Benatar, newlyweds, Casablanca, early 1920s.

the Vichy anti-Jewish laws, Benatar went out of her way to keep Sultan afloat financially. In 1945, Sultan became the first head of the fledgling Moroccan Communist Party.[17]

We do not know precisely why Nelly Benatar decided to study law, but it may have been the influence of friends like Sultan who turned her in that direction. The Faculty of Law at Bordeaux in France had a special arrangement with the Protectorate's Ministry of Education whereby qualified holders of the French *baccalauréat* could acquire a law degree by correspondence. Ten years into her marriage, already in her thirties and the mother of two young children, Nelly Benatar began the study of French law. In October 1933, she received her degree and passed the French bar, at the age of thirty-five becoming modern Morocco's first licensed woman lawyer.

Her aptitude for the law was immediately apparent. She had "a passionate and persuasive tongue, with the gift for both reporting the facts and weaving a story, of never raising her voice, and of firing off a mockery—but never a spiteful one," according to Serge Lapidus. She opened a law office on rue Nationale, a few steps from the family home, and became a member of Casablanca's Cour de Cassation, the final court of appeal in the French legal system—a prestigious post for a beginner, signaling her competence in the

FIGURE 1.4 Benatars' apartment facing the Banque du Maroc, Casablanca, 1930s.

details of French jurisprudence. Occupied by her legal work and her growing family, her life fell into a pattern of constant movement among three different worlds—Jewish, Moroccan, and French—and she found pleasure as well as disenchantment in each.

In the 1930s, Moroccan Jews of the educated class were caught in a web of contradictions. Culturally French, they were part of a colonial system they could not claim as their own—not even people like Nelly Benatar, who was legally French and held French nationality. Like her other Jewish friends who were French nationals, Nelly Benatar did not enjoy the full benefits of French

FIGURE 1.5   Nelly Benatar, back row, at the Cour de Cassation, Casablanca, 1930s.

citizenship. Socially excluded from settler society, elite Jews inhabited a no-man's-land, regarded neither as truly "Moroccan"—a category applied only to Muslims—nor as genuinely French. The only label with which they felt secure was "Jewish," and that, too, had its disadvantages. The old designation of *dhimmi*, "protected person," with its subaltern overtones, still clung to them, making them lesser beings in the Muslim scheme of things. Despite years of education and upward mobility, modernizing Jews resented their treatment as inferiors.

The "Jewish problem" was firmly rooted in the legal sphere. After 1912, the old consular courts where Jews used to seek justice were abolished, forcing Jews without foreign nationality to resort to Muslim courts that operated under shari'a law, where the testimony of non-Muslims did not carry equal weight to that of Muslims. Jews who claimed French nationality were allowed to use French courts, but they were such a tiny minority, that privilege hardly mattered. And although they were still formally under the protection of the sultan, the vast majority of Jews derived little benefit from it.[18] Caught in a state of legal in-betweenness, what Jews desired most was equality with Europeans, but what they got instead was a vague promise of "protection" that could be easily set aside. From the outset of her legal career, the problem of unequal access of Jewish Moroccans to the protective qualities of the law must have weighed on Nelly Benatar's mind.

Frustration with the unsatisfactory status quo drove the educated Jewish elite to seek new avenues of expression. The modern doctrine of Zionism, of building a Jewish homeland in Palestine, was fertile ground. Emigration to the Holy Land for religious motives was a long-standing tradition among Maghribi Jews, but in the 1920s, a new variety of Zionism appeared in Morocco, preaching a message of Jewish renewal through education, physical strength, and communal solidarity.

Samuel Daniel Lévy (1874–1970), director of the AIU school in Casablanca, led the neophyte Zionists of Casablanca, providing an example of how to reach a compromise among their various aspirations. Born in the northern town of Tetuan into a Sephardic family of modest means, Lévy attended the local AIU primary school where his brilliance as a student won him a place at the ENIO (École Normale Israélite Orientale), the teacher-training institute of the AIU in Paris. After a posting to Tunisia as a teacher and a ten-year sojourn in Argentina, he became director of the AIU school in Casablanca. A lifelong Zionist and civic leader, Lévy's influence over the generation of the Benatars was paramount. Following a short trip to Palestine in 1935, Lévy returned home singing the praises of "the plantations rising up in the middle of the desert," but he did not lose sight of those Jews still living in poverty at home. Under the influence of Samuel Lévy, Zionist discourse in Morocco downplayed the issue of emigration, concentrating instead on themes of modernization, social integration, and communal reform.[19]

The small circle of Jewish intellectuals drawn to Zionism was carefully watched by the Residency. Lyautey had vigorously opposed the spread of Zionism in Morocco, and his successors followed his lead. His fear was that an energized Jewish youth would seek equality with Europeans, upsetting the careful balance of social forces that was the axis of his native policy. He was determined to squash any thoughts of repeating in Morocco the "error" of the Crémieux decree of 1870 that enfranchised Algerian Jews and set off rolling waves of civic unrest. According to the historian Daniel Rivet, at the heart of Lyautey's strategy was the concept of indigeneity, that is, upholding the fiction that Jews and Muslims were at parallel stages of social and economic development.[20]

Zionist ambitions proved impossible to contain, however, especially among the new generation who saw Zionism as an opening to greater personal freedom. Signs of enthusiasm were Jewish sports clubs, scouting groups, and summer camps for boys and girls organized under Zionist auspices. In 1935, Morocco even sent a delegation organized by Léon René Sultan to the second Maccabiah Games in Tel Aviv.[21]

European Zionists lent momentum to the local movement. In 1924, the Polish Jewish journalist Jonathan Thurscz settled in Casablanca and two years later established a weekly pro-Zionist newspaper, L'Avenir Illustré. In no time at all, L'Avenir became required reading for educated Jews of Casablanca, bringing them local news, a sampling of international goings-on, and a taste of the endless ideological debates raging within European and American Zionist circles. Readers were soon on a first-name basis with Albert Einstein, Judah Magnes, Henrietta Szold, Ze'ev Jabotinsky, and Menachem Ussishkin. L'Avenir also brought the latest news from Europe, Palestine, Britain, and the Americas, blending current events with commentaries on antisemitism, world economic collapse, and fascist deceit.[22] Through the newspaper's pages, Casablanca Jews traced rising tensions in Europe, from the ascent of Adolf Hitler in 1933 to the invasion of Poland in 1939, and every tragic misstep in between.

A steady stream of European Zionist activists added Morocco to their speaking tours. In the mid-1930s, the French jurist Sasia Erlich and the French Zionist Federation's Fanny Weill both visited Casablanca, introducing Nelly Benatar to the model of the politically engaged woman. Impressed by these encounters, Benatar took on a more public role. In 1936, she joined the Moroccan branch of WIZO, the Women's International Zionist Organization, and soon became its president. Finding her public voice, she recruited new members among the "lethargic" (her term) women of Casablanca; in December 1937, WIZO in Casablanca counted fifty-three members.

Her WIZO work had other benefits. Benatar was the only woman invited to join the governing board of the all-Morocco Zionist Congress that convened in Casablanca in January 1936. Described by Jonathan Thurscz in *L'Avenir* as a "young militant," "brilliant," and "full of enthusiasm," Benatar began to write regular columns for his newspaper, mainly on Zionist topics and the question of resettlement in Palestine. "The construction of a national home in Eretz Yisrael is necessary and indispensable," she wrote, "for the Jewish people are now facing the worst crisis in their history." She urged Jewish women to "join with their husbands, fathers and sons, to support a struggle that is ardently in favor of the ideal of social justice." Her Zionist work energized her, but she feared she was ahead of her times: "In Morocco, women do not yet understand their role as Jews, and are rather too apathetic."[23] This assessment was not completely accurate. In reality, Zionist discourse had seized the imagination of educated Moroccan Jews, giving them an outlet for frustrations made worse by the inequalities of colonial rule.

On the global scale, the Nuremberg Laws of September 1935 deprived the vast majority of Germany's Jews of their citizenship, unleashing a flood of refugees from the Reich. By stripping citizens of their nationality, Germany had created a new category of "stateless" people no longer welcome in their own homeland. These latest victims of Hitler's fury posed a new kind of problem for Western democracies: What to do with the hordes of people anxious to escape Europe? Whose problem was it to protect them? The League of Nations, weakened by internal divisions and faltering under a frontal attack from

Hitler, was unable to act, and the generous protections it had once offered to refugees had become a thing of the past.[24] Thousands of homeless people began to take the road of exile, tipping the demographic balance on the continent and sending shock waves across the Mediterranean to North Africa.

In Morocco, the signs were ominous. The election of the Jewish socialist Léon Blum in May 1936 to head the new Popular Front government in France offered a brief glimmer of hope. Blum appointed General Charles Noguès (1876–1971) as resident-general in Morocco, replacing Marc Peyrouton, whose ultraconservative views were no longer in favor in Paris. Noguès was a polished politician who was comfortable in liberal circles. Born in a small village in the Pyrenees, Noguès, through a combination of talent, ambition, and shrewd choices, had reached the top rungs of the French military hierarchy. After graduating from the prestigious École Polytechnique, he joined the army and was sent to the Morocco-Algeria border, where he met his future mentor Lyautey, Morocco's first resident-general. Lyautey transmitted to Noguès his love of Morocco as well as his firmly held ideas about native policy. Because of his longtime association with Lyautey, Noguès had the reputation of being an "old Moroccan hand." Noguès seemed an ideal choice for the top post in the Protectorate administration, but his sterling qualifications did not necessarily endear him to progressives in Morocco, who remained skeptical of his ability to control a society heading into turmoil.[25]

Almost immediately, Noguès turned on the nascent Moroccan nationalist movement, singling it out as the most potent threat to French control. In 1937, after months of struggle, Noguès abruptly sent the most prominent Moroccan nationalist leaders into exile, giving the false impression that order had been restored. But of course, it had not. The last days of the Popular Front in 1938 in the Protectorate brought an avalanche of confusion, accelerating the polarization of peoples, parties, religions, and classes, and leaving the Moroccan people poorly prepared to face the coming crisis.

As an antidote to the mounting disorder, the Benatars threw themselves into volunteer work for the Casablanca Jewish community. The AIU Graduates' Association was the forum where they met with friends to discuss the rapidly deteriorating political situation. In 1934, Moyses Benatar had become president of the association, with Nelly joining him as vice president. From that vantage point, in late 1938, they decided to put forward the "Plan of Reform" for the Jewish community.[26] Moyses studied the community budget and made the surprising discovery that communal taxes fell most heavily on the poor. Outraged by this revelation, the Benatars made their move. Their plan, published as a pamphlet, called for open elections for a community council, a program of job training for Jewish youth, and the overhaul of community finances, including reassigning most of the tax burden to the wealthy. But given the timing of the report and the general mood of impending disaster, the Benatars' recommendations fell by the wayside. Inspired by the Popular Front and the vision of Léon Blum, the Benatars tried to mobilize their friends and associates for revolutionary change—but it would take a war to bring their ideas to fruition.

CHAPTER 2

1939

The Undesirables

IN SEPTEMBER 1938 at Munich, the prime ministers of Britain and France, Chamberlain and Daladier, signed away Czechoslovakia to Hitler. Chamberlain famously announced that he had achieved "peace in our time," but of course he had not, because Hitler would soon strike again, knowing that the democracies of Western Europe were not willing to fight. Already in a state of high anxiety, Moroccan Jews like the Benatars read the news as an omen of worse things to come. Signs of Europe's torment had already reached Casablanca, as boatloads of panicky refugees inundated the port and crowded the narrow platforms of the main railroad station whenever the train from Oran pulled in. Casablancans suddenly came face-to-face, in real time, with Europe's impending war.

At this moment of anxious waiting, a personal tragedy upended the Benatar household. In early January 1939, at the age of thirty-nine, Moyses Benatar was struck down by an illness that began with a simple cold and moved with lightning speed to an acute bacterial infection. Dr. Blanc, a specialist from the Pasteur Institute, was called in, but it was too late. Within two days, Moyses was gone. His funeral was an orgy of grief, attended by hundreds of Moroccans and Europeans. Samuel Lévy gave the eulogy, later printed in *L'Avenir Illustré*, noting Moyses's work for young people, his efforts for reform, his partnership with his wife.[1]

Nelly was inconsolable. Words offered no comfort. She buried herself and her two young children in sorrow to the point that she inflicted on them a "cruel and destructive" melancholy.[2] Friends tried to help her, hoping that work would distract her from her loss. They insisted that she take over the presidency of the AIU Graduates' Association, which had been vacated by Moyses's death. Nelly hid her sadness and returned to work. But for years, loss hung over her like a pall.

Soon her personal tragedy meshed with misfortune on the grand scale.

On September 2, 1939, Hitler invaded Poland and swiftly dismembered it. Benatar collected all her jewelry and brought it to city hall, where she made the *grand geste* of handing it over for the war effort. As if this were not enough, she added a large gift of cash and implored the rest of her family to do the same.

Her next actions were meant to demonstrate the readiness of Casablanca's Jews to join the war effort. Using her status as head of the AIU Graduates' Association, she orchestrated a politically charged endeavor to enlist Moroccan Jewish men into the French army, using the graduates' association as her headquarters. Posters appeared overnight throughout the city that invited "Moroccan Israelites" to sign up for the duration of the war. Jewish men flocked to a hastily arranged recruitment bureau on rue Lacépède to fill out the necessary forms. "Within 48 hours," she wrote, "two thousand young men enlisted, with about 800 of them ready to go to the front."[3] But the question of how the Jewish volunteers would actually be used was not yet resolved.

The problem was partly a legal one. Moroccan Jews were not French and therefore could not be integrated into the regular army. Nor were they aliens, so the Foreign Legion was not an option. Once again, they were trapped in a legal no-man's-land. If a solution was to be found, it had to happen quickly. Yet the Residency, despite all the public enthusiasm for the Jewish gesture, dragged its feet.[4] Resident-General Noguès was torn between his own conscience and what he saw as the demands of empire. He was sympathetic to Jewish youth who wanted to play their part in the defense of the motherland, but he was also mindful of his mentor Lyautey's warning to maintain parity between Jews and Muslims as a cornerstone of French policy in Morocco. He thought that an all-Jewish fighting unit would tip that sacred balance, overlooking the fact that more than one hundred thousand Moroccan troops were already on their way to France.

The idea of an all-Jewish fighting force within the French army was not a new one. It had come up earlier in the year, when the Zionist leader Chaim Weizmann had proposed the formation of a "Jewish Legion" along the lines

of a unit that had been created during the Great War. Following Hitler's invasion of Poland in September, the French Ministry of Foreign Affairs circulated
a memo supporting the idea of "[grouping] men together who are joined by
blood and are close together in beliefs, values, and common experiences." The
memo optimistically foresaw 100,000 to 150,000 Jewish men from Europe
and the Americas joining the force. But a negative response from the British
government, arguing that a Jewish fighting unit would arouse the jealousy of
Muslims, blocked the idea. Once again, the fear of disrupting an imaginary
balance got in the way. Lacking British support, the French backed away.[5]

Although thousands of Jews who were not French citizens had already enlisted in the French army as volunteers, they were integrated into units made
up of nationals from all over Europe. For this reason, their engagement was
not viewed as specifically "Jewish." These Jewish volunteers had signed up as
EVDGs, "volunteers for the duration of the war," with no promise of acquiring citizenship at the end of hostilities. The EVDGs would play an important
role throughout the war in North Africa, where, as we shall see, the French
military hierarchy took advantage of their anomalous status by shamelessly
exploiting them for the war effort.

Robert Montagne, a close adviser to Noguès and a highly regarded expert on North African affairs, was handed a thick dossier entitled "Using
Israelites in the War" and asked to write a report on his findings. After careful study, Montagne offered a nuanced approach. He was sympathetic to the
Jewish point of view, recognizing that at that moment, Jewish Moroccans—
and especially the young men under the wing of the AIU Graduates'
Association—did not want to be spectators on the sidelines. Algerian Jews
were "covered with glory" because of their military engagement, and Moroccans Jews wanted the same. Montagne also realized that the desire to
volunteer was not a completely selfless one but at some level was premised
on the hope of changing one's legal status. Behind the issue of Jewish recruitment was the larger question of giving full citizenship to Jews within the
French nation. When considered in this light, the proposal was too freighted
with negative outcomes to make it appealing. So the Protectorate regime did
nothing.[6]

Nelly Benatar was deeply disappointed. She understood the legal implica-
tions of the recruitment episode and why the gesture was blocked. But she
also decided that considering it a loss was to miss the point. It was a brilliant

piece of theater that captured people's attention, reminding them that the younger generation of Jews had a love of country and a sense of purpose that non-Jews had overlooked. Written up in the newspapers and the subject of talk over dinner tables, the "recruitment affair" showed that Jews were ready to fight and that stereotypes of their physical and moral weakness were false. It was a watershed moment. Although there would not be a "Jewish Legion" for Morocco, the public display of hundreds of Jewish youth signing up for combat on behalf of France marked a new stage in the deepening political awareness of Moroccan Jewry as a whole.

People were fleeing Germany and seeking asylum elsewhere. By the end of 1933, more than twenty-five thousand Germans had arrived in France, and by 1939, the number had swelled to ten times that.[7] Meanwhile, French public opinion underwent a change from welcoming asylum seekers to treating them as pariahs. In the right-wing press, refugees were depicted as crooks, spies, freeloaders, and speculators, and even more colorfully as "vermin," "swindlers," and "rogues."[8] The label of "undesirable" attached to refugees was a new component in France's lexicon of fear. According to historian Julian Jackson, the intense xenophobia circulating in France in 1939 prefigured in every way the institutionalized violence against foreigners that would reappear with even greater force under Vichy.[9]

Anti-Semitism, a phobia that had deep roots in France, was another disorder that had spread quickly in France in the late 1930s. The fact that Léon Blum, head of the flailing Popular Front, was a Jew, only made matters worse. After 1936, Blum became the target of a withering outpouring of anti-Jewish vitriol in the French Parliament and the press, when native-born French Jews joined refugees in the category of "undesirable." As war approached, universalist values fell away, racism and nationalism gained ground, and the boundary between reason and irrationality blurred. What it meant to be truly French was no longer a matter of high-minded republican values; instead, it had come to involve birth, lineage, and nebulous physical attributes.

In 1938, the French government issued a law aimed at interning foreigners in concentration camps. One did not have to commit a crime to be thrown into jail—it was enough to be foreign and to catch someone's eye. Aliens were required to hold identity cards issued by the police, but many refugees lacked formal papers. If they were caught, they could be jailed or expelled.[10]

The definition of "undesirable" soon expanded further; in the first months of 1939, nearly half a million people—men, women and children, remnants of the Catalonian army—streamed across the Spanish border into France. Sick, hungry, and debilitated, this human flood was greeted at first with compassion, but they were soon reduced to interlopers. More than 350,000 Spaniards were housed in makeshift camps inside France, guarded by truncheon-bearing colonial soldiers. Conditions in the internment camps were terrible. Prisoners had no clothing, blankets, or shelter, and they cooked their meager rations over open wood fires. The journalist Janet Flanner visited the camps in February 1939 and called the scene "unforgettable except for those living in it. They had been in the war itself and seemed to notice nothing."[11] What Flanner did not know was that these camps would become the model for a system of internment that grew exponentially under Vichy, reaching as far as North Africa and into the Sahara.

More French internment camps were created after the outbreak of war, when German and Austrian males between the ages of seventeen and sixty-five were ordered to report to "reception centers" set up around France. Eventually, women too were interned, more than fifteen thousand people in all. These internees were mostly Jews fleeing Nazi-dominated territories. They had no intention of aiding the enemy. Locking them up was further evidence of the confused state of mind among French officialdom at the outset of hostilities. One detainee noted that "France was starting its war against Hitler with a war against the enemies of Hitler."

Meanwhile, an aggressive policy of "selections" (*criblage*) sorted people out according to their "usefulness." Older people were let go, and young men willing to join labor units of the French military were released to join the army. Even so, as Jews, they did not lose the stigma of being "undesirable." Some were organized into work battalions attached to the Foreign Legion in France, while others became EVDGs, assigned to labor units that eventually found their way to North Africa. Zosa Szajkowski surmised that a total of about sixty thousand Jews served in the French military in the years 1939–1940, many of them as volunteers.[12]

Thousands of these civilian "undesirables" were looking for an escape route out of a defeated France to the West. The major obstacle was having the right papers—an exit visa, or permission to leave, transit visas for the countries to be traversed, an entry visa for the country of destination, and most important of all, a ticket on an outbound ship. All these documents had to line up with proper timing. All of them were difficult to obtain, if they could be gotten at all. Finding ship passage from Europe to the New World became increasingly difficult, especially after war was declared in September. The US State Department ordered American liners to restrict their bookings to American citizens. Ships chartered by the United States Lines, a private shipping company, were ordered to carry refugees from European ports, but they were leaving half-empty because of the citizenship requirement.

Other routes were possible for the inventive traveler. A regular steamship service connected Marseille with Algeria; boats belonging to the Compagnie Paquet departed twice weekly for Algiers and Oran. [13] Before hostilities began in September, they had carried mainly tourists and colonial officials. Now they had become conveyors of refugees. At the Algerian ports, the traveler would disembark and then hop onto a train of the trans-Maghrib railroad connecting Tunis and Casablanca. If papers were not in order, the traveler could get off the train at the Algerian-Moroccan frontier and simply walk across to Oujda on the other side. From Oujda, travel would resume by train, bus, or taxi to Casablanca, where, with good luck, passage could be booked to Lisbon and from there to the New World. Other refugees arrived in Morocco covertly from Spain via fishing boats, crossing the strait in the manner of the ancient Phoenicians. The Spanish foreign minister Francisco Gómez-Jordana y Sousa remarked that refugees would pass through Spain "as light passes through glass, leaving no trace."[14]

The sudden influx into Morocco was alarming. Casablanca was already in the throes of a decade's long crisis of overdensity. From a small fishing village in the mid-nineteenth century, the city had grown into the principal port of Morocco, its population increasing from 10,000 in 1900 to 257,000 in 1936. The city sprawled like a giant octopus along the Atlantic shore. There was a critical shortage of housing.[15]

One reason for Casablanca's rapid growth was the tide of rural people, including Jews, arriving from remote villages of the Berber-speaking south. Most poor Jewish migrants headed straight to the mellah. It seemed like home, with its tiny, cavelike synagogues, and its dark, winding alleyways and windowless houses. From a population of 5,000 in 1907, it ballooned to 36,000 in 1936, with a density of 1,400 people per hectare.[16] Wooden shacks

FIGURE 2.1 A courtyard in the mellah of Casablanca, 1920s.

FIGURE 2.2 Jews and Muslims in the medina of Casablanca, 1941.

covered the rooftops; courtyards and terraces became living space. On the average, families of seven or eight lived in a single room of eight square meters. On nearly every street corner, Jews from the countryside practiced the arts of survival, selling vegetables, fixing broken tea kettles, repairing shoes. A teacher at the AIU school wrote that "sixty percent of our students rely on us for food and clothing." Poverty, sickness, and prostitution were rife, causing a human crisis that the government ignored.[17] Although Casablanca was home to the largest Jewish community in Morocco, it was not an inviting destination or the preferred port of entry for Jewish refugees in 1939. When Protectorate officials temporarily closed the port of Casablanca to refugees late in that year, the flow headed north to the far-smaller port of Tangier, where the conditions awaiting them appeared to be far better.

Tangier's population was about sixty-five thousand people, one-quarter the size of Casablanca. It was also home to twelve thousand native Jews. Many relied on charity, but unlike in Casablanca, the self-reliant Tangier Jewish community took care of its own, having the benefit of a well-organized leadership. In this first year of the war, word got out that Tangier was a welcoming place, and it received the brunt of the Jewish refugee influx.

Tangier was more closely tied to its Iberian neighbor Spain than to France. In 1912, when France created its Protectorate in Morocco, it handed over to Spain a generous slice along the Mediterranean coast as compensation for long-standing Spanish claims to a territorial foothold in Morocco. Because of Tangier's strategic location at the narrow gate to the Mediterranean, the Great Powers decided that the city should not belong to any one nation, but should instead constitute an international zone within Spanish Morocco. The 1924 Statute of Tangier assigned the task of governance to a rotating committee of diplomats representing each of the major powers. Somehow, this arrangement worked, and little Tangier strolled through the interwar years with unusual tranquility while the rest of the western Mediterranean—Spain, Portugal, France, and Italy—rumbled toward disaster.

Tied to Spain through the memory of Sepharad, Tangier's Jewish elite was made up of a coterie of interlocking families vital to the economic life of the town, protected by their international passports, their real estate and capital, and their expertise in banking and business. Jewish communal affairs were handled by a committee, or *junta*, of fifteen members who were elected by universal suffrage. Religious matters were under the jurisdiction of a rabbinical tribunal, and private charities took care of orphans, schools, soup kitchens, hospitalization, and even burial arrangements. "From birth to death," wrote one observer, "the poor are guided and supported by their wealthy coreligionists who are taxed proportional to their wealth."

But the rich Jews of Tangier were not really that rich. The more ambitious ones, like Amram Cazes, had pulled up stakes during the Great War and moved to Casablanca. Others went to New York or Paris or Geneva, leaving behind an old guard that thrived on the slow tempo for which Tangier was famous. *Memorias de un viejo tangerino*, a memorial book by the journalist Isaac Laredo published in 1935, captures the mood. In that year, dark clouds were rolling in from Europe, but one would not know it from the exuberant tone of the *Memorias*. Supposedly a history of early twentieth-century Tangier, it is really a loving compendium of profiles of Tangier's *hombres ilustres*, personalities representing the close ties between Tangier and the rest of the Mediterranean world.[18]

Isaac Laredo was a perfect example of the type. Described as "lyrical and gallant, buoyant and benevolent, hospitable and generous," he scribbled in the Proustian mode, propped up in bed wearing a silken smoking jacket.[19] The theme of the *Memorias*, if there is one, is to celebrate the minor miracle that was Tangier, where people of goodwill, polite demeanor, and sparkling wit came together in perfect harmony. No criminals, cheats, or scoundrels here. All were fine examples of what is meant by *un viejo tangerino*—a person of noble spirit and good manners, steeped in the cadences of an eponymous Castilian mother tongue.[20]

Among the very few women included in the *Memorias* was Nelly Benatar. Don Isaac's note was a brief one: "Tangerina de vasta ilustración . . . ejerce como abogad[a] en los Tribunales del Protectorado francés," or "a woman of Tangier of vast knowledge . . . who serves as a lawyer in the courts of the French Protectorate." The accompanying photograph, taken in the garden of the Palais de Justice of Casablanca, shows a young woman with stylishly bobbed hair and a shy smile, dressed in legal robes. After nearly twenty years of living in Casablanca, Nelly Benatar was still considered a *tangerina*, the incunabula of her youth planted on her brow forever.[21]

Fascism would eventually arrive in Tangier, but in 1939, Tangier's Jews carried on as usual, marrying cousins, taking long siestas, enjoying a glass of

FIGURE 2.3 Nelly Benatar as a young lawyer, mid-1930s.

sherry at "the hour of the café." One thing was different, however; the onrush of hundreds of refugees that began in 1935 had reached its pinnacle in 1939. Tangier was an easy point of entry into a non-Hitlerian world. Packet boats arrived daily from the continent; mixed in with the tourists were many German and Austrian Jews, single and in family groups. It was difficult to tell who was a casual tourist and who was a refugee. Surveillance at the port was light, customs procedures were relaxed, hotel rooms were cheap, and the police of the international city, accustomed to foreigners, were not very attentive. If the émigrés decided to stay, there were schools, apartments, and even the possibility of finding work. In the early days, most arrived with resources, placing little burden on the local Jewish community. They quickly blended into the colorful tapestry of the cosmopolitan city and made themselves indistinguishable in the passing crowd.

In 1936, Jewish community leaders created a special committee to oversee refugees and keep track of their numbers. When French Morocco temporarily closed its doors to refugees in February 1939, Tangier became the only port of entry in Morocco for escapees from Europe. Among them, for the first time, were destitute people who asked the Jewish community for help. Ilya Dijour, an official with HICEM, the international Jewish emigration agency headquartered in Paris, asked the Tangier committee to share the burden and take in even more refugees.[22] In no time at all, seven hundred refugees were living in the city, and two hundred of them were on the community dole.

Joseph Garzon was head of the Tangier Refugee Committee. Courtly and soft-spoken, Garzon turned for help to Samuel Lévy in Casablanca:

> We are facing a distressing situation ... the flood of Jewish refugees into our town, growing from day to day, looking for the right to live denied to them in their homelands ... we made a large subscription for them, but the funds quickly disappeared.... What to do? Send them back? Never! To where? No one wants them. What to do? No one knows ... we are appealing to your humanitarian instincts to help us by asking the men of good will in your city to lend their material support and create in Casablanca, as soon as possible, a refugee Committee similar to ours. It would be an act of piety.... [Now] Tangier is the only haven for refugees in Morocco. Don't you think these refugees should be the responsibility of all the Jews of Morocco, not just the people of Tangier who cannot bear such a burden alone for much longer? We are counting on your support.[23]

The Jews of Casablanca held a charity ball and sent Garzon a check for 10,500 francs. The question of refugees was no longer Tangier's alone; other Moroccan Jewish communities became involved in Tangier's plight. In June, Garzon reported that one thousand refugees were staying in Tangier, many of them supported by the local committee.[24] In July, eighty more refugees arrived, and once again, Jewish communities from other parts of the country came to the rescue. Garzon sent out the word that Tangier could not accept any more refugees, for its ability to absorb them was exhausted.[25]

Besides, other trouble was brewing. The foul odor of anti-Semitism was in the air. Garzon wrote to the head of the Jewish community in Berlin: "The arrival of all these refugees without a means of support, looking for work and settling down, has already provoked bad feelings within the foreign colony and among the natives. The latter have repeatedly expressed hostile feelings toward Jews. This immigration could awake hatreds . . . that could quickly give way to behaviors having very serious consequences, both for [the refugees] and for the Jews of our town."[26] Garzon believed that the balance of native Jews, Europeans, and native Muslims in Tangier, carefully preserved for generations, was about to fall apart. Dr. Augusto d'Esaguy, chair of the Portuguese Commission for Assistance to Jewish Refugees and representative of the Jewish emigration agency HICEM in Lisbon, visited Tangier in August 1939 and reported that a war was brewing in Tangier between the city's Jewish elites and its German Jewish newcomers.[27]

Tangier journalist Carlos de Nesry viewed the conflict as "the beginning of a laborious symbiosis having multiple vicissitudes." What he meant was that Tangier's tranquility was being upset by the arrival of "debris from a world that is no more. Never has the Jew of Tangier felt more Spanish, more Sephardi. Never has he so much felt so strongly the powerful lifeblood of his heredity." According to de Nesry, in food, habits, and dress, even in hairstyle, the Sephardi and the Ashkenazi Jew were worlds apart. When the sacred hour of the *apéritif* rolled around, "the shrill and incomprehensible babble of the Czech ladies filled the air" of the outdoor cafés on Boulevard Pasteur, reducing ever further chances of "national reconciliation." A genuine *Kulturkampf* was taking place in Tangier under the stress of the refugee overload. At a moment when solidarity was most needed, Tangier was being torn apart.[28]

Suddenly, a savior came forward in the shape of Jules Braunschvig, member of an affluent Tangier family of Alsatian origin that had settled in Morocco in the late nineteenth century. Only thirty years old, Braunschvig was already a figure of repute, an Ashkenazi Jew raised in Morocco who knew the local ethos and could serve as a mediator between the warring factions. Recruited in 1932 to join the governing council of the AIU in Paris, he had a broad network of friends throughout the Jewish world. Suave and charming,

Jules Braunschvig's manner was self-assured, his voice calm. He was the ideal choice for brokering a truce.[29]

In August, Braunschvig wrote to Morris Troper, Paris-based director of the American Joint Distribution Committee (JDC) for Europe. The JDC, known as "the Joint," was an American philanthropic agency that was sending token aid to Tangier, making its first hesitant steps into North Africa.[30] The JDC was the "right" address to receive Braunschvig's request.

Formed in New York during World War I to aid Jewish war victims, the JDC represented the coming together of three poles of relief within the American Jewish community: the "Labor socialists"; the "Orthodox" Jews, represented by the Union of Orthodox Congregations; and the American Jewish Committee, whose leadership was mostly wealthy German Jews. Its mission was to raise funds from American Jewry to bring humanitarian aid to less fortunate Jews outside of the United States. In the interwar period, the JDC's European headquarters was in Paris; after the fall of France in 1940, its headquarters moved to Lisbon, where it remained throughout the war. In 1939, more than one hundred thousand Jews were still stranded in Europe, having fled from Nazi-occupied areas. The JDC teamed up with HICEM, the most important Jewish emigration agency on the continent, providing it with financial support. Cautious in its approach to policy matters, the JDC tended to move in tandem with State Department directives and was slow in responding to the European emergency. Eventually, its position changed and it became a major force in contributing millions of dollars to refugee relief during and after the war.[31]

Leaving aside the cultural aspects of the problem, Braunschvig focused directly on the question of finances and asked the JDC for more aid: "I insist that [more] relief be given to M. Garzon as soon as possible. I will not repeat again the perfect organization of the Tangier Committee or the economies they have adopted, you have all the numbers and they are sufficiently eloquent in that regard. . . . Tangier is the only town where refugees . . . can enter freely. But for that to happen, the benevolent neutrality of local officials is required."[32]

Swayed by Braunschvig's argument, as well as the realization that North Africa could become a major theater for humanitarian relief in the not-too-distant future, the JDC agreed to help. By 1943, the "Joint" was providing the Tangier Refugee Committee with the hefty sum of $4,250 a month.[33]

The importance of Tangier as a sanctuary for European refugees continued throughout the war. The foreign population remained stable—whoever landed in Tangier before the war would remain for the duration—making the town a golden cage for refugees as well as for its civilian inhabitants. But even in the middle of the storm, Tangier never lost its orientation as an international city and a haven for the uprooted. After Spain's dictator Franco took over the town in June 1940, Jews, British, Americans, people of every provenance and stripe, were allowed to stay. Wartime Tangier was a fascist stronghold that tolerated an Allied presence. In March 1941, Spain permitted Nazi Germany to open a consulate in Tangier. The Germans used the town as a listening post, reporting on maritime movements through the strait. The Americans did the same, running intelligence operations out of their legation, an elegant old palace deep in the medina. In no time at all, Tangier was transformed from a colorful tourist destination into the foremost center of espionage on the African coast, overrun by snoopers of every type. But for refugees who had landed in Tangier, that was irrelevant. For them, Tangier was a secure mooring in a roiling sea.

Farther south, Nelly Benatar was swimming in another sea, a sea of refugees headed toward the West. It was her self-appointed assignment to help them find a friendly shore.

CHAPTER 3

1940

Refugees and Resistance

THREE SNAPSHOTS SELECTED AT RANDOM from a box of old photos: at first, no hint of a narrative. Then, on closer inspection, a story coalesces. The first photo, a group of young women on a gray winter day, most looking happy, some not. One of them, older than the rest, peers at the camera, unsmiling. The second snapshot, a clutch of refugees newly arrived at an internment camp—men, women, children, all dressed for another clime—a few squinting in the hot sun, others too weary to look up, except for two little boys, one of whom sticks out his tongue at the camera. To the side, a mysterious-looking woman dressed completely in black, her back to us. The third image is a passport-sized photo of a woman with severely cropped hair wearing military garb, her shirt tightly buttoned at the collar, her look as disciplined as her dress.

Three photos, each reminding us of what Roland Barthes meant when he talked about the "infinity" of the photographic image: how the camera captures a fleeting moment, but thanks to the art of photography, that image becomes fixed for the duration of human time.[1] The referent in each of these photographs is Nelly Benatar, magically brought to us through the click of a lens, caught at various stages of her journey through that first full year of war.

During the *drôle de guerre*, the six-month-long "phony war" that followed the German invasion of Poland, while most of the world stood still, Nelly Benatar was on the move. Dropping her legal practice, she enrolled in a Red

Cross nurses' training course at the Military Hospital Colombani in Casablanca. The only Jewish woman in a class of forty, she threw herself into the strenuous training. From early morning to late at night, and often overnight, she was at the hospital learning the basics of nursing: how to assist in surgery, how to bandage and apply first aid, how to minister to the sick. After more specialized training, she was even qualified to care for victims of a gas attack.

Benatar reveled in the intensity of the training, and she looked forward to the prospect of going to the front. She enjoyed the military discipline. The French branch of the International Committee of the Red Cross was a conservative organization dominated by ultraroyalist Catholics, mostly retired army officers. Benatar fit into the multilayered organization of the hospital, where medical hierarchies were clearly defined and everyone knew his or her assignment. During the early months of 1940, when most people were frozen in a state of anxious waiting, Benatar was busy learning a new skill.[2]

FIGURE 3.1 Refugees arriving in Casablanca; Nelly Benatar's back is to the camera, 1940.

FIGURE 3.2 Red Cross Nurses' Training Program, Colombani Military Hospital,
Casablanca. Benatar is fourth from right, front row.

Early in June, she received her nursing certification, along with orders to prepare to leave for France in two days with an ambulance unit.

That assignment never came to pass. With Hitler's armor in the outskirts
of Paris, the new head of the French state—the eighty-four-year-old war hero
Maréchal Philippe Pétain, the "Lion of Verdun," doddering but still lucid—
called a stop to the fighting. When his voice came crackling over the airwaves
saying that he would seek an armistice, there was an audible sigh of relief. For
many French people, Pétain was the savior who would rescue France from
disaster. But for Nelly Benatar, he had committed an act of treason.

An eerie calm overtook the metropole, now divided into two parts: the
Occupied Zone held by the Germans in the north and the Unoccupied Zone
in the south, still in French hands. On July 1, Pétain set up a provisional capital at Vichy, a French health resort famous for its thermal baths, and began
to govern by edict, surrounded by what was left of the French state, the

military, and the Catholic Church. The American diplomat Robert Murphy, dispatched by President Roosevelt to report on the situation at Vichy, described it as "an assortment of bewildered Frenchman staggering under a catastrophic military defeat."[3]

In Casablanca, the heat of summer had arrived, and beaches and swimming pools were full, but the mood in the streets was anything but festive. "Casablanca has become a small Tower of Babel," quipped a local newspaper, noting the sidewalk parade of soldiers and strangers who clogged the cafés on the Place de France. The city was hosting a new kind of visitor, the "refugee," most of whom never imagined they would set foot on this corner of Africa. The face of the city had changed. Street corners were piled high with sandbags in anticipation of air raids. The civilian population was warned that sirens could go off at any moment, but only "if the risk of a bombardment was imminent." Somehow, curiosity won out over fear. If by chance an airplane flew overhead, instead of descending to the underground shelters, people climbed to the rooftop for a better look.[4]

The refugee situation quickly got out of hand. The police were issuing directives they could not follow. When convoys arrived, they were told to separate soldiers from civilians and to provide food and shelter—impossible tasks given the numbers of hungry and exhausted.[5] Contrôleur Civil Contard, the government's representative in Casablanca, threw up his hands in despair. Citing "serious difficulties" with the relief operation, he pinpointed a "lack of liaison" among those in charge. On June 29, in the early hours of the morning, a group of 129 Polish refugees arrived at the main railroad station. No one had been told of their coming, and the police were completely unprepared. A few hours later, another trainload pulled in, mostly families. Not knowing what to do, officials bedded them down in the station's waiting room. Two weeks after the Germans entered Paris, more than a thousand refugees had arrived in Casablanca by land and sea.[6]

Then there was the question of security. Fearing that among the motley hordes were dangerous characters, the police attempted to sort them out on the spot. They were especially concerned about refugees from Eastern Europe, some with papers, some without, who were speaking a medley of unknown languages. French nationals, more easily pigeonholed, were allowed to exit into the crowded streets, but foreigners were sent directly to

Aïn Chock, an army camp on the outskirts of Casablanca that had been hastily converted into a reception center. Within days, the facility held hundreds of people living in deplorable conditions.[7]

Suspicion enveloped all strangers, but especially those labeled as "undesirables." A police report noted that among the arrivals were those "who were planning to continue in Morocco the work of economic and social sabotage they had practiced in France. Many are Jews [whose] flight was facilitated, if we are to believe the gossip, by paying an elevated price for their ticket."[8] The authorities were in a state of panic, no one knew how to deal with the crush. Casablanca's hotels were already full, and there were no organized relief efforts. A committee of volunteers headed by the wife of the *contrôleur civil* was the only organization providing refugee relief, but it was completely overwhelmed. Besides, it could not help those detained at Aïn Chock or held inside the port. The authorities were stymied about what to do.

The story of how Nelly Benatar became involved with refugees comes to us in two versions. Serge Lapidus tells us that in her capacity as a nurse, she was summoned to duty at the holding center at Aïn Chock and was sickened by what she saw. At first, she was denied access, but when she returned in her Red Cross uniform and brandished her lawyer's identity card, she was allowed to enter. Conditions inside were frightening. People were sitting on the bare floor or on straw mattresses crawling with cockroaches, the very sick were mingled with the not so sick, and basic hygiene was nonexistent. No officials were to be seen. Profoundly moved, she decided to take action.[9]

Benatar's own version of events is even more dramatic. On Friday, July 5, she was sitting at home when a port worker knocked on her door and presented her with a letter addressed to her deceased husband, along with a piece of moldy bread. The author of the note was Ferdinand Marburger, a stamp dealer from Paris who had done business with Moyses and was unaware he had died the previous year. It contained a pathetic appeal: "Come to our aid! We have fled Europe ... for fifteen days they have been holding us on board like carriers of the plague, refusing to let us disembark. We are close to dying from hunger and thirst. Here is a sample of what they give us to eat ... the number of sick among us, especially the children, is growing."[10]

Benatar rushed to the office of Contrôleur Civil Contard and learned that thirty passenger ships from Europe were tied up in the port, each one packed with refugees. Contard had no idea what to do. She told him that the Jewish community was ready to help and placed on his desk a plan to create the Committee of Assistance to Refugees—under the presidency of Nelly Benatar. Thirty leading members of Casablanca's Jewish community had already signed up to help with lodging, food, and other necessities. Surprised and relieved, Contard agreed to hand over responsibility to her committee, if Benatar would take the lead.[11]

Benatar swung into action. Under her direction, schools vacated during the summer months were converted into dormitories for refugees. Zeide Schulman, a furniture manufacturer, supplied hundreds of beds and mattresses. Jewish families volunteered to take refugees into their homes, and a kitchen at the AIU Graduates' Association began dispensing three hot meals a day. Leopold Greenberg, an American Jewish businessman, had sixteen refugees sleeping in his warehouse. Others donated food, clothing, blankets, and utensils. A loan from the Jewish community chest covered expenses, while private persons, Jewish and non-Jewish, made generous donations to a rescue fund amounting to 130,000 francs.[12]

Benatar borrowed automobiles from friends to transport refugees, and she petitioned for and received an extra ration of gasoline. She had offers of free medical help from Casablanca's Jewish doctors. She personally took sick people to the military hospital where she had completed her nurses' training, and she transferred people from Aïn Chock to more suitable quarters. By August 9, the insalubrious holding pen was nearly empty.

The issue of onward emigration came next. The head of the Office of Political Affairs, an arm of the Residency, was specific on this point: "Their settlement in Morocco is not desirable, and their rapid emigration abroad, according to their ethnic groupings, should be arranged as soon as possible."[13] But leaving Casablanca in the last months of 1940 presented nearly insurmountable obstacles. The last functioning port of departure for the Americas was Lisbon, but there was no way of getting there. In addition, the price of a ticket was exorbitant; five hundred American dollars for an adult was not unusual—a sum beyond the reach of most refugees. For the time being, the problem of transmigration would have to wait.

Meanwhile, the incoming flow showed no sign of letting up. By late August, a new surge of Central European Jews arrived overland from Spain. This group seemed to be of a more desperate sort, raising new fears in the popular mind. A newspaper reported that the Casablanca residence of Thami el-Glaoui, Pasha of Marrakech, had been invaded by a refugee. A gardener chased the man into the garage, where he climbed into the Pasha's Rolls-Royce, began blasting the horn, and shattered the windshield with his fists. He then fell to the ground in a stupor. At the police station, his identity was established as Egon Grunwald, lately of Vienna, who had taken leave of his senses.[14]

Similar stories appeared regularly in the press. Refugees were bicycle thieves, carriers of disease, parasites.[15] Even sensible people resented them. Cora Goold, the wife of Casablanca-based US consul general Herbert Goold, complained that her husband was exhausted by the daily mob of refugees in his office and needed a break: "They are awful whiners," she grumbled, "one woman tried to commit suicide in the Consulate—took poison when told she would have to go to a concentration camp."[16] A gradual reclassification was taking place, transforming refugees from victims of circumstance into social pariahs.

In August, 813 refugees were registered with Benatar's committee and scattered about town in temporary quarters.[17] Desperate about what to do next, the authorities were readying former military camps in the countryside as longer-term internment camps. Families with small children and the elderly were assigned to Sidi El Ayachi, a former army camp at Azemmour, not far from Casablanca, while people considered a political risk were to be sent to even more remote locations. Benatar's committee was given the task of sorting them out. Formed as a humanitarian venture, the Committee of Assistance to Refugees was ineluctably drawn into a system of triage and confinement, deciding the fate of people who had lost the right to make such decisions for themselves.

Benatar recognized the problem as one of disempowerment and made the decision to defend the few rights remaining with the refugees. Her main concern was the question of refugee assets. Some migrants arrived with large amounts of cash, gold, and precious gems.[18] They had to declare their assets on arrival and hand them over to the authorities for safekeeping. Deposited in blocked accounts in the state bank, these assets were supposed to be returned to the transient upon leaving Morocco. But something went wrong. Benatar learned that the blocked accounts were not operating as promised and that assets were returned only after being converted into the much-devalued local currency. Indignant, she wrote to the state director of finances, demanding that the practice be discontinued because it "represents their only fortune they have managed to preserve, often at considerable personal risk."[19] She argued that the migrants would need assets to settle into their new homes. Her appeal was based on the refugees' situation as victims of circumstance whose lives had been unfairly interrupted. By contextualizing their predicament, she called on the bureaucrats' sense of fairness, as well as their practical desire to move the refugees onward. She won her point, and the practice was discontinued.

Actions like this enhanced her reputation as an advocate for refugees and an all-around expert on refugee affairs. As word of her successes circulated, her workload increased. Her staff consisted of one person, Célia Bengio, a trusted friend, but she needed more help. In the last months of 1940, Benatar was joined by Jonathan Thurscz, former editor of the Zionist newspaper *L'Avenir Illustré*, which had been shut down by Vichy. Thurscz had skills that Benatar lacked, such as fluency in German, Polish, and Yiddish. His assignment was to interview people and identify those most ready to move onward. Having a sponsor abroad, a valid passport, or an entry visa to a final destination put a transient in the best position. Thurscz was even able to procure new identity papers for some of his clients from friendly consulates, especially useful for those transients who had become stateless.[20]

Thurscz was a useful addition, but there were drawbacks to working with him. His attitude toward Benatar was patronizing and self-important. He considered Benatar a rank novice in political affairs, and after fifteen years of living in Morocco, he was convinced that Sephardim and Ashkenazim had "different ways of thinking." His interactions with European Zionists over the years had given him an international network that Benatar lacked. Thurscz resented Benatar's status as a lawyer and her position as president of the Committee of Assistance to Refugees. Time and again he wrote letters posing as its head and, even worse, insisted on cosigning her correspondence.

In reality, they were not at all compatible. They had different styles of solicitation, different ways of using words, different priorities. Thurscz was evasive and diffident to authority; Benatar was quick, bold, and precise. While Benatar traded on her qualities as a lawyer, Thurscz enjoyed playing the role of a *macher* (Yiddish for "a person of influence") with his antennae out in every direction. When the refugee committee opened a new line of communication with the JDC in July, they each wrote letters to its European headquarters in Lisbon that contradicted the other.

By the end of 1940, Thurscz's writ had run out. Frightened by a rumor that he would soon be arrested, he quickly arranged visas to the United States for himself and his family. Benatar was not sorry to see him go. She inherited Thurscz's international contacts, hired German and Yiddish speakers to take his place, and solidified her position of leadership over the refugee aid committee.[21]

Another important milestone in Benatar's consolidation of ownership over refugee affairs in Casablanca took place in July, when she opened relations with the American Joint Distribution Committee, the JDC. The JDC was already sending small sums to support Tangier's local refugee committee, but French Morocco was still unknown territory to the organization. Joe Schwartz, the JDC's European representative in Lisbon, had learned through the grapevine about the Aïn Chock center and the plight of the eight hundred Jewish refugees detained there. Some of them held valid American visas; Schwartz did not understand the delay in releasing them. He was told that the local committee "was not equipped to handle the problem."[22]

While the existence of a Casablanca committee to help refugees was news to the JDC, the opposite was not true. Benatar was already informed about the JDC and its capacities. She described it to Contrôleur Civil Contard as an American Jewish organization having "huge influence," capable of providing aid "on a grand scale" to Jews in other countries, especially in the area of emigration. When the JDC offered the Casablanca committee the paltry sum of five hundred dollars, Benatar refused it, to Joe Schwartz's astonishment. "Believe it or not," he cabled to New York, "Casablanca does not need our funds and is able to raise sufficient funds in its own community to provide adequate relief." Benatar was after a bigger prize. She quickly followed up with a note to Schwartz, telling him that she alone was the address for Jewish refugee matters in Casablanca. Her message contained a precise request: "We would like for you to redirect your efforts to quickly resolve the problem of emigration from both the financial and diplomatic perspectives . . . and to use your influence with the representatives of the various countries to obtain the necessary visas. We shall take on the task locally of getting exit visas . . . you might also look into the question of transport, since Morocco is totally without direct communication by sea with the United States."[23] Benatar promised to send the JDC office in Lisbon "complete records and dossiers" of the hundreds of refugees in her care. Still puzzled by exactly who she was, Joe Schwartz saw the advantages of having a contact in Casablanca, where refugee issues were beginning to draw international attention. Their correspondence was a first hesitant step toward a strong working relationship that would last for the duration of the war and beyond.[24]

Nelly Benatar was off and running. Within the first six months of her committee's existence, she had established herself as its unrivaled head, raised large sums of money for refugee relief, developed useful contacts throughout the colonial administration, and opened a conversation with the richest and most important American Jewish aid organization. At the same time, she carried on a secret life hidden from the view of everyone who knew her, including her closest friends and family.

The Resistance movement in Morocco enters our story because of Nelly Benatar's intense involvement. The connection began in 1940 and continued until 1942, when her resistance cell was exposed and destroyed. But in every sense, her engagement is best understood as a single, seamless episode. Her clandestine work was a direct result of her work with refugees—two interrelated activities that complemented each other.

In France, the Resistance encompassed many things, from organizing cells and distributing propaganda to waging armed struggle against Nazi occupiers. Morocco was also the setting for displays of defiance, but on a more modest scale. Unlike France, where the Resistance achieved near-mythical stature in the postwar era, in Morocco, it has been completely forgotten.

Membership in the Moroccan resistance was heterogeneous, embracing a spectrum of left-wing political dogmas from communism to republicanism, with many shades between. The single unifying element among its various members and manifestations was the desire to disrupt Vichy and to help the Allies. Its main adversaries were the arch-Pétainists in the colonial administration who enforced Vichy's orders; its main allies were the officials who played a double game by ignoring those same orders.[25]

Recruitment was a problem. Morocco lacked organized parties on the left to draw on for new adherents. The European settler population was far more pro-Vichy than not. Moroccan Muslims tended to be off-limits because of their anti-French, pro-nationalist tendencies, and Moroccan Jews were for the most part apolitical. Expanding the ranks of resistance in Morocco was slow work. Lacking a ready-made pool of recruits, organizers had to forage among the weak stalks of civil society to find adherents. Refugees were a promising resource, but on the whole, it was difficult finding committed people capable of attracting others to carry out acts of defiance.

Morocco's geographical setting at the gateway to the Mediterranean was another defining factor. In 1940 and 1941, clandestine activities focused on assisting people to cross the heavily guarded strait in both directions—helping some to leave the continent and reach the relative safety of North Africa, helping others to return to Europe and the war. In 1942, attention shifted to planning subversive acts in preparation for the Allied landing later that year.

Benatar's role in these exploits appears to have been more than a minor one. As an expert on refugee affairs, she knew about the comings and goings of all sorts of people. Still, details about her secret war are sparse. She did not keep documents about her activities, for fear that they would be discovered and used against her. In her archive, there are just a few hints—a name dropped here and there, a hurried note written years after the fact. She confided her exploits to no one, not even to her trusted aide, Célia Bengio.[26] Thus, the overall picture is a fragmented one, composed of bits of information from the main actors, Benatar's own scattered remarks, and the testimonies of others who were often peripheral to the story.

An anti-Vichy resistance congealed in Morocco almost as soon as the Armistice was signed. Benatar began her clandestine work immediately after the fall of France by helping people to escape the country by sea. She was aided in this work by some influential actors. In her own words: "Thanks to the help of Contrôleurs civils Gromand and Boniface, to officials in the British consulate until its closure, and after that, to the American Consulate, and under the cover of the Committee of Assistance to Refugees, we were able to help people in the Resistance to hide weapons and documents. We also sent out, by sea in small craft, many *resistants* who went to Lisbon and from there to London."[27]

Her clients in 1940 were mainly soldiers sitting on board ships in the port of Casablanca, ex–Foreign Legionnaires, French officers loyal to de Gaulle and determined to defeat Vichy, and stray British pilots. Some had lost their papers and were stateless; others were banned from entering Moroccan territory because they presented a security risk. These men had to be secretly repatriated. With the help of complicit port police, escaped Allied soldiers were taken off ships and handed over to Benatar, who hid them at the AIU Graduates' Association until small boats became available.[28] Then they were taken by night in groups of eight or ten to a secret landing spot on the coast to begin their journey to neutral Lisbon. If the escapees were intercepted and returned to Casablanca, Captain Gauthier, a judge in the maritime tribunal in Casablanca and an ally of Benatar's, would hand them back to her for another try.[29]

US consular officers could be counted on to provide false papers. Philip Bagby, US vice-consul, was generous with visas and let her use the diplomatic pouch to send messages. She was also in contact with French officials opposed to Vichy. Colonel Herviot, director of the State Security, a secret Gaullist, looked out for her; Guiramand, director of the Office of Political Affairs, was another ally; Commandant General Jacquot, head of the Deuxième Bureau, the state intelligence service, was on her list of accomplices.[30] Benatar did not act alone but was part of a larger network that crystallized in Casablanca in 1940, when the western Mediterranean was drawn into the widening European conflict.

MENGIN'S STORY. Resistance activities began to coalesce around the figure of Roger Mengin in late 1940. An engineer working on the Casablanca docks and an ardent anti-fascist, Mengin built an eclectic organization composed of refugees, Algerian and Moroccan Jews, anti-fascist colonial police, and French civil servants. How this organization came into being is a story of Mengin's single-minded dedication. It is also a tale of undercover ploys, foolish gambits, and in the end, betrayal.[31]

Roger Mengin came from a liberal bourgeois background; his British intelligence profile lists him as an "atheist" and his politics as "republican, left-wing." Born in Paris to French parents, he moved with his family to Chile when he was six and spoke fluent English and Spanish. Called up in 1914, Mengin was wounded and transferred to an airborne unit as a mechanic for the duration of the war. After he was demobilized, he completed his education, graduating from the prestigious École Nationale d'Arts et Métiers in Paris. He then began a career as a mechanical engineer.

When war broke out in 1939, Mengin was assigned to a factory in Oran that manufactured spare parts. But he was restless to get into the fight. When the Armistice was signed in June 1940, Mengin went to the British consulate in Oran and tried to get to England, but he was told to "be patient" and "go home." Depressed by the pro-Vichy mood at his Algerian factory, he decided to leave for Casablanca, where his brother lived. His plan was to make his way to England to join the Free French, but this proved far more difficult than he had imagined. At the US consulate in Casablanca he was once again rebuffed. Everyone, including his cousin, Robert Mengin, a well-known liberal French journalist working in London, told him to drop the idea of leaving North Africa.[32]

Mengin was not easily deterred. He found a new position with the Casablanca shipbuilding firm of Huyghes and promptly began using it as a cover, gleaning crucial information about French shipping from his fellow workers at the port and passing it on to the Allies. A friend introduced Mengin to Robert Schumann, a French Jewish lawyer living in Casablanca, and brother of Maurice Schumann, the London-based spokesman for the Free French.[33] Robert Schumann, also a friend of Benatar, was the organizer of a secret, British-run cell in Casablanca, though not a very successful one. When seven thousand kilos of raw rubber arrived on a ship docked in Casablanca's port, he received orders from London to blow up the ship, but he failed to execute the command. Discouraged, Schumann quit his post in early 1942, leaving Mengin in charge.

Under Mengin's leadership, the organization became an "American operation," repurposed to help with Operation Torch, the long-awaited Allied invasion of North Africa that was already in an advanced stage of planning. Robert Murphy, President Roosevelt's special envoy in North Africa, was put in charge of assessing the French reception to the operation. Within days, David King, one of Murphy's operatives, contacted Mengin. King's official title was vice-consul at the US consulate in Casablanca, but his real job was passing on information in preparation for the Allied landing. King gave Mengin two wireless transmitters and secret codes so that he could begin sending messages about maritime activities directly to Gibraltar. Sheila Joan Clark, King's "Girl Friday," was assigned to "encouraging" Mengin to broaden his network.[34]

The next recruit was a Hungarian Jewish refugee named Alexander Perenyi, who was brought in to operate the new wireless equipment. Perenyi was joined by an Algerian Jew, Albert El Koubbi, who used the equipment to transmit coded messages to Tangier and Gibraltar. The twosome of El Koubbi and Perenyi changed their hideout daily to avoid arrest, packing up the transmitters in suitcases and carrying them to their new hiding spot. Their information was of value not only to the Americans, who were trying to keep track of French shipping passing through the British blockade, but also to people like Nelly Benatar, who was running her own escape operation. El Koubbi invited Benatar to join the Mengin group, and she agreed, expecting that by joining forces, she would have access to intelligence information useful for "passing" people to the "other side." It is highly unlikely Benatar ever met Mengin in person, because he was in deep cover, but she was good friends with El Koubbi, her primary contact with the Mengin organization. Throughout the first months of 1942, Mengin increased the size of his group, and by June, it had grown to 480 members. He did not know names, but each new recruit had a number. He kept up a continuous flow of information to the Americans about port activity, airfields, and military installations. David King took credit, but it was Mengin's people in the field who did the actual reconnaissance.

Late in June, Mengin's organization was fatally exposed when Albert El Koubbi and his friend François Klotz were arrested by police in Marrakech. Still in deep cover, Roger Mengin went into hiding. On August 3, he learned that King had arranged for his escape to England. He went to Casablanca's port, where he received false papers, and boarded a Portuguese fishing boat to Gibraltar. After three weeks in Gibraltar, Mengin was flown to England; eventually, he joined the Free French. With his departure and the arrests of Klotz and El Koubbi, the Mengin organization fell apart and the Moroccan resistance came to an end.[35]

When Mengin arrived in England, he was interrogated by British intelligence . He claimed to have little knowledge of the membership of his organization. His handlers were very disappointed. They thought he was disorganized and not terribly smart. The British felt that they had been upstaged by the Americans. A British intelligence report concludes with the following terse comment: "Very little is known about [Mengin's] organization and few of the names of the people he has worked with have come to our notice . . . he was lacking the fire and energy usually associated with people engaged in clandestine and dangerous activities. Mengin's organization is undoubtedly an American-sponsored project."[36]

The final chapter in Mengin's story is worth retelling. After joining the Gaullist forces, he was promoted to captain in June 1943. Assigned as a liaison officer in 1944 to Allied troops retaking the English Channel ports following the Normandy invasion, he entered Calais with Canadian troops in late September. Mengin was hit by friendly fire and died on his way to a first-aid station. His exploits in Morocco have been forgotten, but in France, he is a hero. A street in the center of Calais is named for him. El Koubbi was sent by the US Army to Calais in 1945 to recover Mengin's personal effects. bringing the wartime relationship between the two men to full circle.

But there is more. We also have the testimony of Albert El Koubbi.

EL KOUBBI'S STORY. In a memoir written in the 1970s, Albert El Koubbi offers a personal view of the resistance movement in Morocco, written from the perspective of the refugee-turned-resistant. El Koubbi was an ideologically committed, physically resilient Jewish leftist who understood the complex social makeup of his group and the repertoire of beliefs that motivated people to join it. His story, filtered through memory, is an important document for re-creating the grand outlines as well as some of the more precise details about the Moroccan resistance.[37]

El Koubbi was born in 1904 into a Jewish family in Tlemcen, near the Morocco-Algeria border, and he spent his youth in Morocco. He loved soccer, but other personal facts are unknown. At some point, he and his family moved to Paris, where they were living when the war began. Educated and worldly, El Koubbi listed his occupation on a military form as "salesman." He was mobilized in France in September 1939, at the age of thirty-five, and was sent to the front with a work unit. After the Armistice, he rejoined his family in Paris, intending to go to England to join the Free French. But he had no luck getting across the channel and decided to leave instead for Morocco, where he heard his chances might be better. In December 1940, he arrived in Casablanca and befriended François Klotz, "my fighting comrade in the resistance," an Alsatian Jew who had also escaped from France. The two of them began building an anti-Vichy cell in Casablanca.

El Koubbi found work as a night clerk in the centrally located Hotel Majestic, where the busy bar was a magnet for gossip and intrigue. He kept his eyes and ears open and began passing information to Sheila Joan Clark, David King's associate at the US consulate. Smooth and gregarious, El Koubbi made friends among the military officers, journalists, and relief workers who showed up nightly at the hotel bar. At some point, he was introduced to Benatar, and he later described her as "the first woman to take a stand in July 1940." They began sharing information and contacts.[38]

El Koubbi and Klotz expanded their field of action, scouting out beaches in the environs of Casablanca for suitable places to launch landing craft. Through Henri Darrot, a French engineer, El Koubbi met Roger Mengin. Darrot also knew Robert Schumann; they often played tennis together on the private court of Raphael Benazeraf, a wealthy Casablancan Jewish businessman who was a member of Benatar's refugee committee. As the circle of like-minded activists widened, Schumann and Mengin decided to form a clandestine organization with specific objectives. The two were natural allies: both were ardent republicans, both had close relatives in London working for de Gaulle, both were graduates of *grands écoles*. Schumann was a Jew and Mengin was not, a fact that took on greater significance later on. Together, they began to plan how to take their network to the next level.

El Koubbi's contacts and local knowledge were vital to the expansion of the group. El Koubbi found employment as a bookkeeper at the busy publishing house of Fortin-Moullet in Casablanca. There he met Ermanno Colombo, a Swiss national, as well as a Moroccan Jewish couple named Benaim, and a Jewish refugee, Samuel Rosenberg, all of whom joined the nascent cell.[39] Using the printing plant as the center of their activities, they secretly began producing pamphlets supporting the Allied cause.

Printing and distributing propaganda was a quintessential resistance activity. It made a statement about a network's existence, and it was a means of disseminating alternative versions of the truth. The pamphlets secretly distributed from El Koubbi's publishing house carried pro-Allied war news that diverged sharply from the propaganda of Casablanca's right-leaning press. Roger Mengin wrote: "People are sick of hearing the same things from 'the big man' [i.e., Pétain] . . . they have a horror of speeches and want to hear precise facts."[40]

With the approval of Mengin, El Koubbi decided to reach beyond Casablanca for new recruits. While Mengin took the credit for enlarging the organization, it was El Koubbi who did the actual footwork. Mengin had credibility with French professionals, engineers, and officials in the military, while El Koubbi, who was fluent in Arabic and familiar with the local culture, was closer to ordinary people. Mengin inspired admiration, and El Koubbi inspired trust. El Koubbi accepted Mengin as his chief because of his links to high places, but he made sure that the organization attracted new recruits from all walks of life. Moreover, he understood the risks people were taking, especially his Jewish friends.[41]

El Koubbi and Klotz traveled to Marrakech in June 1942 to organize the local resistance and to prepare for the Allied landing. Their mission was derailed when El Koubbi and Klotz were arrested in Marrakech's main plaza while looking for a bus to return to Casablanca. The police knew all about their plans. The two men had been betrayed by a fellow worker at the printing plant.

The police put them into filthy cells, where they spent the night. The next day, June 22, they were handcuffed and driven to police headquarters in Casablanca, where other members of the Mengin group were already assembled, including Colombo, who had carelessly left in the printing plant a list of the people in their organization. Colombo was terrified he would crack under interrogation, according to El Koubbi. El Koubbi whispered to Colombo to lay all the blame on him. "For me," he wrote, "that was the rule of the game, the law of sacrifice."

So began El Koubbi's "long and sad ordeal." During fourteen days and nights, he was mercilessly tortured, mainly by a police inspector named Fiori, who applied electric shocks to his feet and his anus. According to El Koubbi, his tormentors called him "a dirty Jew" and shouted at him "France for the French." He shouted back, calling them "dirty Nazis." "I never gave up any information," El Koubbi declared, despite hammerlike blows to his body that caused a hernia, split eyebrows, a lacerated mouth that exposed his teeth beneath his lower lip, a broken thumb, and wrists permanently scarred by handcuffs. Finally, El Koubbi gave them the names of two men he knew had already fled Morocco. This "confession" allowed him to sign a deposition that ended the torture. He was then moved to a civilian hospital in Casablanca, where he spent the next four months recovering from his wounds. Neither El Koubbi nor any other member of the Mengin group participated in the Allied landings of November 1942.

François Klotz, like Mengin, died a hero's death. After he was released from jail by the Americans in November 1942, he joined the Free French in Tunisia. In June 1944 Klotz parachuted into southern France to help prepare for the Allied invasion of France from the south. He was captured and handed over to the Gestapo, and his body never recovered. That same month, Klotz's father, two sisters, and seven members of his immediate family were deported to Auschwitz. Klotz received the American Silver Star posthumously, as well as the French Croix de Guerre.

THE JEWISH ANGLE. From handwritten notes in her archive, we can re-construct something about Nelly Benatar's life in the Resistance. She reveals that it was a natural result of her involvement with escapees and their seeking a way out of Morocco. Benatar's entry into the Mengin group gave her access to British and American intelligence useful for "passing" people to the "other side"; at the same time, information gleaned from the escapees, newly arrived from the continent, could be important. Often the escape route began at 4, rue de Tunisie, in central Casablanca, where Benatar's refugee committee maintained a hostel for refugees.

Benatar's commitment to the resistance movement deepened as Vichy turned toward the violent persecution of Jews. In October 1940, a first set of anti-Jewish laws were promulgated in Morocco. The Vichy regime considered all Jews pro-American and a potential fifth column in the event of an Allied landing. A surprising number of people caught by the French police in the dragnet that followed the arrests of El Koubbi and Klotz were Jewish, leading the authorities to believe that they had uncovered a "Jewish" action. It is a wonder that Benatar escaped the dragnet, raising the question of who might have protected her.

The Vichy police thought that El Koubbi was the head of this organi-zation and did not discover Mengin until later: "We [the police] are not dealing here with patriots, but rather with a full-scale nest of Jews [une juiverie]. Those Frenchmen who are involved are for the most part leftists, nostalgic for the defunct [republican] regime," reads a police report. Of the chief culprit they wrote: "El Koubbi, even though he is a Jew, has a very strong personality and only said what he wanted to say. He did not reveal the heads of the movement, so we should not rejoice too much in this 'coup de filet' [catching this fish]; the ultra-American danger is not past." The sneer-ingly racist tone of the report specifies that El Koubbi and his associates were not brave defenders of a suffering France but a miserable pack of "Jews, leftists, and incompetents."[42]

When El Koubbi wrote about his experiences in the resistance, he expressed the belief that Jews had a special responsibility to join despite the danger, because they had a historical role to play. They had to stand up for decency and humanity, he declared, in order to demonstrate their right to defend those values. Through his exploits in the resistance, El Koubbi believed he was acting as a proud Jew, demonstrating his defiance to the humiliation of Vichy's race laws.[43]

El Koubbi's position was not universally appreciated. Even inside Mengin's heteroclite group, anti-Semitism had shown its ugly face. Mengin wrote:

> It would be impossible to pass over in silence the terrible influence that anti-Semitism exercises over the French mind in Morocco. A French person could be completely Anglophile and Americanophile, and still be anti-Semitic. For example, the head of our group before me [Schumann] was a person of inestimable value, with an advanced intelligence, masses of good will, and remarkable skills, but he was a Jew and doors closed in his face . . . I could name hundreds of our friends who would never have agreed to join a group directed by a Jew. Immediately after I took charge, our ranks tripled in size within a few days because I was not a Jew.[44]

How did members of the Mengin group respond to these barely disguised prejudices? Neither El Koubbi nor Benatar speak of them, perhaps out of a sense of solidarity with their non-Jewish comrades. After the war, when El Koubbi sought redress from the French government to receive the pension denied him, non-Jewish survivors of the Mengin group such as Ermanno Colombo stepped forward and demanded justice for him. Mengin's confession that anti-Semitism was rife within his organization adds yet another layer of complexity to the riddle of the resistance and how Jewish people like El Koubbi and Benatar imagined their role in it.

BENATAR'S PERSPECTIVE. We began with three photographs, the third a headshot of Benatar in military garb, her expression taut and attentive. This was the disciplined Benatar, her expression stern, her costume austere. Like many women who served during the war, she adopted some version of male dress to show her identification with archetypical male traits: dedication, courage, and stoicism in the face of death.

FIGURE 3.3 A wartime identity-card photo of Nelly Benatar, date uncertain.

There were very few women in the Moroccan resistance—El Koubbi mentions only three: Nelly Benatar, Sheila Jean Clark, and an unknown French woman, Madame Kerouedan. Women did not see themselves as resistance fighters, according to the historian Olivier Wieviorka, not in France and not in Morocco. When they joined the French underground, they usually stood on the sidelines and performed jobs like typing, running errands, and the like—tasks not recognized as a "true" acts of resistance.[45] Signing up with the underground for a woman was a transgressive act. Women were not supposed to be present at scenes of violence or caught up in police round-ups, or inserted into the shadowy world of espionage. The underground required stepping away from traditional female roles and showing a disdain for conformity.

Nelly Benatar was used to breaking the mold. As a lawyer, a male-dominated profession, and as a nurse, an unusual choice for a proper *bourgeoise*, she defied convention.[46] Had her husband been alive, he may have objected to her joining up, but he was not, nor was anyone else guiding her decisions. Perhaps, like her friend El Koubbi, she was motivated by a hatred of Vichy and everything it stood for, along with a sense of pride in her Jewishness. This may explain her single-minded participation in dangerous activities. During the entire period of Vichy rule in Morocco, between 1940 and late 1942, she ran the risk of being exposed and suffering the dire consequences.

For Benatar, for El Koubbi, for Klotz and Mengin, to resist was more than a confluence of interests; it was a declaration of personal values. Nelly Benatar's membership in the resistance opens another small window onto her inner life.

CHAPTER 4

1941

The Casablanca Connection

"THE PLACE WHERE EUROPE ENDS and the sea begins" is how the German Jewish writer Anna Seghers described Marseille, where she languished for weeks in early 1941 waiting to leave "a continent that was closing down." In her novel *Transit*, the male protagonist wanders aimlessly through the streets along with other dog-faced strays—from the post office to a consulate to a dingy café—consuming endless cups of ersatz coffee. The Marseille of her story is a repellant place, dirty, cold, rife with rumors, a repository of bewildered souls. The main thoroughfare, the Canebière, is a funnel through which "people from the camps, the displaced soldiers, the army mercenaries, the defilers of all races, the deserters of all nations," stream, finally ending at the sea, "where there would be at last room for all, and peace."[1]

Varian Fry (1907–1967) was an American journalist who arrived in Marseille in the summer of 1940 intent on helping refugees flee from a darkening continent. Working under the auspices of the New York–based Emergency Rescue Committee (ERC), Fry helped many hundreds of refugees escape from Europe.[2] His list reads like a who's-who of European cultural icons: Marc Chagall, Max Ernst, Lion Feuchtwanger, André Breton, Hannah Arendt, and Franz Werfel and his wife, Alma Mahler Gropius Werfel, who crossed the Pyrenees carrying an original score of Bruckner's *Third Symphony* in her suitcase.[3] Fry kept his operation running for more than a year, until he was shut down by the combined pressure of Vichy, the Gestapo, and the US

State Department.[4] After returning to the United States in 1941, he was placed under surveillance by the Federal Bureau of Investigation and spent the rest of his life in the shadow of disgrace. It took years after his death for his name to be cleared and his contributions finally recognized. He was the first among five Americans to be posthumously recognized by the State of Israel in 1996 as one of the "Righteous among the Nations," an honorific awarded to non-Jews who risked their lives to help Jews during the Holocaust.[5]

Fry was his own best publicist. His book, *Surrender on Demand*, tells the story of his short career with the ERC. Much about it resembles the work of Nelly Benatar, who also walked a fine line between legal and illegal activities, collaborated with Vichy officials when necessary, undertook dangerous missions and visited refugee camps. She, too, was a travel agent, booking passages, arranging berths, providing shelter and pocket money, chasing down visas, and relying on friends and the charity of others. And like Fry, she found herself physically threatened because of her work. Missing from her profile, however, is recognition of her deeds at the level of formalized rituals of memorialization. Fry has become a celebrated hero; Benatar is hardly known.

In 1941, Nelly Benatar and Varian Fry worked together. Their link was forged because of an abrupt change in escape routes from Europe. Suddenly, and for no apparent reason, in January 1941, Vichy decided to be more generous in issuing visas, and once again hopeful emigrants could exit France.[6] Representatives of international relief agencies flocked to Marseille, the last functioning French port for the transatlantic route. The American Friends Service Committee, or AFSC, known as "the Quakers," Varian Fry's Centre Américain de Secours, and the European Jewish emigration service HICEM all set up offices in the city. Each organization had its own methods and clients: the AFSC concentrated on political refugees, Fry's clients were cultural and scientific luminaries, HICEM took care of Jews.

HICEM was by far in the most important agency because of its size, handling 35,000 cases per year, as opposed to 1,500 for the AFSC and less than that for Varian Fry. HICEM claimed the status of "official" agency for Jewish emigration, and so it was regarded by the other players. The name was an acronym composed of the names of several different agencies that had joined together to facilitate Jewish emigration from Europe after Hitler's rise to power. Its main office was in Paris, and there were branch offices established in thirty-two other countries. When the German Jewish exodus began, migrants found a HICEM representative to whom they could turn for assistance in almost every country where they landed. Big American Jewish organizations such as the JDC worked closely with HICEM, knowing that it had the most accurate information on all aspects of emigration. When refugees were unable to pay the costs of emigration, HICEM, through its cooperating donor agencies, was usually able to provide the necessary funds. Careful to maintain a legal countenance, HICEM rescued Jews while operating under the ruse of helping Vichy to "rid itself" of its "least desirable" elements. The arrangement worked, with reservations: Vichy bureaucrats helped to smooth emigration procedures while dropping racial slurs that tested one's patience and composure. In the years 1940–1945, Nelly Benatar developed a close working relationship with HICEM's representatives in the western Mediterranean region.[7]

Presiding over the Marseille office of HICEM was a Russian Jew named Raphael Spanien. A heavy-set man with flowing mustachios, Spanien was a presence that some thought overbearing. Big, loud, and bossy, he fit the stereotype of the "uncultured" Jew. Sophie Freud, trapped with her mother in Marseille, took a special disliking to him. Eighteen years old and already entitled, the granddaughter of the inventor of the Id was unsparing: "This Spaniel [sic] . . . is full of himself, Mr. Big Shot. Everyone hates him because he has offended everyone in some way."[8] But for Nelly Benatar, Raphael Spanien was a larger-than-life personality with a no-nonsense approach to getting people out. In 1941, Benatar and Spanien began a productive relationship that lasted more than a year and resulted in the transmigration of many hundreds of stranded refugees from Europe to the New World.

Spanien's priority was to find escape routes out of Europe, both legal and illegal, for his clients. It was an ongoing project, since safe routes came and went with shifts in Vichy's moods and the gyrations of international politics. The usual routes were overland through Spain to Lisbon, but the Spanish border could open and close without warning. Furthermore, Franco's Spain was off-limits to veterans of the International Brigades, socialists, communists, and Spanish republicans. So long as Spain was the only pass-through, exit from Europe would be limited and extremely dangerous.

The new route from Marseille to the French West Indies that opened early in 1941 had a direct impact on emigration from the western Mediterranean. Now ships departing Marseille, especially those chartered by HICEM, could travel directly from the French port to Martinique. Furthermore, they had the option of stopping at Casablanca to pick up additional passengers and often did. The trickle of migrants escaping France by sea became a flood, as Marseille turned into a transit camp for refugees awaiting ships that left every four or five days.[9] Blocs of berths on the Martinique-bound vessels were bought up in advance by HICEM and paid for with funds provided by the JDC. Once ships reached Martinique, those passengers with ongoing visas would head south to Latin American countries or north to the United States. The "Casablanca route" offered several advantages: it avoided Gibraltar, which was closely watched by the British; it was safe for refugees who could not transit Spain; it allowed boats to stop in Casablanca to take on additional passengers, and because of HICEM's patronage, it was the preferred route for Jewish emigration.[10]

Benatar's interest in refugees was diversifying and deepening, as the politics of transmigration became a matter of high concern within the Vichy administration. Along with her involvement with Jewish refugees, Benatar was also helping Spanish republican parliamentarians and other stranded political figures who were coming under increasing pressure from Vichy. The Spanish political exiles posed a whole new set of problems for Benatar, testing her legal skills, raising her profile as an advocate for refugee rights, and extending her reach into the upper echelons of the Protectorate's governing hierarchy. The story of Spanish republican politician Alonso Major demonstrates some of these developments.

Alonso Major, former governor of Seville and Granada, was among the many high level officials who fled Spain for Moroccan safety following the republican defeat of 1938. In 1941, a crackdown on Spanish refugees by Vichy-controlled police landed him in jail. The threat of extradition back to Spain, where he faced certain imprisonment and perhaps even death, hung over him. Major heard about lawyer Nelly Benatar and appealed to her for help. Benatar was not familiar with the facts of Major's situation, but she was perturbed by what she considered the illegality of imprisoning political refugees. She decided to take her case directly to Resident-General Noguès. The introduction to Noguès most likely came through his wife, Suzanne Delcassé-Noguès, who met Benatar through their mutual involvement in refugee work. The two women became friends.[11] The daughter of Théophilé Delcassé, one of republican France's most distinguished elder statesmen, Madame Noguès was at home in the political arena and was said to have considerable influence over her husband, often serving as an informal adviser. Resident-General Noguès and Nelly Benatar met face-to-face for the first time at the end of January 1941.

Benatar's agenda with Noguès was to discuss the matter of the hundreds of Spanish political refugees in Morocco being harassed by Vichy. Her objective was to gain his support for the renewal of a decree dating from 1928 banning the extradition of political exiles. We know about their conversation not from her archive, but from another authoritative source: the official court transcript of Benatar's testimony at Noguès's trial for treason in 1956.[12] Accused of "national indignity" for his alleged collaboration with the Vichy regime during the war, General Noguès was found guilty in 1947. At a second trial in Paris in October 1956, Noguès was hoping to clear his name. Again at the insistence of Mme. Noguès, Nelly Benatar was summoned from Casablanca to Paris to testify on General Noguès's behalf. Here is her testimony about her first meeting with the head of the Protectorate regime:

> I was in contact with Général Noguès in 1940. At the time I was President of the Committee of Assistance to Refugees. This committee took care of all the refugees who transited Morocco, regardless of their nationality or religion. In 1940, there were many demands for the extradition [of political refugees]. I was asked to defend Alonso Major, former governor of Seville and Granada being held in a prison in Casablanca as a common criminal, when in fact he was a political refugee. I met with Noguès and asked him to promulgate a *dahir* [decree] preventing the extradition of refugees. I became rather heated during our conversation, explaining all the reasons why the Spanish parliamentarians who had sought refuge in Morocco [should not be] subject to extradition. The Resident-General answered me as follows: "You can leave in peace, Maître, you will have your law and you will be able to defend your clients." The *dahir*, promulgated on March 7, 1941, in the *Bulletin Officiel* saved many thousands of lives.[13]

Benatar's approach to Noguès and her vigorous advocacy for the Spanish refugees introduces a new dimension to her wartime persona. Given the mounting vitriol in France against Spanish political exiles, her démarche was a courageous one—a rebuff to Vichy carried out in the public eye, complementing her secret work with the resistance. In March 1941, an official decree banning the extradition of political refugees was published in the *Bulletin Officiel*. It was signed by the sultan, but the hand of Noguès was clearly behind it.

Why did Noguès respond so quickly to Benatar's request? Rumors were flying in Morocco that Noguès had fallen out of favor with Vichy and that his grip on power was loosening. The promulgation of the anti-extradition decree was a bold demonstration that he was still in charge and capable of managing Morocco's severe refugee problem. As for Benatar, although her role was less public, her motives were even more transparent. The question of refugee rights was her constant preoccupation. Renewing the legal barrier to extradition was a clear statement of her intention to protect refugees from Vichy's abuses, regardless of the provenance or religion of her clients. It was a victory for both Benatar and Noguès, and it strengthened the bond between them.

Benatar's closeness to the Residency was critical for carrying out her refugee work with any degree of success. They were strange bedfellows—Nelly Benatar, HICEM's Raphael Spanien, and General Noguès—cooperating to keep the tide of humanity moving forward. As the refugee volume increased, it was only a matter of time before forces opposed to its unimpeded flow would try to stop it.

The relentless Nazi war machine began to envelop Nelly Benatar in a very personal way. The trouble began in February 1941, when Roosevelt's special envoy, Robert Murphy, signed an agreement with General Maxime Weygand, Vichy's top military man in North Africa, allowing the United States to send nonmilitary goods to the local civilian population to relieve critical shortages. In the Germans' eyes, the Murphy-Weygand agreement upset the political balance in the region by giving the Americans—who were not yet at war but were suspected of strong pro-British sentiments—a decided advantage.[14]

The German Armistice Commission, created in the wake of the 1940 Franco-German Armistice, was supposed to oversee the situation on the ground in Morocco. Its assignment was to check on military supplies, keep track of economic resources, and generally discourage anti-German activities. Initially, the size of the commission was quite small. But as the months went on, and over Resident-General Noguès's objections, its numbers grew. In March 1941 there were 62 Germans in Casablanca; by April, 140 additional inspectors had arrived, and in June, the commission numbered 204 Nazi operatives. Unleashed and roving at will, they seemed to be everywhere. Casablancans got used to seeing smartly dressed German officers strolling on the avenues and relaxing in cafés, taking in the passing scene.

Noguès feared that the sight of so many Germans would undermine French authority. Already rumors circulated about pro-Axis sentiment among the working classes. Police reports claimed "that the majority of Muslims of Casablanca admire Germany."[15] Noguès forbade anyone on his staff to meet with Theodore Auer, the recently arrived head of the German Armistice Commission, much less socialize with him. Noguès wanted to keep the Germans isolated, "as if in a glass house," but that proved to be impossible. Soon they were appearing everywhere, in Rabat, Fez, Marrakech, and even in Fedala, a coastal town near Casablanca.[16]

A pompous gadfly who spoke excellent French and English, Auer began making the diplomatic rounds. He launched his campaign with a note to Robert Murphy, reminding the American envoy of their meeting in Paris before the war, and inviting him to a "rendezvous."[17] Cora Goold, wife of the US consul general Herbert Goold, crossed paths with Auer at dinner parties and felt he was a threat. She believed that Auer had taken a special dislike to her husband because of Goold's openly pro-British sympathies at a time when US policy was one of strict neutrality. By Goold's own account, he took a strong interest in shipping and he may have been among those people who were supplying information on sea traffic to the nascent Moroccan resistance movement. Auer was reportedly telling people that "Goold must go."

No surprise when Goold was relieved of his duties in early 1941. Cora believed it was Auer who was behind her husband's recall, and her suspicions were not unfounded. A letter in Goold's State Department personnel file indicates that Resident-General Noguès was under pressure to get rid of the irksome American diplomat. Noguès wrote to Vichy that Goold "facilitated pro-British propaganda" and aided "certain agents, exceeding the terms of his mission." Word about Goold's "indiscretions" was passed to Murphy, who was worried about maintaining a strict American neutrality, and Goold's fate was sealed.[18]

Buoyed by this success, Auer continued to cast his nets widely, poking everywhere for signs of anti-Axis sentiment. He did not have to go far. Small fish were as good as big ones, and in no time at all, he was trolling for Nelly Benatar. He complained to French police that a "campaign" against him was centered on Benatar's refugee committee.[19] On April 23, the ax fell. Benatar became the target of a coordinated attack by Nazi officials and Vichy bureaucrats to put her out of business. Her office was ordered closed, and the authorities demanded a list of the names and addresses of all her refugee clients, by then numbering in the thousands. She refused to hand it over, declaring that she had none. To round out her troubles, she was told by Poussier, the new *contrôleur civil* and a confirmed Vichyite, that her committee had to be dissolved because it was "opposed to state security." Ordering her to "cease all activities," he threatened her with deportation to Bou Denib, a notorious Saharan detention camp, if she did not comply.[20]

Stripped of her official status, Benatar decided to continue operations under cover. She could no longer raise money openly because of the ban, but a small monthly stipend from the JDC kept her going. In spite of her precautions, her law office was repeatedly broken into and searched by French police accompanied by Gestapo agents in civilian garb. Luckily, these searches yielded nothing, as all compromising papers, lists, records, and notes in her archive were hidden behind a false wall or had been destroyed.[21]

Benatar was intimidated, but she was not about to give up. She decided to use her access to Noguès to again ask for his help. Her first concern was not for herself, but for her refugees: "Having nothing to lose, I decided to appeal to the Resident-General and tell him, these people have to depart from Morocco quickly, because lists authorizing their deportation [back to Europe] have been prepared by the [German] Armistice Commission."[22] On June 24, Benatar met with Noguès a second time to discuss matters of a "personal nature." Her real intentions, however, concerned a démarche on behalf of refugees. Hundreds of transients were sitting on ships being held up in Casablanca port, waiting permission to move. Presenting herself as the local representative of HICEM, she told Noguès about all the services she could provide—creating emigration dossiers, obtaining visas, booking onward travel, making arrangements with shipping companies, transferring payments from HICEM—that no one else could offer. She pointed out the importance of working at top speed because visas would expire, leaving the transients permanently stranded in Morocco.

Noguès's response once again was to reassure her that she could continue her work—under his protection. "You should go," he said; "if you have any trouble, do not go to Casablanca [i.e., to the *contrôleur civil*] or to the Office of

Political Affairs, but come directly to me." Two days later she was summoned to the office of Colonel Herviot, director of public security, who handed her his personal calling card, giving her authorization to restart her committee.

Armed with the guarantee from the influential Herviot, Benatar started anew. Finding a new office was her first order of business. Her brother-in-law, Raphael Benatar, offered her space in a half-finished building he owned in the city center. This address became "refugee central" when both HICEM and the JDC also moved their offices into the building. Soon its rough cement courtyard became a waiting room filled with refugees looking for assistance. Under the new regime, the title Committee for Assistance to Refugees was also banned, so Benatar had to hang out a new sign, "Hélène Benatar— Refugees." She also hired more people: Marguerite Fux, an ex-Austrian, and Ernest Baden, a young, multilingual dentist from Berlin, joined her staff. The endorsement of the lawyer Moretti, the head (*batonnier*) of the Casablanca bar, offered yet another layer of protection.[23]

Benatar was back in business. Her personal connection with Noguès had given her the defensive shield needed to carry on, empowering her to move with discretion among disparate factions, including refugees, local Jewish groups, international organizations like HICEM, and French officials ranging from devout Pétainists to closet Gaullists. Just as this was happening, a sudden halt in the flow of traffic on the Casablanca route became a crisis of international proportions.[24]

Refugee ships began piling up in Casablanca's port in mid-1941, creating a fresh emergency. The Marseille-Martinique route had transformed migration patterns, but it also had led to confusion and dire mistakes, bringing it to a sudden halt. One problem was that ships used on this route were old freighters unequipped to carry hundreds of passengers. Henry Blumenfeld, a precocious teenager from Paris, remembered the *Monte Viso*, the ship that carried him and his family out of Marseille, as "not a luxury liner . . . but closer to Conrad," a reference to the dilapidated steamboat made famous by Joseph Conrad's *Heart of Darkness*.[25] Accommodations were basic: a narrow bed in a cargo hold designed to transport packing crates, not people. Crews were composed of rough deckhands, unprepared to deal with crowds of overwrought and frightened European Jews in flight. When the passage went according to plan, it was tolerable, but when something went wrong, it turned into a living hell.

FIGURE 4.1 Passengers aboard the SS *Monte Viso* departing Marseille for Martinique on the "Casablanca Route," May 1941.

In late January, the *Alsina*, en route from Marseille to Buenos Aires and carrying almost seven hundred refugees, was detained for four months in Dakar because of the British blockade. The boat was finally rerouted back to Casablanca. Two other aging ships, the *Monte Viso* and the *Wyoming*, which departed in May 1941 on the Marseille-Martinique route with a total of 676 refugees aboard, were halted in the open sea by French and German submarines and turned back to Casablanca. By mid-June, all three ships were languishing in the port of Casablanca. After days of waiting, 1,200 refugees were herded onto trucks and closed railroad cars and transferred to internment camps in the interior of Morocco. Four hundred and fifty people from the *Wyoming* were sent to the camps at Oued Zem and Sidi El Ayachi. Among them were sixty clients of Varian Fry.[26] Some passengers carried documents that raised the suspicions of port officials and were sent to "forced residence" in even more remote settings, far beyond the reach of diplomatic or humanitarian help.

Treated as though they were illegal aliens, the incarcerated foreigners sent up howls of protest and began sending scores of telegrams to New York, Lisbon, and Marseille, looking for an exit from their misery. In mid-June, Varian Fry wrote directly to Vichy, demanding that his people be considered "travelers in transit" and be brought back to Casablanca, where they could meet with consular representatives to plan their ongoing travel. But the Vichy police were adamantly opposed to releasing them. The Americans were not much better. The US consulate in Casablanca declared that refugees with relatives in Nazi-occupied countries would not be allowed to renew their American visas, which meant that about 90 percent of those passengers held in detention would not be leaving Morocco anytime soon. Officials at Vichy raised the temperature even more by denouncing the influx of "the Hebrew element" into Morocco, where "anti-Semitism is always ready to take on a violent form."[27]

For Nelly Benatar, the sudden wave of displaced people arriving on her doorstep presented a windfall of opportunity.[28] As the sense of panic mounted, Benatar got a nod from the Noguès administration to swing into action. She made lists of the refugees brought ashore and the dates of their visa expirations; she contacted shipping lines; she set up access to their bank accounts to finance their onward journey. "Independent of this work, I have to obtain American visas, Portuguese visas, Spanish transit visas, exit visas, and to avoid as much as possible the expiration of one kind of visa and the delivery of another. . . . This is long and delicate work for which a special office and necessary staff are needed," she wrote.[29] Benatar became a one-person emigration agency, determined to solve the problem of the interrupted voyages.

At the top of her list were Varian Fry's protégés, some of whom found themselves penniless in a strange land. Fritz Rogge, a German movie actor, and Benjamin (Victor) Peret, a poet and companion of Remedios Varo, a surrealist painter and friend of André Breton—celebrities rescued by Fry now locked up in Morocco—were completely out of money. Working in cooperation with the Fry organization in Marseille, Benatar set up the "Compte Amercour" that allowed her to receive funds already sent to Martinique, redistributing them to Fry's destitute clients. With Benatar's prodding, Casablanca's Jews also rallied to assist the stranded luminaries, raising 210,000 francs in a matter of days—more than $4,000—to tide them over.[30]

Within this crowd of transients, some people stood out. Not simply "refugees," but refugees *in Morocco*. Three refugee accounts from that summer of 1941 reveal how different each of their stories was, yet how a series of disasters created a semblance among them—the escape from Marseille, the interrupted passage, the miseries of the internment camp, their eventual return to freedom.

Erwin Blumenfeld was born in Berlin in 1897. During World War I, he served in the German army as an ambulance driver and became familiar with death. After the war, he befriended Dadaist artists in Paris and, through the medium of photography, won attention as a high-end fashion photographer until the war interrupted his career. Interned in various French camps, he, his wife, and their three children left Marseille aboard the *Monte Viso* in May, bound for Martinique. Detained for three months at Camp Sidi El Ayachi, thanks to the combined efforts of HICEM, the JDC, and Nelly Benatar, they left Casablanca in August aboard the SS *Nyassa*, headed to New York City. Here is Erwin's story:

> The rickety freighter *Monte Viso* had cabins for twelve passengers at most. Four hundred and forty migrants were crammed into two holds of this death ship. A floating Vernet. Bow: *Hommes*. Stern: *Femmes*. We were not even out of the harbor of Marseille, safe from Hitler's clutches, when an unholy battle broke out between the eastern Jews ("the filthy Pollacks") and the German Jews ("the

filthy assimilated Jews"). Only the vigorous intervention of the crew—the boat was manned by jungle gorillas—prevented them all from throwing each other overboard.

We went, much too quickly, past Oran, through the Straits of Gibraltar and along the coast of Africa to Casablanca, where no one was allowed on land: quarantine. An order from Hitler via Vichy. For weeks they left us to fry like eggs on the red-hot iron ship in the boiling harbor during which, as in the concentration camp, the social classes crystallized into different layers. As the heat increased daily, both the people and food became increasingly odious [and] the shits increased. . . . The water stank, you could hardly even wash in it. The captain did not deign to speak a single word to any one of us. . . .

On June 22 . . . the *Monte Viso* steamed out of Casablanca with an escort of French torpedo boats, heading for America. Passengers sobbed and embraced—SAVED! I didn't feel like spending the night in the boiling hot cargo hold so I stayed up on deck, hoping to see the Southern Cross at last. What I did see at midnight, to my horror, was the Pole Star doing a 180 degree turn. We were going back! . . . The next morning the *Monte Viso* once more lay at anchor in the very same spot in the hell of Casablanca harbor. A few days later the *Alsina* . . . anchored alongside us.

. . . [On July 1] the order came to move us . . . to Moroccan concentration camps . . . people with small children [went] to [Sidi El Ayachi]. Amid the scorching sirocco heat of the desert . . . behind barbed wire, in miserable mud huts, plagued by stable-flies and watched over by Senegalese guards (much more human than the *gardes mobiles* in Vernet) we groaned as if our end was nigh . . .

When, however, we had overcome the initial shock, . . . Sidi turned out to be almost a romantic idyll. . . . The camp commandant, another German ex–foreign legionnaire, invited me to drink peppermint tea in his harem. . . . The guards could not read, but they were happy to accept a Paris metro ticket as a *laisser-passer* . . . [and] opened the gate to fairyland.

On a black rock high above the chocolate-brown river we discovered Azemmour, a gleaming white dream-town straight out of the *Arabian Nights* with caliphs, storks, veiled houris, dervishes, and miracle rabbis. We ran through cactus groves where camels, with their young beside them, walked around in circles turning idyllic water-mills, then through gentle green dunes to the warm ocean. While we were swimming, Arab boys ran off with our last pair of shoes.[31]

Erwin's son, Henry, offered his own version of his family's Moroccan "idyll":

> One afternoon I walked with Perf [his father] to Azemmour. We looked a bit around the casbah and then we came upon a mysterious cave, full of glittering phylacteries and colorful embroidery in dim candlelight, which was a Jewish shrine to a great medieval rabbi. . . . Most people in the camp were suffering from some disease or other. Maman had a big abscess on her chest, which was treated with one of the new sulfa drugs, but finally had to be punctured and drained. Lisette [his older sister] had bleeding gums from vitamin C deficiency, and Yorick [his younger brother] had a fluctuating temperature with plateaus, which was diagnosed as being typical of typhus fever. I was in relatively good shape. . . . The only edible food was watermelons.[32]

Lilli Joseph was born in Berlin in 1922. Her father, Walter Joseph, was a well-known impresario who wrote musical scores for German cinema. He knew Marlene Dietrich and worked on *The Blue Angel*. Her parents' friends were

FIGURE 4.2 Blumenfeld family with friends at the Sidi El Ayachi
internment camp, Azemmour, Morocco, summer 1941.

FIGURE 4.3 Refugee children guarded by Moroccan soldiers, Sidi El Ayachi internment camp, Azemmour, Morocco, summer 1941.

mostly show business people and musicians. In 1933, after the rise of Hitler, they fled to Paris, where her father earned a living playing the piano in a Parisian nightclub. Lilli attended a private high school, learned French, and created her own jazz club. During the exodus from Paris in June 1940, her family was separated; she and her mother were sent to the internment camp at Gurs, and her father went into hiding. By sheer luck, they were reunited and acquired entry visas to the United States. They boarded the *Wyoming* in Marseille, headed for Martinique, but the ship was turned back to Casablanca. Loaded onto a sealed train with eight hundred others, the Joseph family arrived at Oued Zem, a deserted Foreign Legion post hastily prepared for their arrival. Retelling her story seventy years later, Lilli's voice still shook with emotion:

> We were taken to an Arab camp by Senegalese soldiers who made us stand outside in the sun in a line, it was 140 degrees. The barracks had tin roofs that never cooled off; there were rats everywhere, with Arabs living among us in the barracks, with men and women mixed together. Disastrous!
>
> We did not know where we were. They did not take away our passports or visas—they ignored them. Men and women died of malaria . . . Slowly people

disappeared, our number fell from eight hundred to six hundred. In the front were French, but in the back, the Germans were pulling the strings. I said to myself, 'I am going to make it!' I did not give up, there was nothing to eat, I contracted amoebic dysentery.

I worked at the camp hospital, full of syphilitic Arabs . . . I brought them tea. One day a French officer came in, thumping his leg with his stick. He said, would you help me with something? For this, every so often he gave me a piece of cheese. I asked him, would he allow me to send telegrams to the outside world? . . . We sent telegrams to France and the U.S.A., The HIAS [HICEM] went into action and got the JDC to hire the boat *Guiné*. . . . Our family in America paid $2,700 for our tickets. We were stopped in Bermuda by the British. They took away our few remaining family photos. They finally let us go and we landed on Ellis Island on August 26, 1941.

Even when deathly sick, Lilli was always "extremely optimistic." "Life has to be lived. I had some experiences with French soldiers, lieutenants, I felt, I'm seventeen, I may never have a chance. They were very nice . . . absolutely very loving." When she arrived in New York, she found a job as a cashier in a Manhattan restaurant, bought a fur coat, and earned a business degree from New York University. Lilli, a successful entrepreneur, lives in Palm Springs, California, where she is a leading patron of the arts.[33]

Hans Cahnmann was born in Munich in 1906. His father was a factory owner and his mother a housewife, and Hans had five siblings. At university, he studied biochemistry and pharmacy. With the rise of Hitler, he moved to Paris and worked for a pharmaceutical company until 1940, when he was interned. Through word of mouth, he learned about the Casablanca route ("Rumors, you live on rumors when you are a refugee!") and escaped, heading to Marseille, where he stayed "in a lousy hotel full of bedbugs." Meanwhile, he contacted Varian Fry, "a wonderful man, very helpful," who gave him pocket money and helped him to get an "emergency" visa to the United States reserved for scientists. After paying "a lot of money," he secured a berth on the *Wyoming*. When the ship arrived in Casablanca, Hans, like Lilli Joseph, was transferred to Oued Zem:

The conditions were terrible, we had to clean the toilets. Men, women and children were separated according to barracks, and we saw that we would stay a while . . . I opened a little water stand. From time to time, we went into the town: It was very interesting. It was half Jewish, half Arab—[Jews wore] black and [Arabs wore] white. The Jewish community said prayers for us and put on a concert for people from the camp . . . I talked to people in the market, they were primitive, simple Jews. I was never invited to the home of a well-to-do Jew . . . after two months, the HIAS [HICEM] organization sent a small boat to pick up passengers with a paid ticket . . . Beautiful sea. Dolphins jumping. We enjoyed it. We told jokes. A nice voyage. We arrived in Staten Island on August 6, 1941.

Hans worked as a scientist at the National Institutes of Health. His father died before the war; his mother died in Auschwitz. His siblings live in the United States and Israel.[34]

For the majority of refugees stranded in Morocco in 1941, the interlude did not last long. Most of those detained in the spring left by the end of the year on one of three ships, the SS *Guiné*, the SS *Nyassa*, and the SS *Serpa Pinto*, all sailing under the Portuguese flag. In August 1941, a press release from the JDC trumpeted news of the arrival of the *Guiné* in New York, highlighting the JDC's role in rescue:

> Two hundred refugees from Nazism rescued through the efforts of the American Jewish Joint Distribution Committee, will arrive aboard the *SS Guiné* which docks this morning at Pier 8, Staten Island, after a fifteen-day voyage from Casablanca, Morocco. The Joint Distribution Committee arranged to have the *Guiné* stop at Casablanca. The J.D.C. is the major American agency for rescue, relief and rehabilitation of distressed Jewish populations overseas. These refugees had faced the prospect of being stranded indefinitely until the J.D.C. came to their rescue. Another 200 are scheduled to arrive soon aboard the *SS Nyassa* which, also at the instance of the J.D.C., called at Casablanca.[35]

The JDC press release failed to mention that the success of the Casablanca route was the result of coordinated effort among European, Moroccan, and American aid organizations. The HICEM representative Raphael Spanien arrived in Casablanca in May and worked day and night with Benatar to move people out of the detention camps and onto ships chartered by the JDC. Spanien, unlike the JDC, acknowledged that Benatar's help was crucial to the operation: "Madame Benatar, in complete agreement with us, organized the housing of those in transit, in addition to taking charge of refugees remaining in Morocco to whom she distributed financial aid." The admiration was mutual. Benatar remembered Spanien in her archive: "We must not forget the name of Raphael Spanien, representative of the HIAS [HICEM] who came to Morocco and confronted great dangers with courage."[36]

Seven more convoys transited Casablanca in the final months of 1941, even though conditions were becoming progressively more difficult. Between May and December, the JDC, Benatar, and HICEM brought more than seven thousand refugees to safety. Fluctuations in Vichy's mood, coupled with the American declaration of war against the Axis in December, complicated matters. French officials working under German scrutiny tightened surveillance of all refugees transiting Casablanca. Yet throughout this turmoil, the "Casablanca route" remained open.

A new and bleaker reality enveloped Moroccan Jewry in 1941 that penetrated into the pores of daily life. In France, the Vichy regime steadily increased restrictions on its Jewish population, reducing their rights and feeding an already-virulent anti-Semitism. In Morocco, Resident-General Noguès was determined to hold onto his authority over Jewish affairs without directly challenging his superiors in Vichy. The Moroccan sultan, though lacking any real political power, was anxious to preserve his considerable moral authority as "protector" of the Jews. On the periphery of this struggle were Moroccan Jews, watching with trepidation as each of the main actors considered how "the Jewish question" might play out in its favor.

Vichy's anti-Jewish legislation (*Statut des juifs*) came to Morocco in stages. In October, 1940, the first anti-Jewish decree was promulgated in France, excluding Jews from the civil service, the judiciary, and influential positions in cultural life. A few days later, it was signed into law by the sultan in Morocco. More racial decrees followed in 1941, establishing strict quotas for Jews in the liberal professions, including medicine and law.

The psychological impact of these decrees on the professional classes was calamitous. Some Jews panicked, pleading to be excused and claiming that they were "apolitical" and "distant from the exercise of power," while others appealed for special exemptions based on ancestry or service to the state. But it was impossible to halt the forward momentum of the discriminatory laws, especially after Xavier Vallat, head of the Vichy's newly created General Commission for Jewish Questions was given the mandate to enforce them. Restrictions that a few months earlier had been unthinkable were by then guidelines for everyday life. An upsurge in anti-Semitic speech in the press,

FIGURE 4.4 On board the SS Serpa Pinto, departing Casablanca
for the United States, 1941.

on the street, and in other public places caught Moroccan Jews by surprise and deepened their despair.[37] On August 5, 1941, a census of all Jews, native and foreign, and a list of their property was carried out under orders from Vichy. The census was understood as a first step toward banishing Jews from active involvement in economic life.

Two weeks later, Vallat arrived in Morocco on an official tour of inspection, with the intention of studying "a certain number of delicate problems raised by the Jewish statute." But his real purpose was to exercise his personal control over the "Jewish problem" in France's North African dependencies. Before his arrival, Vallat made it clear that the new statutes were part of a state-supported ideology promoting hierarchies of "racial purity." Perhaps he did not realize that in Morocco, the statutes countered the long-standing principle of indigeneity that supposedly maintained a balance of strict equality between Jews and Muslims. Nevertheless, he forged ahead. Following an official audience with the sultan, Vallat went to Fez, home to Morocco's most revered rabbis and the seat of Moroccan Jewish learning. The war-injured Vallat walked the cobbled streets of the Fez mellah on foot, leaning heavily on his cane. He was followed by a large and noisy retinue of local Jews, baffled by the reason for his visit, not knowing whether to be flattered or afraid. At the main gate to the mellah, Vallat was met by a delegation of the grand rabbis of Fez who welcomed him respectfully and humbly promised "never to became mixed up in French politics." At the end of the day, despite the courtesies, no Jew felt reassured; on the contrary, Vallat's visit underscored Vichy's dire intentions.

When Vallat left Morocco the next day, everyone was glad to see him go. Noguès understood that the visit was meant to shore up Vallat's position as the vicar of all things Jewish, demonstrating that his authority reached into the heart of the empire. Shortly thereafter, Vichy asked the Residency to pay for a permanent representative of the General Commission for Jewish Questions in Morocco, but Noguès flatly refused, leaving the day-to-day management of Jewish affairs firmly in the hands of the Residency. Vallat may have been spurned, but the anti-Jewish laws still went into effect.[38]

The new decrees made a direct hit on the Benatar household.[39] Nelly Benatar was in a vulnerable position; she petitioned by letter for an exemption, arguing that because of her work with refugees, she should be excused. Noguès wrote a marginal note on her letter in support of her appeal, but the request was denied at Vichy and Benatar was promptly disbarred. The name "Cazes Benatar," along with twenty-five other Casablancans, appears on a list prohibiting them from practicing law because they were Jews.[40]

The final blow for Benatar was the requisitioning of the headquarters of AIU Graduates' Association on rue Lacépède. This was the "house" that she and Moyses built—the setting for their boldest ideas and aspirations. She felt that she was being specifically targeted for punishment. It is possible that the harassment was increasing not only because of her refugee work but also due to suspicions about the clandestine activities that went with it. It was rumored that her name was high on the list of people that the Reich's consul general Auer wanted "eliminated."

Benatar's response to the cumulative blows of 1941 was to build around herself a protective barrier of supportive relationships. She began by reinforcing her ties to the world beyond Morocco—to the JDC and to HICEM, and to a widening circle of international philanthropic agencies. Most important, however, was her connection with Noguès and the Residency.

Benatar aligned herself with the Residency through the avenue of refugee relief. This alliance had its dangers as well as its benefits. Noguès represented the French state—a state embodied by Vichy, whose animosity toward Jews was unequivocal. Benatar knew that collaboration with a fascist regime and its philosophy of top-down rule required a strict obedience to authority. However, she also knew that in Morocco, things worked differently—not so much through brute force, but rather through carefully negotiated relations of loyalty and reciprocity. This meant the pursuit of mutually beneficial bonds up and down the ladder of exchanges, at all levels of interaction. Understanding the exercise of power in Morocco and how to navigate it came naturally to her. She calculated that relying on Noguès was still her best chance for survival.[41]

Noguès was not always an easy man to follow. He was subtle in his thinking and variable in his decision making. Obedient to Vichy on most matters, he was highly unpredictable in others. Noguès's first loyalty was to the safety and prosperity of French Morocco and to the longevity of the colonial order that he and his predecessors had so painstakingly built. He surrounded himself with a "brain trust" of senior colleagues who shared his philosophy of rule. Surrounded by "his" people, Noguès was ready to act independently, even when his judgment differed from his distant *chefs* in the metropole.

Noguès chose his battles carefully. He accepted the organizational changes dictated by Vichy, the redefinition of norms, and the proliferation of authoritarian policies. He did not publicly oppose the exaggerated militarism, although he may have chafed in private. He did not countermand the racial quotas imposed from outside. But he did send forward petitions to Vichy, requesting exemptions for individual cases such as Benatar's—almost always to no avail. How much of Vichy's anti-Jewish legislation he actually enforced is a matter of debate. Noguès bowed to some *diktats* but definitely worked at cross-purposes to others.[42]

Certain policies, however, he simply would not accept. Noguès strongly believed that Vichy's suppression of economic activities involving Jews was wrongheaded. He knew that Jews were tightly woven into the fabric of the Moroccan economy. He also understood the sanctity of Jewish communal life and made sure that its basic institutions were not disrupted. Throughout his wartime tenure, Jewish religious schools, rabbinical courts, places of worship, and communal organizations continued to function with little or no interference from the state. The AIU schools remained open and absorbed students ejected by fiat from the Vichy-controlled state schools. Thousands of Jewish refugees were allowed to transit Morocco, for the most part unmolested. And, as we shall see, while the Protectorate administration could do nothing to quell the worst abuses of the forced-labor camps, foreign and domestic aid organizations, including Benatar's, were given access to them to provide relief.

Meanwhile, the mass of Moroccan Jews were left alone to live in relative tranquility. Jacques Dahan, prominent member of the Jewish community of Rabat, remarked on the gap between the harsh nature of the anti-Jewish laws and the respectful behavior of the resident-general and his entourage toward people like himself: "By their use of coded language, we were made to understand their disapproval [of the race laws] and asked for our patience while waiting for the 'final victory.'"[43] Noguès had a vision of Moroccan society under French protection as a place where Jews had a specific role to play; indeed, Morocco as he knew it was unimaginable without them. This was the meeting point where he and Nelly Benatar converged to broker their wartime alliance.

The attitude of key figures in the Protectorate administration was also consequential. The more harmful anti-Jewish legislation promulgated by

Vichy in Morocco failed to be applied, not only because of Noguès's purposeful foot-dragging, but also because of resistance at the highest levels of the Protectorate government. His closest advisers—Robert Montagne, an "old Morocco hand"; Roland Cadet, chief legal counselor; Pierre Voizard, secretary-general of the Protectorate; Roger Thabauld, director of primary education—circumvented the uglier aspects of Vichy's plan for the Jews. Roland Cadet reported that Noguès told him to "to avoid in Morocco the excesses of the policies of the metropole" and not to add more restrictions "than those that are already in place."[44]

Benatar knew these men and depended on their goodwill. With their support, she continued to work directly under the noses of her antagonists, speaking her mind, indifferent to personal danger, knowing that behind the scenes, she had influential friends and a powerful protector.

CHAPTER 5

1942

Stateless in Morocco

"WE DON'T LIKE TO BE CALLED 'REFUGEES,'" the German Jewish philosopher Hannah Arendt (1906–1975), herself a refugee, wrote in an article entitled "We Refugees," published in the *Menorah Journal* in 1943. In this brief, poignant essay, she summed up the existential condition of the contemporary European refugee, stripped of all legal rights, cast out from the protective arms of the nation-state, dependent on the charity of strangers. Naked before the world, the stateless refugee, she declared, was a "a new kind of human being."[1]

Jewish refugees were a special instance of the type, according to Arendt. Forever optimistic, they tried to assume new identities while coping with the stigma of being eternal outsiders. Beneath the surface positivity, dark specters from the past haunt them, encouraging "a dangerous readiness for death."[2] With masterful irony, Arendt identified the dilemma that made mockery of 150 years of false promises that Jews could meld into the mainstream of the modern secular state. The bitter truth was that "through proving all the time their non-Jewishness, they succeeded in remaining Jews all the same." In just a few pages, Arendt's essay measured the teetering balance between hope and despair that ran through refugee lives.

Through a careful reading of Nelly Benatar's archive, we discover that defining refugees as "a problem" and describing their situation as "a crisis" does an injustice to the complexity, ingenuity, and wholeness of their lives. Amid the daily struggle for existence, most refugees learned to exercise a nimble agency. No single factor was decisive in shaping their actions or their ability to survive. Refugee status demanded a constellation of life-affirming skills in order to resist the invisibility that statelessness implied.[3] In the archive, we discover the extremes of feeling experienced by refugees wandering in unfamiliar places. We wonder how refugees made a life for themselves without legal status, local knowledge, family, or friends; how they found housing, fed and clothed themselves, maintained their health, communicated with the outside world, and held onto the belief that someday, normalcy would return. By imagining a refugee in a specific environment, we introduce fixity into a transient state. Let us now turn once again to Casablanca, that archetypal refugee setting.[4]

THE CITY. The first assignment was to become familiar with the place. Refugees learned quickly how to negotiate the complex geographies of Casablanca and to locate the essentials. Even before Hollywood appropriated its image, Casablanca had a certain aura: "Fraught with all that modern industry can provide," was one view. "The spontaneous phenomenon of French energy," another.[5] The city was quintessentially modern, built of steel and cement, dynamic in form and spirit.

In the first years of the Protectorate, Lyautey's planner in chief Henri Prost laid down the outlines of the new French town—a carefully partitioned urban space separate from the old medina, mapped into commercial, residential, and administrative zones joined by a network of modern roadways. Commercial areas near the port boasted hotels and skyscrapers, shops and markets. Residential areas to the west offered lush gardens and modern villas. The monumental government zone at the city center housed the central post office, the state bank, the law courts, and city hall. Important buildings were conceived in a restrained but graceful Hispano-Moorish style, using local materials and motifs such as arches, fountains, and green-tiled roofs.

Excluded from Prost's plan for Casablanca was the old city, with its crenellated walls guarded by hulking cannons, stretching along the waterfront. But even this section was imaginatively absorbed into his overall scheme, reappearing as two distinct quarters: a Jewish town, the mellah, and a Muslim one, known simply as the medina. Otherwise identical, these two halves differed mainly in their religious makeup. Over time they merged into one

extended neighborhood, dense and insalubrious, a remnant of another Morocco both premodern and pre-French.[6]

Newcomers saw the city in their own way. Refugees were not tourists.
Compelled to register with the police while still in the port, the refugee was
already under surveillance.[7] Any indiscretion could mean banishment—to an
internment camp, to "forced residence" in a distant provincial town, or even
worse, to a labor gang in the Sahara. But for those who passed the test, Casablanca could be a pleasant surprise. The city seemed clean and new. In the
central Place de France, gleaming apartment buildings built in the 1920s and
early 1930s catered to a wealthy, international clientele. The Assayag building
on Avenue de la Marine, designed by architect Marius Boyer, was a stunning
example of modernist architecture, with its subterranean parking garage,
ground-level shops, and expansive rooftop terrace.[8] High-rise buildings in
the city center had spectacular views and tasteful interiors, making them the
housing of choice for refugees who could afford them.

But most refugees could not, and modest accommodations were hard to
find.[9] Benatar's lists show that single men preferred cheap hotels in the city
center, while women and families lived in apartments or private homes.[10]
Rents could be low: 25 francs a month for a room, 150 francs for a small apartment. Casablanca's well-to-do Jewish families sometimes took in refugees as
an act of kindness. Clark Blatteis's family from Berlin stayed with a Jewish
family in "an elegant apartment house" near the US consulate in Place Verdun
for a few days upon arrival. Then they moved to a one-room rental, where
they spent the next eight years.[11]

After housing, the most pressing need was food. The ration card was a
necessity, even for refugees. Long lines in front of food shops were a fixture
of daily life. Meat, butter, milk, and potatoes were a rare sight, and sugar, tea,
and coffee practically nonexistent. A heavy dark loaf of bread made of wheat
mixed with barley was the staple of the native diet. By mid-1942, just about
everything was rationed: soap, rice, chocolate, fuel, sausages, eggs, and even
horsemeat. Ordinary folk suffered from hunger constantly, according to the
sociologist Jacques Berque, and "an appalling inequality divided the rulers
from the ruled."[12] Ration cards were stamped with a letter designating one's
status, and quantities were adjusted according to hierarchies, privileging "true
French" above everyone else.[13] Social networks, word of mouth, and sheer invention were needed to get enough to eat. Even Nelly Benatar depended on

her extended family for food. Her brother owned a dairy farm at Tit Mellil, south of Casablanca, that provided her with milk and butter throughout the war.

Along with rationing came the black market. Food stocks vanished from the shelves of the neighborhood *épicerie* within days of the Armistice. Gossip had it that food was being shipped by order of Vichy to Nazi Germany.[14] People resorted to the black market, either directly or through intermediaries. Black marketeers were usually normal vendors who sold items at a higher prices, "but you had to know the vendor."[15] Clark Blatteis, our young German Jewish refugee, remembers that his mother's chief supplier was a Yugoslav woman who worked at night as an "exotic" dancer. People caught selling goods on the black market were denounced by name in the local press. When shopkeepers were arrested and cited, guilty Jews were singled out by the prefix "Israelite." Resident-General Noguès offended Rabat's Jewish leaders when he ordered them "not to take advantage" of the situation of scarcity.[16] While no more guilty of black marketeering than anyone else, Jews fit neatly into the stereotype of dishonesty and lack of civic responsibility. Whether one was a native Moroccan Jew or a Jewish refugee did not matter—it was believed that violating the rules came more naturally to the Jew.

Health was another sector in which survival skills came into play. In the popular mind, refugees were thought to be carriers of disease. Coincidentally, the war years saw an increase in epidemics that rolled across the Maghrib; cholera, typhus, plague, and smallpox were ordinarily held in check, but with wartime scarcities of medicine and the increased mobility of people, they hit especially hard. In 1942, a severe typhus epidemic struck down more than fifty thousand people in Casablanca alone, with a 20 percent mortality rate. In reality, the death toll was probably much higher, but families feared that if they reported a death, they would lose a ration card.[17] Vala Roublev, the child of Jewish refugee doctors from Odessa, had memories of constantly washing her hands. Her family drank boiled water and ate fruits soaked in a turgid soup of potassium permanganate that turned apricots, bananas, and raisins a queasy yellow. At the hairdresser, clippers and scissors were subjected to a blast of purifying flame.[18]

After years of wandering and physical neglect, many refugees needed medical help. They suffered from all sorts of maladies, including skin eruptions, heart disease, dental problems, "women's troubles," and tuberculosis.

Those who were afflicted with tuberculosis, a widespread disease, presented a special problem, because they had to be isolated. Benatar tried to settle tubercular refugees in rural towns, but with little success. The state-run sanatorium at Azrou was reserved for the French.[19]

Many documents in the Benatar archive concern health matters, including hundreds of copies of pharmaceutical prescriptions for treating everything from aches and pains to the disorders of old age. Benatar paid for medicine that refugees could not afford. Some prescriptions called for simple herbal remedies, such as bismuth, garlic, foxglove, and Vaseline, while others prescribed the new sulfa drugs. Until mid-1942, the number of Jewish doctors in Casablanca was adequate, and some treated refugees without charge.[20] But when the Vichy regime began to enforce professional quotas, a dozen Casablancan Jewish doctors had to shut down their clinics.

Among the local doctors was a Jewish refugee couple, Sofia and Alexandre (Sacha) Roublev, who had fled Russia after the revolution and settled in Paris. In 1930, facing increasing difficulty finding work, the Roublevs migrated to Morocco and set up a practice in Casablanca that was an instant success. Patients filled their waiting room: Russian exiles, French settlers, Moroccan Jews and Muslims. After the Vichy race laws came into effect, they were forced to close their practice, yet they continued to see patients under cover, working with Benatar to process refugees in need of medical clearances.

The Roublevs lived in a spacious villa with a garden that became a gathering place for Russian émigrés. Vala (Valentine) Roublev, born in 1921, spent her childhood amid "an uninterrupted parade" of Russian-speaking visitors. On Sundays, a large crowd would gather, seeking medical advice, hearty food, and conversation in Russian. The Roublevs' cook, an Austrian refugee, would prepare an enormous goulash for twenty or more. After lunch, guests would disperse in small groups throughout the garden for more talk, along with ice cream, cakes, and patisserie in "industrial" quantities. According to Vala:

> My parents held open house for a whole cohort of refugees who came to recount their troubles and seek advice. Russian doctors, Romanian psychiatrists, Hungarians of no defined profession, stateless dentists, former Austrian businessmen, now stateless and penniless. They were birds of passage who, in the course of their migrations, landed for a few days and installed themselves like cuckoos in our nest. Friendly but tyrannical, my mother—trailing a cigarette—oversaw this small world, arranging every detail with manic attention.

Nostalgia for home was often the topic of conversation. I remember a German Jewish refugee who spoke to everyone in German, whether they understood him or not. Perhaps it was better not to understand. He commented in a loud voice on the victories of the *Wehrmacht*, calling it *unsere* [our] army, and described the detention center from which my father had recently rescued him as "very dirty," not like "our" concentration camps.

Most of these people stayed for a time in Casablanca, waiting for a visa to the United States. All of them had to pass through my father's clinic for the medical examination required of new immigrants. It was there that Sacha recruited the regulars who came to our villa. It took at least a year to obtain a visa. Then, for the most part, we lost sight of them forever.[21]

The Roublevs represent a special, but by no means unique, example of the refugee experience. Some long-term refugees were bystanders, silently awaiting their fate; others were just the opposite—engaged actors who rendered valuable services to their fellow refugees when they saw an opportunity.[22]

Clothing was another necessity that loomed large in refugee lives. With the onset of war, cloth was no longer imported into Morocco, and it was not long before ordinary people began walking about in something like rags. "Textiles of all kinds are now almost non-existent . . . the American Consulate has been unable to buy even a pair of bedsheets," one aid worker complained. Following the November 1942 landings, US soldiers who bivouacked in the countryside noticed that their canvas duffel bags would disappear overnight, only to reappear a day or two later as the baggy breeches worn by Moroccan workers. The lack of white cotton for burial shrouds was a special hardship for the Jewish community.[23]

Refugees tried to keep up appearances, but eventually, their wardrobes deteriorated. Clothing was so precious that some refugees survived by selling off their apparel, piece by piece. A German Jew named Mauer, confined by police to "forced residence" in Marrakech, wrote to Benatar that he was desperate: "I sold a shirt and two weeks later, a jacket belonging to my wife for 1150 francs."[24] The shift from comfortable bourgeois status to indigent refugee was devastating. An unshaven European hawking neckties on a street corner would not draw much attention.

Finding work was another challenge. Most refugees could not get work permits, but some managed to find employment "under the table." Clark Blatteis's father, a shoe salesman in Germany, barely made a living wage cutting

FIGURE 5.1 A refugee street vendor in Tangier, Morocco, 1940.

shoe leather in a mellah workshop. Refugees with special skills were snatched up, but men formerly in trade had a more difficult time. Albert El Koubbi, ex-salesman, worked in a print shop where most of the employees were Jewish refugees; during the day, they filled customers' orders, and at night, they used the same presses to print anti-fascist leaflets. Social networks, solidarities, and information shared by word of mouth were the main means for finding a job.

The refugee population of Casablanca was not a stable one. People were constantly on the move, arriving and leaving. Refugees with valid entry visas to western countries were eager to get on their way, and those arriving without documents or visas were grateful for a place to rest while awaiting a change in fortune. Casablanca was a *plaque tournante*—a vast hub—for refugee activity. The city offered all the services needed for moving onward, including consulates, doctors, telegraph offices, and charitable help. In 1942, the Marseille-Martinique route was finished, but there were other options. The JDC purchased space on four Portuguese-registered boats, the *Serpa Pinto*, the *Guiné*, the *San Thomé*, and the *Nyassa*, all sailing out of Lisbon and stopping at Casablanca before crossing the Atlantic. Nearly eight thousand refugees left Europe in 1942 on one of these ships. Half of that number boarded at Casablanca.[25]

This activity brought international aid workers in search of a base for their operations to Casablanca. In August 1942, Leslie Heath opened a new AFSC (Quaker) field office in the city. A large, warmhearted man, Heath quickly recognized that Casablanca, with its large floating refugee population, offered an unusual opportunity. Before leaving the United States, Heath had contacted Benatar's cousins, wealthy international businessmen Jack and Abraham Pinto, who had an office on Broad Street in Manhattan's financial district. Heath made a favorable impression, and the brothers Pinto offered to contribute to the AFSC's program in Morocco. On arrival in Casablanca, Heath contacted Benatar, and almost immediately they began sharing information and consulting on how to best handle troublesome cases.[26]

Benatar admired the Quakers. She thought they were disciplined, trustworthy, and resourceful. Their selfless good works and their measured approach to problem-solving appealed to her. It was not long before Heath came to appreciate Benatar as well—someone "who knew the ropes," was honest and unafraid, and had connections in the Protectorate administration, something he did not have. He described her to his fellow workers as "very courageous and efficient and able." They were a good match.[27]

Joe Schwartz, the JDC's representative in Lisbon, also made note of the increase in activity in Casablanca; expenses were adding up and the list of recipients of aid was growing. Casablanca was a place of interest, where relief operations both current and in the planning stage began to coalesce. Schwartz noticed that Benatar had begun serving an entirely new clientele—prisoners in Vichy labor camps on the edge of Sahara. Alerted to the idea that these camps might house Jews, Schwartz wrote to Benatar asking for clarification: Who was being held in those camps, and how did the Saharan camps differ from other sites of detention? How many of the inmates were Jews? Schwartz was asking pertinent questions, and Benatar felt obliged to answer them. It did not take long for her to realize that she was slowly and reluctantly being drawn into the surreal world of the Vichy forced-labor camps.[28]

Word of Vichy prison camps in North Africa where Europeans were being held against their will had leaked out in the early months of 1941. Surprisingly, first notice came from distant America. Cora Goold was the source. Cora wrote to a friend, who passed the news to another friend, who passed it on to the JDC, that "in the mountains of Morocco" were "about 1000 Jews, mostly Poles and Austrians, who had enlisted in the French Foreign Legion at the outset of the war, and were now suffering extreme hardship." Joe Schwartz confirmed this information to the New York office, adding that he had asked his "Casablanca Committee"—that is, Nelly Benatar—to look into the situation. But he doubted that Benatar could do anything about it, as access to the camps was "very strict" and the local committee also "lack[ed] the experience to cope with the situation."[29]

Schwartz underestimated Benatar. She already knew about the Saharan prison camps. An inmate at the Bou Arfa camp in southern Morocco named Cysner, an ex-Legionnaire, wrote to her in March 1941 asking for help. Her response was abrupt and negative: "I regret that we cannot come to your aid, our commission only takes care of refugees in Casablanca." Benatar was already on a list of "dangerous individuals" compiled by the German Armistice Commission. She may have felt that an inquiry into the Saharan camps would fall outside the bounds of her weakened mandate.[30]

The subject of the Vichy camps did not go away. Under pressure from

American donors, the JDC refused to let it drop. A month later, reporting on "the situation in Morocco," a JDC press release said that Madame Noguès, wife of the resident-general, was trying to help ex-Legionnaires imprisoned in Morocco, and that most of them were Jews. In June, the subject again came up, when disturbing articles appeared in the American press. A story in the *Nation* by a German refugee, the journalist Heinz Pol, announced that "thousands of German, Austrian, Czech, Polish, and Spanish refugees... are today kept by the Vichy government as slaves in the Sahara desert in a flagrant breach of international law." Vichy officials in Algeria flatly denied the charges, saying that they were "exaggerated" and "inexact." Moreover, they claimed that conditions in the Saharan camps for these "semi-militarized" workers were "less severe than those imposed on the Foreign Legion." The report did not mention that many of the workers were Central European Jews. They were identified only as "Spanish."

The story would not die. Julius Wolf, a refugee from Vienna and a former lawyer, told people at the JDC about the "frightful" conditions in the Saharan camps, where "a thousand Jewish former Legionnaires were working as slaves."[31] As evidence mounted, the JDC's Schwartz once again turned to Nelly Benatar, promising her an increased budget if she could research the needs of inmates. That was all the incentive that she needed. In November 1941, Benatar received authorization from the Protectorate government to visit the camps.

But she did not go, not then. She had no idea where the camps were located, how many men were involved, and under what conditions.[32] In a report to the JDC, she mentions only four camps, when in fact there were fourteen, either already operational or in the making. She was vague about their purpose. Oued Zem was a *camp de triage*, a sorting operation; Missour, where political internees were held, a camp for "people with a weak constitution"; and Bou Arfa, one of the worst hard-labor camps, "under the protection of the Legionnaires Commission." Perhaps she was withholding cruel facts until she herself could verify them. One thing is clear: she did not yet realize that the Saharan camps had a dual purpose: to serve as the cornerstone for Vichy's project of ethnic and social cleansing and to fulfill Vichy's commitment to collaborate with the Nazi war effort.

Vichy's program of racialized injustice unfolded through edicts and practical steps that targeted particular groups in society. The Moroccan and Algerian concentration camps were part of this plan. Their location in remote sites far from population centers allowed Vichy to practice unobserved some of the more brutal aspects of its program of "purification." The camps were meant to serve as a dumping ground for "unwanted" people purged from the metropole. At the same time, the potential of the camps to act as a reservoir of slave labor compensated for the organizational burden they imposed. Following closely the Nazi model, the Saharan labor camps were used to align Vichy's racialist objectives with its economic needs.[33]

The roots of the camp system are found in prewar France. In 1939, many foreigners volunteered to fight the Axis, including Spanish republicans and German, Austrian, and Polish Jews. After the June 1940 debacle, foreigners in the French military, many of them EVDGs, "volunteers for the duration of the war," were screened to establish their suitability for further service. Demobilized men found fit to work were often sent to North Africa, but they were not set free. Instead, they were transferred to the Ministry of the Interior and reorganized into companies called *groupes de travailleurs étrangers*, foreign workers' groups or GTEs, and reassigned to the Office of Industrial Production, the government unit responsible for overseeing "essential" war work. More than eight thousand ex-soldiers were assigned in 1940 and 1941 to various work camps in southern Morocco and Algeria, where they lived under extreme physical and climactic conditions: badly paid, stripped of their legal rights, imprisoned behind barbed wire, enduring harsh military discipline.

Each work camp was unique, with its own cadres of command, its own tasks, its unique physical setting. Men from the GTEs—one estimate is between three thousand and four thousand—were assigned to two interrelated projects: some were sent to work on extending the Trans-Saharan Railway, while others were sent to camps where iron ore, coal, and other minerals needed for the war effort were mined and then shipped by rail to continental destinations.[34] Certain uniformities existed across the camp system: the noncommissioned officers were usually German ex-Legionnaires who imposed stringent rules and punishments, while the French officers in charge were indifferent to the behavior of their subalterns and worked hand in glove with Vichy's Office of Industrial Production to extract maximum labor at minimal cost. The entire system reeked of cruelty and corruption.[35]

Most of the work camps were paired with satellite punishment camps where men were sent for the slightest infraction of the rules. Conditions in the punishment camps were even worse than at the work sites. Men died from malnutrition, abuse, and torture. The entire system was controlled from Algiers, where a Colonel Lupy, inspector of North African internment camps, was headquartered.[36] From time to time, voices were raised about the poor conditions in the camps, but rumors of ill treatment were rejected as "pure invention." In May 1941, Resident-General Noguès informed the Ministry of Foreign Affairs that "no one in our GTEs is complaining" and that the workers received a salary that was "the equivalent in similar professions." The statement was entirely misleading.[37]

Yet another type of camp was designated for high-value political prisoners. Detention camps were different from the forced-labor camps. Though equally remote, they were not intended for punishment; instead, the inmates were left alone and did not perform hard labor. Vichy police usually made selections for these camps at dockside, guided by their instincts. A police report states that lurking among "decent people" arriving by ship are "shady characters from the national point of view, who might be attached to a country whose politics would someday be opposed to that of France."[38]

The infamous Bou Denib, where Contrôleur Civil Poussier threatened to send Nelly Benatar, was the most remote detention camp. After traveling hundreds of kilometers through the Middle Atlas Mountains on narrow, winding roads, the visitor discovers a rocky escarpment in the middle of the desert. Reaching the actual camp calls for a half-hour hike up a steep path more suited to goats than people. At the top, on a wind-swept plateau, are the remnants of a Foreign Legion fort, suspended in an immense, unbounded space. A more lonely, isolated place can hardly be imagined.[39]

At Bou Denib, inmates were a mixed bag of socialists, communists, and Gaullists. Pierre Jalée, a former inmate, wrote that most prisoners at the camp were resigned to their fate and bonded together in a "homogeneous paté":

> This concentration camp had nothing to do with a Nazi camp . . . the absence
> of freedom was certainly total, the climate harsh, food was scarce, the living
> conditions rugged, but we were forced to work only to maintain ourselves,
> not a lot, not terrible, and we were able to make use of our free time as we
> wished . . . The odious aspect was that this camp was French, and that the
> sole reason for our internment there was our having a bad reputation vis-à-
> vis an authority that hoped to have a good reputation with Hitler.[40]

Another camp for political detainees was Missour, a remote town in the

Middle Atlas, where about 150 communists, labor agitators, anti-fascists, petty criminals, spies, "debauchers," and miscellaneous other social pariahs languished in makeshift quarters around a miniature train station, their life-line to the outside world. The manufacture of sandals from esparto grass was the inmates' principal occupation. They were otherwise left on their own.[41] Each camp differed from the other; the single constant was Vichy's underlying desire to put French assets, even its "unwanted," to work.[42]

The forced-labor camps were part of Vichy's scheme to mobilize the colonial economy to help fulfill its obligations to the Nazi war effort. During the period 1940–1944, it is a well-documented fact that vast quantities of goods, agricultural products, and raw materials were shipped to the Reich from France under the Armistice agreement. According to Robert Paxton, "France became the principal foreign furnisher of labor power, raw materials, and manufactured goods to the Nazi War machine."[43] But it is less well known that the colonies also had their orders to fill.

An integral part of economic collaboration was Vichy's reorganization of the Moroccan economy along corporatist lines that duplicated a similar reorganization in France, where state control meant replacing laissez-faire practices with policies that shored up "nationalist" values. In the Protectorate, the Moroccan Cooperative Union, composed of a small group of elite Muslim merchant families, took control of the export of all agricultural products. This top-down "cooperative"—a brash misnomer, because it was clearly organized along corporatist lines—made huge profits "by selling wheat, barley, palmetto fiber for the manufacture of explosives, salt, fish and eggs to Germany. Five to six ships left Casablanca each week for Marseille ... experts believe that about 80 percent of this was transshipped to Germany," according to a US government report.[44]

The Germans were especially interested in iron, zinc, manganese, cobalt, and molybdenum, all mined in Morocco and used in the manufacture of armaments. During the war years, Germany received almost one million tons of Moroccan phosphates, quantities of coal and iron ore, as well as smaller amounts of strategic metals. Pierre Voizard, secretary-general of the Protectorate, confirmed the strategic importance of the Moroccan mineral production and verified that "rare metals used by the military" were sent to Germany, including, in his words, "about forty tons of cobalt."[45] Most of these products came from remote settings in the Sahara. In the desert, there were few roads, no bridges, no electricity, and a scarcity of water. Transporting raw materials from the southern region to the coast was a problem that had to be

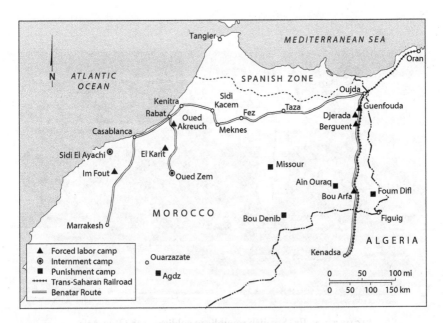

Benatar's Camps Tour, February 1943.

solved quickly.[46] The solution was to extend the Trans-Saharan railroad line deep into the mineral-bearing regions of Morocco's south.

The idea for a Trans-Saharan railroad had a long history. The project was conceived in the nineteenth century as a means of tying together France's West African colonies with the Mediterranean coast, but it stalled during the Great War. In the interwar period, the track along the stretch between Oujda and Bou Arfa in Morocco—a distance of about 260 kilometers—was completed. A second leg between Oujda and the Algerian town of Port Said was also finished. By 1939, when World War II started, the railroad line extended from the Mediterranean coast to the pre-Saharan region, and then stopped.[47]

When Vichy came to power, the idea of extending the railroad farther into the desert was revived. A new company, the Mer-Niger, was formed with the ambitious long-term goal of completing the entire distance of 3,650 kilometers between Algiers and Dakar by 1947. However, an immediate aim was far more pressing—to extend the roadbed a mere 160 kilometers south from Bou Arfa into the coal-rich region of Kenadza in Algeria. Despite the heat,

FIGURE 5.2 Ex–Spanish republican soldiers at the Bou Arfa
forced-labor camp, 1941.

FIGURE 5.3 Forced laborers working on the Trans-Saharan Railway,
1941–1942.

FIGURE 5.4 Prisoners at the Im Fout dam site, south of Casablanca, 1942.

FIGURE 5.5   Ex–German Jewish prisoner Rosenthal at Im Fout dam site, 1942.

sandstorms, and equipment failures, new track slowly snaked its way across the desert, built mainly by forced labor.[48]

In December 1941, the railroad line between Bou Arfa and Kenadza was completed, and a "magnificent reception" in the desert celebrated the event. A sumptuous banquet was laid out on the sand dunes for the honored guests—Resident-General Noguès of Morocco, the governor-general of Algeria, and from Vichy, the minister of communications Paul Berthelot. Minister Berthelot ceremoniously nailed in the last bolt and blew a whistle, signaling the departure of a train carrying four hundred tons of coal to coastal ports. Nowhere in the extensive press coverage of the event was there a hint that the majority of "workers" were ex-soldiers, Spanish republicans, political detainees, and Jews, sentenced to hard labor for practically no pay. Nowhere was it mentioned that the final destination of the material on board was somewhere in Hitler's Reich.[49]

The secret of the camps was impossible to contain. Muslim populations living in proximity to them were curious and began to ask questions. With no newspapers or radios, country people had limited information of the outside world and almost no knowledge of current events. Unable to follow rapid turns in the war, they knew little of Vichy and even less of de Gaulle. The name *Hitler* was vaguely meaningful. Colonial rulers were the *fransis*, who spoke another language. The camps' inmates they saw by the roadside were equally inscrutable. What *nasranis* ("Europeans," in Moroccan Arabic) were doing in the desert performing heavy labor ordinarily reserved for Moroccans was a mystery. Townspeople often referred to the workers as *Alleman*, "Germans," because of the prisoner-of-war camps located in the Moroccan desert during World War I. They were very surprised to hear that some of the *Alleman* were Jews. For them, the Jew was a peddler, a shopkeeper, a craftsman—not one of these pathetic, ragged specimens who had no money, no possessions, no language in common with them. One thing was clear, however: Hitler was winning the war and did not like Jews. This, too, came as a big surprise and only deepened the conundrum.[50]

Inmates in the camps began to seek contact with the outside world. As conditions worsened, they wrote letters that remarkably reached their intended destinations. Some inmates even managed to escape, crossing hundreds of miles of empty desert, finding their way to Casablanca. Among the men left behind, a rumor began to circulate throughout the camps system about a Jewish woman lawyer in Casablanca named Benatar who advocated for refugee rights. Some of the men wrote directly to her asking for help.

BERGUENT. The camp at Berguent held special interest for Benatar, especially when she learned that the inmates were almost exclusively Central European Jews.[51] From late 1940 to mid-1943, the Berguent labor camp was a vital link in the project of extending the Trans-Saharan Railway. The camp's population fluctuated wildly. At one point, it held more than four hundred European Jews, but the usual complement was about half of that. The workers' camp was located near the main railroad line between Oujda and Bou Arfa, on a flat plain about a kilometer from the town. Berguent began as a French military outpost at the beginning of the Protectorate. Border demarcations in this region were vague, and there was even some question as to whether this remote place was in Morocco or Algeria. A civilian population slowly grew up around the military outpost, and by the 1930s, a small Jewish community had settled there. In 1942, the wealthiest person in town was a man named Cohen who owned the local petrol station. Colonial-era postcards show a settlement of several rows of mud-brick houses and a wide main street, looking like a frontier outpost of the American Old West.

During the war, work at the Berguent camp involved cutting, crushing, and moving heavy stones for the railroad. Workers moved huge rocks from the top of a nearby cliff to the plain below, where they were broken apart by hand. The material was then pushed in handcarts along the railroad track to the railhead some distance away, where other workers used the crushed stones as ballast between the newly laid tracks. A Polish Jewish prisoner named Morice Tondowski, who spent a year and half at Berguent, said the work was very hard. In addition to transporting stones to the worksite, he had to carry all his tools with him. Every day, as the track crept forward, the distance from the campsite to the railhead grew longer.[52] The rigors of the fierce climate, broiling hot in summer and frigid in winter, added to his misery.

In July 1942, Dr. Edouard Wyss-Dunant, North African representative of the International Red Cross, visited the Berguent camp on a tour of inspection. Wyss-Dunant reported that conditions were deplorable. The work was arduous, the men lacked warm clothing and blankets, and they slept out of doors. Food was scanty: ersatz coffee in the morning, some soup and bread in the evening, with six men sharing a single loaf. The basic ration was 500 grams of bread a day, 150 grams of meat a week, a quarter liter of wine twice a day. They worked ten hours a day, six days a week, and were paid, according to the report, an average of 5 francs a day, or about 10 cents. Wyss-Dunant recommended that the camp be shut down.[53]

But the camp was not closed. Anti-Semitism was the reason behind the extremely punitive conditions at Berguent, according to Leslie Heath of the AFSC. When one of the inmates was offered a job as a baker in Rabat that would mean freedom, the authorities refused to let him go "because he was a Jew." When Jewish men in other camps complained about their situation, they were told that if their protests did not cease, they would be "sent to Berguent."[54] In March 1942, the JDC's Joe Schwartz asked Nelly Benatar specifically about Berguent. Her response was to dispatch two boxes of food to Oujda, with a request to the head of the Jewish community there that they be delivered to the camp about seventy kilometers away. The person who received them turned out to be an unreliable postman. The boxes sat in Oujda for more than three weeks, and when they finally reached Berguent, most of the contents were rotten. The gesture, however, had an effect, and letters from Berguent began to arrive at Benatar's office asking for foodstuffs, cigarettes, and permissions to leave the camp. She responded with more food packages, straw mats for sleeping, and cash allocations for the most destitute.[55] She also began a steady correspondence with one inmate, ex-German accountant Adolf Besmann, who agreed to "represent the interests of his comrades" by reporting on their needs.[56] Benatar had become a presence, if in name only, in this remote and cruel place.

Surprised that someone was finally listening, other men at Berguent came forward with requests. Bernard Leska wrote that he had been receiving money from France, but his family "was sent to Poland," leaving him "without resources." Benatar sent him a pullover and a cash allotment of 150 francs.[57] Max Brakl wrote vividly about his trials:

> The work—a road is being built with pick and shovel—begins at dawn and ends at dusk. Today, for example, we did not even have time to finish lunch. There is not even water to drink. It is almost impossible to wash our bodies, which is of course very dangerous in this region scourged by typhus. . . . [W]e earn 1 franc, 25 centimes per day and are driven on in our work all day long by veteran Legionnaires. Last week we were deloused and yesterday we walked eight kilometers to the nearest washing facility and eight kilometers to return. Because of that, we had to work on Sunday.[58]

Felix Orbach wrote that "the winter arrives in our region with a harshness that I would never have imagined for a hot country like Morocco . . . we thank you, dear Madame, for your friendship."[59]

Men within the camps system were shuffled around from one locale to another to meet the needs of the Office of Industrial Production. As they moved from place to place, word about Benatar spread. An inmate named Baum at Oued Akreuch, a worksite near Rabat, wrote to her: "Our situation here has become critical. . . . We have no cigarettes, no soap, no clothing. We ask you to come to our aide, because you are the only one who can help us."[60] Sometimes the men did not even know her name but wrote to the "Committee." Walter Brandweiner wrote from the military hospital in Oujda: "I have been suffering for five years and I do not believe I can stand it much longer. I am at the end of my strength."[61] The volume of letters from the Saharan camps kept growing, consuming greater amounts of Benatar's time and emotional strength. More than any official report, the personal messages made legible the breadth of the punishment system and the scale of suffering it had produced. As her preoccupation with the camps increased, Benatar realized she would have to see them firsthand. The journey would be a difficult one, requiring careful planning. But it was not until February 1943 that she became an actual eyewitness to Vichy's vile system of forced labor.

The synergy created by proximity is one of the more intriguing aspects of archival research. Like inert chemical substances that come to life when placed next to one another, pieces of paper, strategically repositioned, speak in new ways. So it is with Nelly Benatar's hundreds of accounts, reports, letters, tallies, receipts, chits, stubs, notes and lists: taken singly, they mean little, but when put into some kind of order, they take on new meaning. A handwritten note by Benatar from 1942, "An Inventory of the Items contained in this Box," directs the reader to bank deposit slips, customs receipts, post office forms, copies of telegrams, and other trivia, with no apparent order or logic. "It would be useful," she wrote, "having the names of the refugees and their date of departure, to locate them and get their testimonies about their passage through Morocco. For this reason, I believe that these pieces of paper are very important and deserve to be closely studied, analyzed, and commented on to serve as a starting point and a linkage between former refugees and ourselves."[62]

Like pieces of a jigsaw puzzle, the contents of Nelly's archive create narratives that conventional histories might overlook. She was not much of a self-explainer; rather, she was the sober eyewitness who chose discretion over wordiness. She berated herself when she became "heated," believing that sudden flashes of anger did not serve her well, not in the courtroom and not in life. Self-discipline was a leading character trait; in cases of self-defense, the well-placed jab was preferable to the mighty slash. She tried to edit out of her archive any evidence of excess—of her own passions, hates, and obsessions—but sometimes, they break through the careful prose, illuminating her character with a laser-perfect light.

It was inevitable that the refugees in her care would see her as a resource and a means to an end. From her clients' perspective, she could make life a whole lot easier. Even with her limited resources, her "allowances" offered them the prospect of better food and housing, small comforts like cigarettes, a cup of coffee, a fresh shirt to replace a tattered remnant. She could get a refugee permission to visit a consulate, or initiate liberation from a camp, or find a job, or even reserve a berth on a ship to freedom. In matters both large and small, she had the power to change refugee lives. She knew that the relationship between the protector and protégé was never an equal one and could engender strong feelings. "If we are saved we feel humiliated, and if we are helped we feel degraded.... We are afraid of becoming part of that miserable lot of *schnorrers* [Yiddish, "freeloaders"] whom we, many of us former philanthropists, remember only too well," was Hannah Arendt's view from the receiving end.[63] But for the protector, too, there was a price to pay: overreaching, favoritism, arrogance, and what the writer Albert Memmi has called "the Nero complex," a power-laden delirium verging on the corrupt. On both sides of the quotient, there were risks—about which Benatar was no doubt aware.

"I solicit you, dear Madame, to kindly intervene with the Casa police, to get me a permission for three days to get my possessions out of customs.... I have no coat, and I suffer greatly from the cold in these wooden barracks," Josef Weingarten wrote from the Oued Zem camp, soliciting an act of kindness she may or may not have been capable of giving.[64] From Missour, that miserable rat hole in the Middle Atlas, a letter from the Polish ex-soldier Joseph Vogel: "Can you send me a little monthly help for cigarettes, for an occasional cup of coffee, for an egg here and there?" The piteousness of the request is hardly bearable. What could she do in response? Hundreds of such missives are found in her archive, sketching the contours of the refugee plight.

Benatar was soft-hearted but could also be very tough. She knew a *schnorrer* when she saw one. Eisik Wiesel, a Czech Jew who arrived in Morocco via Belgium with his family in 1940 (remember the two clowning boys in the photo) was penniless, stranded, and in his third year as a refugee. Wiesel fathered yet another child while interned at Sidi El Ayachi. He plagued Benatar with requests, and she usually complied. But finally, her patience gave out. After the American landing in November 1942, jobs became plentiful. She wrote to Wiesel: "There are many opportunities to work now, we hope that the two extra months [of support] we have given you will allow you to create an independent situation."[65] A quiet, admonishing voice.

Nor was she sympathetic to people who asked for special favors that seemed to her excessive. Moses Pack, a devout Jew, asked her to cover his pay for the Sabbath and for the entire week of the Jewish holiday of Shavuoth

(Pentecost) while he refrained from work. Benatar's response was clear: "I understand perfectly that your religious feelings have created this situation, but this is a problem for which only you can find the solution."[66] At the same time, she attended to the needs of observant Jews, providing special foods at Passover and sending the men at Berguent *siddurim* (prayer books). She was lionlike when French officials punished a rabbi for refusing to work on the Sabbath, berating the chief of the Office of Industrial Production in unmistakably corrective tones: "Rosner is extremely pious and would undergo whatever privation rather than infringe upon a religious law."[67] Religious practice was not a problem for her—after all, she had her own spiritual needs—but seeking special favors that bordered on the *schnorrer* mentality was out of bounds.

She was capable of extraordinary acts of kindness, especially toward women in need. Jeanne Bougerol Martin was a Canadian woman who gave birth to twins while in transit in July 1942. Her husband, a French naval officer, went down with his ship a few months earlier, leaving her a widow at the age of twenty-eight. The family lived with Benatar during their six-week layover in Casablanca. Nelly was completely enamored: "I am extremely attached to these babies, as if they were my own," she wrote. She made arrangements for the family's onward travel and stayed in contact with Jeanne Martin for years, visiting her in Minnesota during one of her trips to America after the war.[68]

A bizarre situation in December 1942 put Benatar's empathy on display. Chaya Schreiber of Lodz, an elderly woman who spent years in French detention camps, died unexpectedly on board the SS *Serpa Pinto* in December 1942, just as the ship was pulling out of the harbor for the transatlantic crossing. Fearful their visas would expire, the rest of her family decided to leave anyway, asking Benatar to take charge of burial arrangements. "Nothing will be neglected to honor her memory," Benatar wrote. She made sure that *yiskor*, the Jewish prayer for the departed, was recited in the main Casablanca synagogue in Chaya Schreiber's memory. A year later, according to Jewish practice, she ordered the headstone placed on her grave.[69]

These displays of good intentions were purposefully left in her archive. Relations with her refugee clients were not always smooth, and she wanted to keep the record straight. Sometimes refugees stored up their anger, releasing it when they no longer needed her help. Manfred Unger, a former soldier, falsely accused Benatar of taking bribes, serving only the rich, and sending everyone else to concentration camps. Benatar responded to this absurd charge in a white heat. She was used to ingratitude, she wrote, but this was the first time anyone had questioned her honesty: "I have not only given to the refugees all my time for almost three years, but I have sacrificed my work, my legal practice, even my children, and I have often spent my own wealth when the need has arisen. I do not know this Manfred Unger . . . but you can tell him from me that I plan to register a complaint of defamation with the court as well as with his superiors."[70]

A close reading of Benatar's archive tells us that, from time to time, the "years of glory" were also years of pain.

The last two months of 1942 were a pivotal moment in the history of the war. In October, in the Libyan desert, the British halted Rommel's advance, pushing the Germans back to Tunisia, while on the Eastern Front, the Wehrmacht was stopped before Stalingrad and began its long retreat back to Berlin. Feeling confident, Churchill and Roosevelt decided to open the long-awaited "Second Front." On the night of November 7, 1942, 110,000 Allied troops landed in force at strategic points on the coasts of Morocco and Algeria. The landing caught the French defenses off guard, and for three days the battle raged, leaving a total of over 800 Allied and 1,500 French dead, before a cease-fire was declared on November 11. Benatar's friend Noguès had stubbornly refused to capitulate, irrevocably besmirching his near-impeccable record. Vichy commanded him to keep up the fight, and good military man that he was, he followed orders. Noguès paid a heavy price for this ill-advised decision. Dismissed from his post in 1943, he and his wife took refuge in Portugal. In 1947, he was tried for treason in absentia by the French High Court, and found guilty of "national degradation for life." He remained in Portugal until 1954, when he returned to France and requested a retrial. In 1956, after a formal hearing in the Palais de Justice where Benatar provided evidence in his defense, Noguès was again condemned to "national disgrace." But this time, the sentence was immediately lifted. The consensus was that Noguès's crime was not one of gross moral failure like those of Pétain or Laval, but a momentary lapse of judgment. The "old Morocco hand" was reprimanded, slapped on the wrist, and summarily dismissed.[71]

At the height of the Allied bombardment, Nelly Benatar and her daughter Myriam took command of a first-aid post to care for the wounded from the port area, where the bombing was particularly intense. During a lull, one of the French nurses let loose a violently anti-Semitic diatribe, clearly aimed at the Benatars. No one said a word, and Myriam, in a rage, left the room. Later, her mother sent a letter of protest to the head of the medical unit. His reply was pallidly ambiguous and unapologetic.[72]

The Allied landing may have stirred up hatred among the European settler population, the bedrock of pro-Vichy sympathy in the Maghrib, but for Moroccan Jews, it was nothing short of miraculous. Jews saw it as an act of divine deliverance, and they let their feelings show. In Casablanca, they poured out of the gates of the mellah onto the main boulevard, lining the sidewalks as victorious American troops filed past. A wild melee broke out, stones were cast, and blood flowed. Leslie Heath complained that "the Jews have celebrated the arrival of the Americans most indiscreetly."[73] In the next days, American GIs paraded through the streets, showering the (mostly) adoring crowds with chewing gum and Tootsie Rolls. Each day that passed, more shiny Dodge trucks piled up in Casablanca's port. After three years of severe deprivation, all this abundance was simply "stupefying," according to André Hardy, a French official.[74] Overnight, the pro-Vichy settler press became a propaganda tool for the Allied cause, touting news of the American success in majuscules. The newspapers were simply reflecting a new reality—the futility of resistance.

President Roosevelt made a public announcement on November 17 calling for the liberation of the North African prison camps, and the American Jewish philanthropic world moved into high gear. A flurry of cables crossed the Atlantic. Joe Schwartz decided that the first step should be to "gain the release [of] all refugees in internment camps [in] North Africa"; following that, the JDC should use its influence to win "the restoration [of the] rights of Jews [in] those regions." Benatar quickly followed up with supportive cables of her own. She wrote to Max Gottschalk, an influential voice in Jewish affairs in New York: "Racial laws unchanged . . . we expect hopefully abolition those laws and liberation of about thousand internees . . . as announced in the speech of President Roosevelt . . . try intervene . . . you can assure authorities our entire devotion to Allied cause." In another series of exchanges with Schwartz, she seized the opportunity to propose a vastly expanded budget for her refugee operation.[75]

After years in the shadows, Benatar had emerged fully as the local expert on refugee affairs. She had the blessings of the JDC, the foremost American Jewish philanthropic agency active in the field. She had the numbers, the contacts, the information. She estimated that more than three thousand people were still held in Moroccan camps, most of them in labor camps in the south. But this was a rough estimate; it was impossible to know exact numbers without taking a census on the ground.

In the meantime, Sidi El Ayachi, the camp closest to Casablanca, became a place of pilgrimage. A steady stream of military officers, diplomats, and international relief workers began to march through on tours of inspection, not realizing that Sidi El Ayachi was hardly a representative example of the Vichy forced-labor camps. Its residents were a handful of stateless Jews with no visas and no immediate prospects for leaving. The true scope of the problem was not yet known. Allied military, French officials, the JDC and other international aid agencies joined in a conversation about the liberation of the Vichy camps, seeking solutions to a problem about which they had only the barest knowledge. The work ahead consisted of fact-checking, tabulating, profiling, evaluating, planning. No one on the scene was better equipped than Benatar to take on this assignment. A new phase in her struggle for refugee rights was about to begin.

CHAPTER 6

1943

Liberating the Camps

THE RAINS CAME EARLY in the winter of 1943, promising an abundant spring harvest. By mid-February, the fields of wheat lining the coastal road between Casablanca and Rabat were an electric green. Armed with a *laisser-passer*—an official permission to travel—signed by the *contrôleur civil* of the Casablanca region, Nelly Benatar and her team set off in late February on an epic journey of 1,700 kilometers, crossing the length and breadth of Morocco to visit forced-labor camps on the edge of the Sahara.[1] In the party were Nelly's daughter Myriam and three others, all refugees: Vienna-born Jacob Klein, lately of Paris, editor of fine art books, driver and auto mechanic; Malka (Marguerite) Fux, ex-Austrian, fluent in half a dozen languages; and Maurice Vanikoff, a Polish Jewish, French-trained human rights lawyer who fled Paris in 1940 to carry on advocacy work from the safety of North Africa.[2]

The four traveled in an aging DeSoto sedan belonging to Dr. Lévy-Lebhar of Casablanca, one of the few Jewish physicians still allowed to practice under Vichy's discriminatory laws. Through friends in the Protectorate administration, Benatar was allotted an extra ration of petrol. With this bounty, they made the trip from Casablanca to Bou Arfa, a distance of almost a thousand kilometers, in just four days. Mishaps along the way included a ruptured tire and a burst inner tube, but the travelers persevered, even though the engine gave signs of exhaustion. Repairs were carried out on the spot under the guidance of Klein, who would curse each time the car broke down in heavily accented French, "Salopie de voiture!" ("What a bitch of a car!")[3]

Moroccan roads in 1943 were of wildly variable quality. In the 1930s, colonial engineers had created a modern highway system in heavily populated areas, weaving together Casablanca, Rabat, Marrakech, and Fez into a single, smooth network. But the rest of the country lagged far behind, served mainly by dirt tracks that gave off clouds of dust in summer and turned into muddy bogs in winter. Of the forty thousand kilometers of roads in 1941, five thousand were considered "good," three thousand were "secondary," and the rest—more than thirty-two thousand kilometers—were *pistes*, "practical for light vehicles, except during periods of rain," according to the *Encyclopédie Coloniale*.[4] Roads through the Middle and High Atlas, the most direct routes to the deep south, were more like widened tracks than actual highways, treacherous in winter because of rain, ice, and snow.

The itinerary was carefully planned to avoid the worst conditions. From Casablanca, Benatar's party headed east to Rabat on the coastal road, then turned north to Port Lyautey (Kenitra) and then south to Petitjean (Sidi Qacem), and from there to Meknes, where they spent the first night. The following day, they headed east through Taza to Oujda, located on the Morocco-Algeria border. On the third day, they drove south to Berguent, where the paved road ended. On the fourth and last day, after bumping along on a rutted dirt track for two hundred kilometers and seeing nothing but desert, they reached Bou Arfa. Along the route, they visited Vichy labor camps and collected information the inmates had prepared in advance. After a week of arduous travel, they returned home with notebooks filled with data to support their campaign to liberate the camps.

The days following the American landing were a time of soaring optimism, as relief funds from US aid organizations poured into Morocco. Benatar estimated that the 250 inmates at Sidi El Ayachi would be liberated first, with the ex-soldiers in the Saharan camps to follow. The JDC promised two million francs to cover costs and counted on Benatar to do the rest.[5] But as the weeks went by, inconclusive negotiations with French officials brought everything to a halt.

The defeated military leadership of French North Africa was not yet ready to open the prison gates, even in the face of mounting pressure. Roosevelt's announcement following the American landing calling for the liberation of the prison camps seemed to have fallen on deaf ears. As it consolidated its foothold on the African continent, the American military wrestled with a colonial bureaucracy sheltering die-hard holdovers from Vichy. Many French officials were openly pro-Allied, but a hard-core remainder still clung to *le Maréchal*. On a visit to Casablanca, the American diplomat James Rives Childs marveled that six weeks after the landings, he found "a propaganda center for the National Revolution still open on a main street engaged in the distribution of violently anti-Allied [material]." Portraits of Pétain still hung in cafés and other public places, and far-right associations continued to stage boisterous, pro-fascist rallies featuring robust youth and bereted old men. It was difficult to detect any turning of the tide expected after such a radical reversal in the fortunes of war. The historian Christine Levisse-Touzé wrote that Admiral François Darlan, the Allied choice for high commissioner for North Africa, had simply replaced "a Vichyism under German control for a Vichyism under American control."[6]

After the assassination of Darlan on December 24, the mantle of leadership fell on General Henri Giraud, a favorite of Robert Murphy's. Friendly enough to the Allies, Giraud was still committed to the Darlan approach, preferring half measures rather than genuine reforms. He kept former Vichyites in place and failed to remove the anti-Semitic laws. "Upright, honest, dim and reactionary," in the words of the historian Julian Jackson, Giraud refused to open the gates of the internment camps, fearing an outpouring of "dangerous fanatics" and "Communists."[7]

The American journalist Drew Middleton, writing for the *New York Times* from North Africa, deftly skewered the attitude of the French high command toward the stale leftovers of Vichy. Legionnaires, settlers, and General Noguès himself were held in contempt by Middleton: "Profiteering, political apathy—worse than any factional strife—distrust of the Americans and lack of faith in an ultimate United Nations victory, are rife in French Morocco," he wrote. "[It] is a confused, dizzy country where the American flag flies near concentration camps and French collaborationists form an inter-Allied club and mix freely with American officers."[8]

The few voices calling for a speedy liberation of the camps were drowned out by a chorus of naysayers who continued to portray the prisoners as a threat. Dr. Edouard Wyss-Dunant, head of the local branch of the International Red Cross, warned not to set the men free until "the bad" could be sorted out from "the good." Wyss-Dunant called for separating out the "friendly nationalities"—Poles, Belgians, Czechs, Greeks, Yugoslavs, and British—from all the rest. He declared that the "friendly" group presented no problem, but the others, ex-Germans and ex-Austrians who were mostly Jews, should be handled "with great care." Friedrich Schnek, an ex-German Jew held at Kenadza camp on the Morocco-Algeria border, summed up the situation: "Having been treated until November [1942] as a *bande de sales juifs* [a bunch of dirty Jews], . . . we are said now to be *sales Boches* [dirty Krauts]."⁹

Movement on the camps was slow but not completely frozen. The Americans' overwhelming need for able-bodied workers to support the Allied war effort was the critical factor favoring the liberation of the camps. The prison population in early 1943 was estimated at roughly three thousand men, a welcome source of manpower.¹⁰ "It was perfectly clear that the only adequate labor to be had was in the camps," AFSC representative Leslie Heath wrote.¹¹ Heath encouraged Nelly Benatar to contact an American officer, Colonel Warren Pugh, head of civil affairs for the US Army, with a proposal. In early December 1942, Benatar made Pugh an offer that was difficult to refuse. She suggested that "stateless persons of German and Austrian origin interned in concentration camps and work camps" in Morocco be released into her custody, to help the Allied cause. She pointed out the absurdity of keeping people locked up when their labor was needed, and she promised to look after them once they were set free: "Most of [them] came to Morocco in July 1940 from France and Belgium as anti-Hitlerian refugees, because of their anti-Nazi views they were placed in camps from which we desire to see them exit. It remains understood that the American Joint Distribution Committee, of which I am the representative in Morocco, will take charge of all the costs of feeding and housing them until they can find remunerative work."¹²

Colonel Pugh looked on the offer favorably and Benatar responded, not with a list of men in the forced-labor camps (a list she did not yet have), but rather with a list of sixty-six people at Camp Sidi El Ayachi. The list included twenty-nine ex-Germans and ex-Austrians, and twenty-seven others of diverse origin, among them Poles, Russians, Yugoslavs, Hungarians, Romanians, and Lithuanians.¹³ Weeks went by in silence while Benatar bombarded French and American officials with letters calling for action. Finally, at the end of January, buckling to American pressure, the Protectorate authorities finally agreed to let the Sidi El Ayachi inmates go——the first detainees to be given their freedom.

Leslie Heath reported that "there was great jubilation among the Israelites yesterday, most of the people on Madame Benatar's famous list of Jews at Sidi El Ayachi have been released."[14] While waiting, Benatar had made an inventory of the professional qualifications of each detainee. She also found lodgings for them even before they left the camp. Her hastily written marginal notes tell the story: "Zalma Grynbaum, pastrymaker, Polish, worked at the 'Viennese Patisserie,' Passage Sumica, can live with friends, no need for aid"; "Jacob Goldstein, Polish, has money to live on, can work."[15] It was a significant victory. Most of the liberated people, both men and women, were stateless and without papers. The decision to make this category of refugee eligible for work permits was a milestone.

The liberation of Sidi El Ayachi, driven forward by Benatar's dogged persistence, sent ripples of excitement through the world of refugee relief in Casablanca. The JDC, the International Red Cross, the AFSC, and other service agencies jumped at the chance to become involved in the push for further prisoner releases. A new phase was opening up, finally turning the page on Vichy's grim history of racially and politically motivated incarceration.

In the background to the campaign to liberate the Vichy camps were important developments in the Mediterranean theater of war. The American public was thrilled by the success of Operation Torch. The landings not only transformed military prospects but also raised new questions about civilian refugees. The Allied military saw North Africa as a giant catchment area for thousands of rootless noncombatants who could easily "get in the way" of progress in the war. Unsure of how to handle the problem, they sought help from "experts," private organizations such as the AFSC and the JDC with credentials for dealing with humanitarian issues. Looking forward, cooperation between nongovernmental organizations and the Allied military made the most sense as the best method for delivering refugee relief. But the contours of how to proceed on that model were still unclear, largely because of hesitancy at the higher levels of policy making.

In Washington, American officialdom was still in denial about the severity of the refugee problem and did everything in its power to minimize it, reassuring the American public that an "invasion" of foreign refugees was not in the offing. Assistant Secretary of State Breckinridge Long, a fierce opponent of immigration, insisted that consular officials keep a tight hold on issuing US visas. To further complicate matters, the State Department refused to allow returning American troop ships to transport refugees, leaving many holders of valid US visas in limbo.[16]

In April, US and British officials met in Hamilton, Bermuda, to consider the refugee question. Perhaps the tropical splendor lulled them into passivity—the diplomats decided that their answer would be inaction. US immigration quotas would not be increased, nor would the British consider allowing more Jews into Palestine. The *New York Times* declared that the Bermuda conference had ended with a "hopeful hint," but American Jewish groups scorned the results, calling them a "cruel mockery."[17] For years, official American sources had used the mantra that the pursuit of "total victory" overrode all other wartime objectives, including helping refugees. When news of mass murder in Hitler's Europe reached American Jews in late 1942, they dropped their customary restraint. On March 1, 1943, more than twenty thousand people gathered in Madison Square Garden at a rally sponsored by the American Jewish Committee, demanding to "stop Hitler now." In Britain, the archbishop of Canterbury spoke out, calling the atrocities "the most appalling horror in recorded history."[18] Jews and non-Jews in the West were finally waking up to the fact that a hecatomb was taking place within the territories held by Third Reich.

State Department officials recognized that the Jewish factor in the refugee crisis could no longer be ignored. Up to this point, US diplomats had carefully avoided saying that most of those seeking asylum in the United States were Jews; instead, they referred to country of origin or "nationality" as the defining category for visa applicants. Now that Hitler's plan to annihilate European Jewry was fully exposed—though not yet labeled as "genocide"— Jewish organizations insisted that refugees be counted, not only in terms of their country of origin but also in terms of their ethno-religious identity. It was a great leap forward from the Jewish point of view, an important battle finally won. The US State Department reluctantly complied, fearful that if it did not, it would be charged with anti-Semitism. Discussion of the refugee issue began to change dramatically.[19] That change was not immediately apparent in the field, but eventually, it would have a dramatic impact on the work of the relief agencies operating in North Africa.

With the Sidi El Ayachi release behind her, Benatar turned her attention to liberating the forced-labor camps in the Sahara. This was a far more difficult exercise than the Sidi El Ayachi liberation. Just counting the Jewish prisoners held in the Saharan camps was a formidable task. In addition, many of the men were working on projects such as the Trans-Saharan Railway that were deemed "essential" for the war effort. French officials from the Office of Industrial Production were still locked in a Vichy mindset and unlikely to make concessions. The transition from a collaborationist mode to one directed toward helping the Allied cause was far from complete.

Benatar decided to begin her assault on the Saharan camps with the long-awaited tour of inspection, visiting each camp to gather data at firsthand. By equipping herself with factual knowledge of who was in the camps, their status and skills, she believed that she could make a better case for their release. She began by knocking on doors at the Residency in Rabat, reaching as high as Pierre Voizard, secretary-general of the Protectorate, in order to get clearance to make the journey. Voizard, who was sympathetic to her plans, issued an *attestation* (official orders) commanding that "all facilities be given her to accomplish her mission, including interviews with the prisoners."[20] The stage was set for an all-out effort to finally liquidate the forced-labor camps. Benatar's timing was perfect, because the Allies were also getting ready to act. In late January, sensing a shift in the international mood and following Roosevelt's lead, Robert Murphy decided to look into a plan to "liquidate the political prisoner problem in North and West Africa" by creating the Inter-Allied Joint Commission to study the status of the forced-labor camps. With the influential Robert Murphy now into the game of liberation, there was no turning back.[21] Word spread throughout the camps system that help was on the way.

The travelers left Casablanca on February 24, reaching Bou Arfa, the farthest point of their journey, four days later "after a strenuous trip on very bad roads." The visit to Bou Arfa became the model for how to proceed. There they found 86 Jewish and 620 Spanish workers still under lock and key.[22] "Their most ardent desire," wrote Benatar, "is to leave this forlorn place as soon as possible and to work in Casablanca." Benatar met with the French camp commandant and exchanged cordialities, and then her team went to work, interviewing, filling in missing data, completing the employment profile for every Jewish inmate, and for many who were not Jewish. They followed the same procedure at each site they visited. Myriam Benatar and Marguerite Fux did most of the interviewing, while Nelly Benatar and Maurice Vanikoff met with camp officials. Notes about the actual proceedings have not survived, but it must have been an emotionally charged experience to finally meet face-to-face with the men who had endured years of harsh confinement.

On the return trip, the party stopped at Berguent and the Guenfouda and Djerada mines, where seventy-eight Jewish EVDGs were employed under very bad conditions. Work at the mines was extremely dangerous and un-healthy. Some of the Jewish prisoner-miners had become radicalized by their Spanish coworkers, and they were in a rebellious mood. The management wanted to keep the men there, but Benatar insisted that if they stayed, they would have to sign work contracts with the mine's management, guaranteeing them the same salary as civilian workers. Only a few expressed a readiness to stay. The group spent their last night on the road in Fez at the elegant Hotel Palais Jamaï, a lavish Moorish-style establishment owned by the state railroad company. From the hotel dining room, they enjoyed a stunning view of the Fez medina at night, the flickering light of gas lamps lighting up the walls of the ancient town. At dinner, they made a toast to their success and to their return to civilization.

Two weeks later, Benatar made another, shorter circuit to Im Fout, where a huge hydroelectric dam was under construction using forced labor, many of whom were ex-EVDGs. Benatar's archive suggests that this trip was not only for work but also for pleasure. Her only companion on this circuit was Jacob Klein, the Viennese "chauffeur." After the visit to Im Fout, they spent three nights in Marrakech at the luxurious Hotel La Ma-mounia, crown jewel of French touring hotels and favorite watering hole of British prime minister Winston Churchill, set within a vast garden of tropical flowers and fragrant orange trees. The purpose of the Marrakech stopover, according to Benatar, was to "consult the regional authorities and the employment services" on behalf of refugees. But there is no evidence in her archive that any such meetings ever took place. Instead, several elegant dinners for two in the hotel's posh dining room, according to a hotel bill casually inserted in her files. A romantic interlude? Perhaps. Benatar and Klein, after weeks of travel together, had become solid companions of the road. The Mamounia interlude must have been idyllic—a beautiful, restful hiatus far from the stresses of war.

The February journey to eastern Morocco—still arduous by today's standards—produced important results. The Benatar team visited all the internment camps where former soldiers were still held and found 391 Jewish ex-EVDGs at thirteen different locations. On her return, Benatar made the rounds of the Residency and left on Voizard's desk a forty-page report containing precise details about all the ex-EVDGs still in Morocco in the former Vichy camps. Voizard had the authority to make decisions quickly, and to force both the Office of Industrial Production and the security services to comply.[23] Within days, he ordered the liberation of a first group of twenty men, promising that as soon as they found employment, another twenty would to be let go, and so on, "until the proposals of Maître Benatar are completely satisfied."[24]

News of Benatar's success traveled fast. In May, David Hartley of the AFSC reported that "amazing changes have taken place in the camp situation here." He credited Murphy's Inter-Allied Joint Commission for bringing to bear official pressure, but he also acknowledged the work of Benatar, "for had not the individual plugging been done and the consequent odor arisen, the Commission probably would never have been appointed."[25] Eric Johnson, another Quaker representative, was even more specific: "Mme. Benatar of the J.D.C. had been doing a sort of underground railroad business of getting people jobs in the U.S. Army. Men would just turn up from the camps, and no one would ask any questions . . . Now the French have agreed to free all those who have work contracts."[26]

The liberation of the forced-labor camps in the spring of 1943 was a high point of Nelly Benatar's war. But not everyone was enamored of this feisty, single-minded woman who was such a fierce campaigner for refugee rights. Eric Johnson of the Quakers, a good friend of Benatar's, admitted that she "had her faults." "Still," he agreed, "she has gotten a helluva lot done . . . I'm perfectly willing that she go off the deep end now and then."[27]

The deep end, unfortunately, was familiar territory when it came to Benatar's relations with the JDC. She suspected that the JDC was stealing credit for her work, intentionally dropping her name from their publicity. At one point, relations between Benatar and the JDC deteriorated so much that Eric Johnson had to be called in to mediate. Through Johnson, she declared that the camps' liberation was "an internal affair," and the JDC should not be involved. Still, Benatar knew that the JDC was a steady source of funding and had to be appeased.[28] The tug of war would continue until June, when Joe Schwartz visited Morocco and he and Benatar had their first in-person meeting. Afterward, Schwartz acknowledged her role as the architect of the camps' liberation:

> She is a person of energy, devotion and great executive ability. Despite the fact that she is one of the leading attorneys in all of Morocco, she has given a great deal of her time to the refugee problem and has performed her services remarkably well. She is held in high esteem by the American, British, and French authorities and is very highly thought of by the local Jewish community. With her energy and with the fine group of young people which she has gathered around her and with the moral and financial support of the JDC, it is felt that something concrete may be accomplished.[29]

The publicity department of the JDC that once refused to mention her name began to regularly refer to her as their official "Representative in North Africa." For Benatar, the taste of victory must have been delectable.

Soon there was more good news. The legal quota imposed on Jewish lawyers was formally revoked in February 1943. While her male Jewish colleagues were quickly reinstated in the first round, Benatar's name was absent from the list. She wasted no time in writing to Resident-General Noguès: "I am waiting impatiently. The ban has hit me hard, for I am a widow with two young children and responsible for their support." Voizard answered back with an apology, reassuring her she would be included in the next general order. She returned to the practice of law with renewed energy, and because of her soaring reputation, found work easily.[30] Her organization, the Committee for Assistance to Refugees, nullified by the German Armistice Commission in 1941, was legally reinstated. Finally, in another show of strength, she brought her long-standing feud with the International Red Cross to a close and had her revenge. She told their Moroccan representative that henceforward, she would take care of "all Jewish refugees seeking help," canceling the International Red Cross's role in Jewish refugee relief in Morocco.[31]

Her relations with the American military were extremely cordial. She made herself indispensable, helping US military intelligence identify ex-German and ex-Austrian former prisoners to serve as informants in planning Allied bombing raids.[32] She befriended Jewish Army chaplains and helped to arrange home hospitality for Jewish GIs.[33] These gestures were motivated by more than political expediency. Benatar was genuinely moved by the role that American Jewish soldiers—more than six thousand of them—had played in the liberation of her country.

Instantly rolling back all the nightmares of the previous few years was not possible, but restoring a sense of dignity to former inmates was definitely within reach. Thanks to the Americans, Casablanca's economy was booming. Thousands of soldiers had to be fed and clothed, tons of war matériel arriving daily had to be sorted, inventoried and redistributed. Requests for workers poured into Benatar's office. In addition to the US Army, mining companies, flour mills, a glass factory, a textile factory, transport companies, bakeries— all required workers. "We have a great need for personnel, and we would like help as soon as possible," came a message from the manager of a soap factory in Casablanca.[34] Benatar made lists of jobs and tried to match them with men who qualified.[35] Her office became an employment bureau for ex-prisoners, sending people out to interview for jobs she considered suitable.

According to a report filed by the Quakers, nine thousand European Jews were employed in Casablanca in mid-1943. Nearly two thousand Jewish men were working on the docks alone, turning refugee labor into a vital component of the local war economy. Benatar's "protégés" were much in demand. To the boss of a trucking company looking for a night watchman, she wrote: "I am sending to you Alfred Schwartz, an ex-Austrian, who seems to me perfectly suited to fill your vacant post." Schwartz, a former EVDG, was a furrier by profession. After three years of incarceration, even the humble position of night watchman was appealing, for it meant a weekly wage and the freedom to walk the streets. If one job did not work out, Benatar would find the ex-prisoner another while providing him with food and shelter.[36] For Benatar, liberation was not a onetime act of emancipation but a sustained effort to get people back on their feet.

A most pressing need at the time was for refugee housing—where to lodge the newly released former inmates who flocked to the city seeking work. The JDC and other aid agencies joined forces to create a refugee center at the "Luna Park," an abandoned recreation park to the east of the city, and put Benatar in charge. Benatar hired refugee workers to renovate the dilapidated social hall, converting it into dormitory space. Using discarded wood from US

Army packing crates, the refugee carpenters turned the scrap into beds and partitions, and the first group of forty liberated ex-EVDGs moved in.

But matters soon got out of hand. Most of this group were veterans of years of incarceration, and they rejected all constraints on their freedom, indeed, supervision of any kind.[37] "Incidents of all kinds are taking place, due to the mix of people of every mentality and morality, to the point where we are unable to enforce even a modicum of the discipline that should prevail in a facility of this sort," Benatar wrote. The root of the problem was a refugee named Epstein, who lit fires in his room, invited women in, and refused to comply with the rules. The conduct of some of the ex-Legionnaires was even worse. They would return late at night drunk, singing at the top of their lungs.[38] Fearing that the JDC would get word of the chaos and lose confidence in her, Benatar hired a director for the center, a recently arrived Austrian refugee named Ganz, who quickly brought the situation under control. A thorough cleaning, more electric lights and hot water, a supply of daily newspapers, and even flowers for the entryway instantly boosted morale. Ganz made a list of bylaws to regulate social relations. Within a matter of weeks, he reported that residents spent the evening "sitting together, reading and writing, playing checkers and chess."[39]

The Luna Park experience made a strong impression on Benatar. The camps' liberation exposed her to a new species of refugee; people with no legal identity, no resources, no family or emotional support, lacking the tools to survive on their own—quite different from the transients who were the vast majority of her clients during the first two years of the war. The days of simple humanitarian gestures were over. The phase ahead would have to take into account the "whole" person—physical, psychological, and aspirational. People damaged by years of turmoil and abuse needed special care, calling for a diversified organizational response, carried out by trained professionals with the deep pockets to pay for it.

In November, forty-four representatives of the new United Nations met at the White House and created the United Nations Relief and Rehabilitation Administration (UNRRA). Governor Herbert Lehman of New York was named director general, signaling that the American government, with strong British backing, was taking the lead in organizing long-term refugee relief. UNRRA was the most ambitious international relief project yet. With its headquarters in Washington, DC, UNRRA's mandate embraced "rehabilitation" as well as relief, broadening its mandate into the postwar era. Organizations like the JDC did not waste time jumping onto the UNRRA caravan.[40]

Benatar understood that UNRRA was the start of something new, and she tried to visualize a role for herself in it. It was a moment for serious reorientation. Many of her old friends within the Vichy administration in Rabat had been replaced by a new cadre of enthusiastic pro-Gaullists. Noguès was gone, swept away in the housecleaning that took place when General de Gaulle arrived in North Africa at the end of May. Finally, the command centers for American-sponsored refugee relief had relocated away from Lisbon, Casablanca and Marseille to new headquarters in Washington and Algiers.[41] For the first time in years, she felt at loose ends.

At this moment, a group of Benatar's liberal friends working for the new French government in Algiers proposed that she join them. They urged her to take on a legal portfolio befitting her skills; namely, seeking redress for refugees whose civil rights had been lost under Vichy rule. Taking advantage of her daughter Myriam's decision to continue her medical training at the Faculty of Medicine in Algiers, Nelly Benatar began dividing her time between her home in Casablanca and the excitement of Algiers.[42]

Algiers in 1943 was a city turned on its head. From a distance, it was a mirage in white and blue, with the chalky shapes of the native quarter tumbling down the steep incline of the casbah like a cascade of pearls. It looked tranquil, even lifeless, but that was deceptive. From within, it pulsated with movement and excitement—people, traffic, and a throbbing energy brought on by swift changes in the progress of the war.

There was no place to rest in this cauldron of activity. People slept in chairs, on camp beds, even in the back seats of automobiles that were not suited for anything else because of the lack of petrol. Finding a meal was equally as trying. Most restaurants had been requisitioned by the military and were overflowing with hungry soldiers. The streets were jammed with jeeps, ambulances, trucks, trams, donkeys, and human porters dodging sleek official cars carrying Allied military officers and French politicians.[43]

Politics was the *menu du jour*, as General de Gaulle began his long, slow march toward a new French nationhood. After the landing in November 1942, the American plan was to put forward the feckless Giraud as the face of the regime, but de Gaulle refused to work with him. Instead, he bided his time, knowing that the French Left and the Resistance were on his side. Even so, his footing in North Africa was not secure. The overall picture was one of "chaos and confusion," according to the French philosopher-pundit Raymond Aron, with many different factions jockeying for position. Yet Algeria represented an opportunity for de Gaulle. There he could dismantle what was left of Vichy and create a new government that would become the cornerstone for a democratic postwar France. For several months, de Gaulle shared an uneasy bicephalous command with Giraud, but the latter's summertime absence gave de Gaulle the opportunity to tighten his grip and create his own political arm—the French Committee of National Liberation (Comité Français de Libération Nationale, the CFLN). By the fall, Giraud was gone and de Gaulle alone held the reins of power.

The atmosphere in which the *épuration*, or political purges, began in late 1943 was a direct result of de Gaulle's abhorrence for Vichy and everything it stood for, as well as the practical need to demonstrate that the CFLN was ready to serve as the generator of a reborn French republic. With de Gaulle's approval, a civilian purge commission was created in August, empowered to impose an array of punishments ranging from dismissal, to prison sentences, and even death for former Vichy officials who stood in the way of a transition. Driven by the passion of the Resistance, yet governed by reference to the rule of law, during its yearlong tenure the purge commission took up nearly one thousand cases of suspect behavior.

Conscious of this fundamental shift, lawyer Nelly Benatar tried to take advantage of the new mood sweeping through the French bureaucracy. As personnel changed from Vichyites to Gaullists, so did Benatar's methods of interacting with them. Overall attitudes were evolving, but the refugee still had to navigate a labyrinth-like bureaucracy. Identity cards, ration cards, and signatures on documents were necessary to establish rights to food, housing, and even a work permit. Benatar's strategy was to advocate for a new way of thinking about refugees as people with rights, taking her case directly to those in charge of designing the new French state.

Her most convincing argument with officialdom was the familiar one that her clients—mostly stateless people—were stateless through no fault of their own. "All these people arrived in France as anti-Hitler political refugees, and their political views should not be doubted," she argued.[44] She would show up with her clients at government offices and argue on their behalf, and usually her view prevailed. Her goal was to transform the category of "stateless" from a term of negativity to a condition having some legal value, and she was beginning to have success.

The case of Enrico Coen, a Jewish ex-EVDG born in Istanbul to Turkish Jewish parents, is representative of her approach. Coen went to the police in Rabat to obtain an identity card but was refused. He found himself in the midst of a bureaucratic muddle and appealed to Benatar for help, fearing that without the identity card, he would be sent back to a detention camp:

> It is with great pain that I come to you again, for I have not forgotten all of your earlier efforts for me, thanks to which I am now free . . . please intervene on my behalf with the Diplomatic Bureau (Cabinet diplomatique) if you have the time. . . . I was born May 12, 1919 in Constantinople to Turkish parents. In 1922 we left Turkey for Italy, where my father became an Italian citizen. He was deprived of that citizenship in 1938, because he was a Jew. . . . In 1939 we went to France and I enlisted as an EVDG, and was sent to Morocco . . . when I was demobilized, I was sent to the labor camp of Bou Arfa. and then to Sidi El Ayachi, from which I was liberated thanks to your intervention. I declared myself to be stateless because . . . my father no longer had Italian citizenship. I fought for France against the Italians. I would like a resolution to my problem in order to live peacefully.[45]

Benatar was unable to confirm Coen's Turkish birth. His Italian nationality, conferred on him by his father, was null and void, making him stateless. She decided to put the question of birth and nationality aside, making the case for him on different grounds. She claimed that his service in the French military and his actions as a soldier demonstrated his loyalty to France, and for that he should be granted French citizenship. Her argument was that his war record had released him from any accidents of birth. She also obtained proof that two of Coen's uncles had heroically fought for France during the Great War; one was twice wounded and the other was killed in action.[46]

The remaking of Coen's claim to French citizenship on the basis of his military service, instead of on his presumed birthright, was a bold move that would allow him to exit from a legal limbo. Ironically, the claim for French citizenship on these grounds was precisely what prewar French governments had tried to prevent. But now, the situation was quite different. Coen was not sent back to prison by the courts; instead, he got new papers, found a job in Casablanca, married a Moroccan Jewish woman, and eventually was repatriated back to France with his family. The times had changed. Benatar had improvised a new pathway to claiming French citizenship, finding a practical solution to the dilemma of statelessness that had followed so many of the ex-EVDGs from the camps of Vichy into liberation.

Benatar joined a tight circle of activists in Algiers dedicated to defending the rights of ex-EVDGs like Enrico Coen. As a group, they were especially keen to redress miscarriages of justice that involved refugees who happened to be Jews. She worked closely with her old friend Maurice Vanikoff, who was also living in Algiers. The dynamic Vanikoff wore multiple hats: as legal counsel for the EVDG Association, as head of the pro-Gaullist Center for Political and Social Documentation, and as a writer for the resistance journal *Combat*. Also in this circle was Léon Marchal, an influential member of the pro-Gaullist government in exile, who helped Vanikoff in his quest to win legal rights for ex-EVDGs.[47] Another member of the Vanikoff group was Robert Schumann, a friend of Benatar from Casablanca and the days of the Mengin resistance organization. A lawyer by profession, Schumann had fled Morocco in 1942, reappearing a year later in Algiers. As the purge trials gained momentum, Schumann was seized by the idea that Jews deserved a special sort of retribution, and he purposely sought instances that exposed examples of the racially motivated bias of Vichy. He wanted to make the case, important but not yet popular, that Vichy's crimes against the Jews were not a sideshow but went to the heart of its strategy of domination. Schumann tried to draw Benatar into his project, seeing her as a capable and useful ally. But his plan turned out to be a flawed one, causing Benatar some grief. The details of this painful episode are as improbable as its setting; nevertheless, they are worth retelling, because they expose yet another well-hidden aspect of Benatar's personality.

Tineghir, a small town in the Draa Valley of Morocco on the far side of the Atlas Mountains, was home to a small Jewish community practically indistinguishable from its Berber-speaking neighbors.[48] Long-standing habits of peaceful coexistence between Muslims and Jews were suddenly disrupted in 1943 by shocking events. The Jews of Tineghir were reportedly being tormented by a local commandant, a sadistic French military officer named Chayrenne. Inspired by Nazi-style forms of persecution, Chayrenne demanded that Tineghir's Jews perform debased acts and wear humiliating clothing as signs of inferiority.

Seeing an opportunity for some eye-catching publicity, Schumann urged Benatar to take on the legal case against Chayrenne in defense of the Jews of Tineghir, opening a new front in Schumann's war against the remnants of Vichy. Benatar reluctantly agreed and wrote a letter to Thami el-Glaoui, Pasha of Marrakech, feudal overlord of the Draa Valley and codependent of the French colonial regime. Benatar sought his intervention in the case, but she soon regretted it. "I am not used to this style," she complained, referring perhaps to the despotic nature of el-Glaoui's rule. She was also unsure about the facts of the case and felt as if she was on shaky ground.

There was more to her discomfort than "style," for two reasons: first, her legal sense told her that it would be a waste of time, and her instincts proved correct. The Jewish plaintiffs of Tineghir, no doubt fearing retribution in their small corner of the world, refused to go to court. But a second reason strikes even closer to home and offers a clue to her own inner feelings. This incident is one of the very few places in her archive where Benatar takes notice of rural Moroccan Jews, who accounted for more than three-quarters of Moroccan Jewry at that time. She had little firsthand knowledge of the people of Tineghir or of their way of life. She refers to them as *barranin*, an Arabic word meaning "outsiders" or "strangers"—a frank admission of their distance from her world. She recognized that the tyrannical system under which they lived held them prisoner, and that there was little she could do to change it. So she abruptly removed herself from the case.[49]

Thus ended Benatar's brief and unrewarding foray into rural Moroccan politics. This disappointing episode had a positive turn, however, for it helped her to redirect her next steps. European refugees were still her cause, and new opportunities to help them were on the horizon.

CHAPTER 7

1944

The Right to Have Rights

FEDALA CAMP was an old French army post located about seventeen kilometers east of Casablanca on the Atlantic coast. Taken over by the American army in 1942, the camp was used as a staging area for troops on their way east. In 1944, it became the first UNRRA camp in North Africa, taking on new life as a safe haven for hundreds of refugees evacuated from Nazi-occupied Europe. With its freshly painted barracks and nearby beach, it had the air of a seaside holiday resort, so long as the onlooker did not notice the barbed-wire perimeter patrolled by armed Italian soldiers. An American flag flew proudly over the gate.[1]

Nelly Benatar spent a large part of 1944 at Fedala, helping to restore refuges to mental and physical health. From her home in Casablanca, she commuted regularly to the camp and became a familiar face to residents as well as to the UNRRA staff. In her role as JDC representative, she perfected her interviewing skills and began to think more deeply about the place of refugees within the framework of a postwar settlement. She understood that the ground had shifted, and that "displaced persons"—a new term coming into use—were the leading edge of a wave of humanity that would have to be reclassified, rehabilitated, and resettled as part of a return to normalcy. The enormity of the task ahead injected an element of grave seriousness into her work.

The idea of creating a transit camp in North Africa for escapees from Hitler's Europe was first raised at the Bermuda Conference in April 1943, but nothing came of it. The American military was lukewarm to the idea and unsure of its ability to run a civilian camp. Among French officials in North Africa, still in disarray due to the change in regime, enthusiasm was even less. In retrospect, it seems certain that without Allied pressure, the camp would never have come into being.[2] But now that the war was going well, a few inspired people in Washington decided to wrest control of the refugee problem from the obstructionists in the State Department. Urged on by the Treasury secretary Henry Morgenthau Jr., FDR created the War Refugee Board in January 1944. The purpose of this entity was to organize Allied efforts to intervene directly in helping Europeans escape from Hitler's grasp. The War Refugee Board was eager to begin operations and viewed the Fedala setup as an opportunity to put its ideas to work.[3]

What exactly "rescuing" meant at that point was rather murky. Did it mean propaganda? Support for partisans, secret deals, help for the resistance? Did it involve rehabilitation for escapees at UN camps, resettlement, family reunification? All these options were on the table, and many of them were eventually adopted after a period of trial and error. Meanwhile, the opportunity to bring to North Africa a large group of survivors presently cooped up in Spanish camps under intolerable conditions was an opportunity not to be missed.[4]

UNRRA was just coming into being in early 1944 and had not yet developed detailed protocols for running a refugee camp. It had to rely on the expertise of organizations already in the field, like the JDC. The security issue was a major stumbling block. Every refugee had to be screened by French police to filter out suspected Nazi sympathizers. Each new resident was obliged to fill in sixteen different forms, with five photographs and eleven sets of fingerprints. The residents began their lives under UNRRA protection in a flurry of inspections premised on establishing their credibility as bona fide "refugees."

Moses Beckelman was chosen as the Fedala camp's new director. Beckelman was a hard-boiled social worker from the Bronx who earned his chops in the Bowery during the Depression. He was no stranger to the miseries of war. After joining the JDC in the mid-1930s, he was sent to the Baltics, Shanghai, and South America to help with the evacuation and resettlement of Jewish refugees fleeing Central Europe. His current assignment was to get the Fedala operation up and running quickly. In February, he went to Spain to recruit candidates, but he ran into trouble when more than half the people he interviewed refused to come to Morocco. Most of them had fled Vichy France and had enough of the French.

Eventually, Beckelman rounded up five hundred people willing to move. UNRRA insisted on calling Fedala a "transit" camp, claiming that its occupants were "in transit" for somewhere else. The French also insisted that camp residents remain completely separate from community life, surrounding the camp with barbed wire to suppress any doubts about its degree of isolation. Meanwhile, a hastily assembled team of UNRRA relief workers, mostly young Americans and British having little direct exposure to victims of war, prepared to receive their "guests."[5] The refugees began arriving in three separate groups. The first group of 40 came via Oran on May 11, the second and largest group of 574 people arrived from Cadiz on June 22, and a third group of 26 from Tripoli in Libya came in July. As of July 31, 1944, there were 630 refugees in Fedala camp, and by the end of the summer, the number had reached 800.

Camp residents were a strange mix. Hardened veterans of the Lincoln Brigade mingled with families with small children who had crossed the Pyrenees on foot. A group of twenty-two Roma people were the objects of special curiosity. The remainder of the residents, with few exceptions, were European Jews. They lived in a collection of tents and makeshift wooden barracks that afforded minimal protection from the weather. As winter approached, harsh winds blew in from the sea, bringing pelting rain, rattling doors, and soaking tar-paper windows. Amenities were few: card games, classes in English offered by a professor from the University of Vienna, sports and "physical culture," a mess hall where C-rations were the *plat du jour*. Also a canteen, where the refugees staged a near riot on their first visit as they scrambled to fill their pockets with cigarettes and chocolate. They did not yet understand that the supply of these items from US Army stores was practically inexhaustible.

Despite the drawbacks, Fedala was an improvement over the internment camp of Miranda del Ebro in northern Spain, where most of the first wave came from, and it was certainly better than Bergen-Belsen, where most of the second wave originated. Letters speak of the copious food, the kindness of the staff, hot water for washing, the opportunity for paid work, and a library. Kate Greene, a young UNRRA staffer from Cambridge, Massachusetts, was happy not to have been assigned to one of the UNRRA camps in Egypt, noting optimistically that "even in midsummer our place won't be hot . . . it's on a little rise and we can see the water from it, so there should always be a breeze to cool us."[6] The residents came from thirty-three different countries and spoke sixteen languages; they asked for eleven different religious services.[7] Announcements were made in French, Spanish, German, and Yiddish. Everyone was required to perform light tasks around the camp, including the kitchen work, in order to reintroduce a sense of a normal routine.

Especially noticeable at Fedala was a group of Sephardic Jews from Salonica, who made up the largest single national cluster. Greek in culture and language, they held Spanish passports that turned out to be their ticket to freedom. Most of them were deported by the Nazis in the last convoy of Jews from Salonica in August 1943 and sent to the German concentration camp at Bergen-Belsen. Though badly treated, they were kept isolated from other inmates, given survival-level rations, and not required to work, which kept them alive. They also had friends in high places. The consul general of Spain in Athens, Sebastián Romero Radigales, pleaded for their liberation and finally won the support of Franco, who threw in his lot with the Allies when he saw that the Germans were losing the war. In February 1944, more than 350 Jews from Salonica with Spanish passports left Bergen-Belsen, moving slowly across wartime Europe by train, accompanied by German guards. When they reached Barcelona, they were handed over to the JDC. After languishing for several months in Spain, they arrived in Fedala in June 1944.[8]

Despite an appearance of normalcy, most of the camp's residents were still deeply traumatized. The excitement that took place when the well-stocked canteen first opened was only one example of an undercurrent of free-floating anxiety. The resident doctor reported that the leading complaint among his patients was hypertension caused by stress. There were also problems about food. Residents refused to eat unpeeled potatoes that were a reminder of the Nazi camps. They were also upset when leftover bread was thrown away and asked that it be given to the "Arabs."[9]

Beneath the veneer of calm were a raft of legal and procedural problems. This is where Benatar's skills became useful. Her official title was "local representative of the JDC," and she used it to make her influence felt. Fedala was the JDC's first major relief project in North Africa in cooperation with UNRRA, and Benatar was invested in making it a success. She took on tasks that drew on her legal expertise and her familiarity with French officialdom.

She knew how to smooth ruffled French feathers, and with her improving English, she was also able to connect with her American and British coworkers.

Benatar's job was to interview problem cases, to identify refugees wanting to emigrate to Palestine, and to begin the process of procuring identity papers for stateless persons to hasten their resettlement. Another task was to reunite separated families. Some residents had left close family behind in Spain. She pestered French officials ceaselessly to admit them to Morocco, and she asked the JDC to arrange for their transfer—not sometime in the future, but "on the next convoy."[10]

She was especially good at adapting to the lexicon of the new era. The abrupt transition from the authoritarian nightmare of fascism to the friendly gestures of the Allies had left many Central European Jews disoriented. For the destitute refugee—and most were destitute—reconstituting one's selfhood was an essential first step to gaining access to UNRRA's generous benefits. Benatar mastered the language of eligibility for refugee status and crafted positive profiles for refugees who had been stripped of their legal rights. Interviewing the applicant face-to-face, using facts from a personal history, and adding her own comments and observations, she would make the case for a client's inclusion in the coveted status of "refugee" under UNRRA protection.

Benatar's understanding of who should qualify for UNRRA's largesse was based on years of experience in the field. It was a skill that her younger coworkers did not always share. Observing that the level of frustration was rising among the staff, she decided to set down clear guidelines for interviewing and establishing the qualifications needed to collect UNRRA benefits. She wrote a short essay about what she had learned, calling it simply "Étude sur les réfugiés," or "An Essay on Refugees," in which she drew on the work of Russian Jewish demographer Eugene Kulischer to organize her thoughts.[11]

In a pamphlet authored for the American Jewish Committee in 1943, Kulischer, an expert on migration, took up the question of Jewish postwar settlement. Proceeding on a country-by-country basis, he used statistics to map the awesome dimensions of the emergency. How to absorb and resettle hundreds of thousands of "displaced persons" (a term that Kulischer is credited with having invented) was the problem. He urged nation-states to consider opening their gates to people from other countries while suspecting this may have been wishful thinking. If states failed to act, then he suggested that international forces take over. Migrations had to be "regulated" by the global community, with people "selected" and "trained" for migration to a specific destination.[12]

Kulischer's work had a resounding effect on Benatar. She saw in it a solution to the "stateless" problem, a way of turning persons with no rights into people having qualities of their own. Her own essay proposed a quasi-legal status to be granted by an international entity to individual refugees that would be independent of the nation-state. Recognizing that many refugees would not return to their "habitual home," she proposed a "home of choice," or *foyer d'élection*, a place of their own choosing that would be recognized by UNRRA.[13] Benatar felt that refugees' humanity had been compromised long enough; what they deserved was the right to protection by the international community.[14]

Like many others, Benatar had reframed her thinking to fit with newly circulating ideas about human dignity—the "right" of all people to basic and commensurate freedoms. Throughout the free world, as the historian Elizabeth Borgwardt has noted, the war had unleashed a belief in "the fundamental freedoms that differentiated the Allies from their totalitarian rivals."[15] Although the modern human rights regime born out of Europe's wartime torment was still in the future, Benatar's work in the UNRRA refugee camps in 1944 and 1945 embodied a belief in new forms of empathy and understanding of the refugee condition that would gain momentum as the war entered its final phase.

Fedala was a short lived but useful experiment in establishing guidelines for postwar refugee relief. It was a proving ground where ideas were tested and new practices were established. However, even before the camp was fully operational, Moses Beckelman predicted that it would not be viable over the long term. Even at its height, the camp was less than half full, uneconomical to run, and a drain on UNRRA's budget.[16] In addition, the hinge of war had moved to the north and east, away from Morocco. By September 1944 there were forty-five thousand displaced persons on the Italian front who needed to be accommodated by UNRRA. Unless something was done quickly, the nightmare of "individual wanderers running into the many thousands" could become a reality. Relief organizations like the AFSC and HICEM closed their Casablanca offices and moved closer to the front. Morocco had become a backwater.[17]

Then there was the question of Palestine, the final, mythical destination for many Jewish refugees. At the other end of the Mediterranean, with little means to get there, officially on lockdown because of the White Paper of 1939, Palestine was formally off-limits to emigrants. Yet groups of refugees were acquiring "certificates" of entry to Palestine recognized by the British Mandatory authorities. At Fedala camp, lists of residents wishing to migrate to Palestine were drawn up by relief workers with the help of HICEM, and some people, including many Jews from Salonica, began the long journey to the Jewish homeland.[18]

For all these reasons, UNRRA decided to move its North African operations from Fedala to Philippeville in central Algeria, where a new UNRRA camp was being readied to absorb the mass of refugees expected to arrive soon from Europe. The Jeanne d'Arc Center at Philippeville was closer to Italy, the Balkans, and Sinai, where large reserves of displaced people were being held. Also, the new camp had much greater capacity than Fedala and far better facilities. In the final weeks of 1944, refugees still at Fedala moved to Philippeville, and Nelly Benatar moved with them.

The political situation within Morocco suddenly gyrated out of control in 1944, propelling what seemed to be a stable colonial regime into disorder. The signs had been there for some time: the fall of Vichy, the resurgence of the nationalist Istiqlal (Independence) party, and in January 1944, a popular manifesto calling for a separation from France. This series of events triggered a panic within the Residency. For a short time, there was hope that political reform would be taken seriously, but that moment passed quickly. The breach between the nationalists and the colonial regime was irreconcilable.[19]

Moroccan Jews were among those swept up in the delirium of change. Unlike the nationalists, they kept a low profile, debating what a "calculated liberalism" might look like. Under colonial rule, Jews had been seduced culturally but smothered politically and shut out from public life. Hidden behind the façade of the modern colonial state was the archaic and lopsided notion of Moroccan Jewry as a faith-based entity held in place by religious values. True, the Protectorate had allowed modern education to reach selected groups of Jews through the agency of the AIU, but in reality, conditions for the vast majority of Moroccan Jews had changed little under French rule.

Progressive cadres of the Jewish community favored radical reform. Their battle would be on two fronts: on one front, facing the repressive colonial regime, and on the other front, against their own archaic leadership.[20] We should recall the Plan of Reform of 1939, placed on hold by the outbreak of war. With the end of the war in sight, it seemed worthy of revival. And finally, after years of immobilism, Moroccan Jews were being drawn once again to the idea of Zionism and emigration to Palestine. "A profound upheaval of ideas and aspirations," is how one Jewish elder referred to the moment.

The Residency's fear of political activism by indigenous Jews was always a potent one, especially as Jews worldwide began to make an accounting of their assets and to organize for postwar recovery. The World Jewish Congress announced the convocation of an emergency meeting to be held in Atlantic City, New Jersey, in November 1944 for just that purpose. Three separate delegations from Morocco, Algeria, and Tunisia were invited to participate . For the first time in modern history, North African Jewry would be represented at a general convocation of the Jewish people.

The World Jewish Congress's (WJC) emergency meeting of 1944 brought North African Jews into the orbit of global Jewry. Though considered peripheral to the business at hand because they were non-Europeans, the North Africans managed to seize center stage while the rest of the Jewish world was watching, by situating themselves squarely within discourses of Jewish renewal. For the Moroccan delegation, the meeting was a watershed moment that exercised a powerful influence over all aspects of postwar planning and action.

The WJC was created in 1936 to serve as the diplomatic arm of Jews everywhere. Its pro-Zionist leanings were apparent from the beginning. The congress operated within a democratic framework and delegates were elected by secret ballot in their home countries. During the war, meetings were suspended until word trickled out about the destruction of European Jewry. Thereafter, the WJC became the most vocal Jewish organization calling attention to the agony of the Jewish people. The emergency meeting in Atlantic City of November 1944 was the world stage on which the WJC came to grips with the enormity of the loss and the problems of the postwar era.

The meeting unfolded in three phases: preparation, the actual meeting, and the aftermath, when delegates returned home. With hundreds of Jews from all over the world in attendance, the Moroccans could have been a bit players. Instead, they made their presence felt by addressing the plenary and meeting privately with key figures of international Jewry. Delegates converged from all parts of the Jewish world; the intense emotional atmosphere deeply affected the North African delegation, who, for the first time, came face-to-face with the full dimensions of the European tragedy. The event was carefully prepared through a steady flow of communications. The overriding purpose was to confront the problem of the European "remnant." The Moroccans willingly joined other delegations to support Zionist goals, adding their voices to the call for an independent Jewish state. However, they also had other ambitions, based on their own particular style of diasporic existence. The reform of communal structures and a change in the legal status of Moroccan Jewry within the colonial framework were at the top of their list.

Choosing a delegation to represent a population of over two hundred thousand Moroccan Jews with no unified voice was a major challenge. After a lengthy and contentious process, Nelly Benatar and Samuel Lévy were chosen as delegates. The rest of the delegation would be filled out by people already in America—Jack Pinto and Haim Toledano—along with Jonathan Thurscz, the former editor of *L'Avenir Illustré*.

Jack (Jacques) Pinto (1896–1979), Benatar's cousin, was a Tangier-born businessman and philanthropist living in New York City. The Pinto family fortune, like so many in Tangier, had its source in the Amazon, where Jack's father, Moses Pinto, had prospered handsomely from the rubber trade. Jack Pinto generously contributed to many projects benefitting Moroccan Jews. In 1940, he was the largest single donor to Benatar's refugee committee. His wife, Luna Toledano Pinto, was his partner in philanthropy. Haim Toledano, also a resident of New York City, was a Tangier-born journalist who served as political correspondent for various continental newspapers until his departure from Morocco in 1903. Like Jack Pinto, he kept up his connection with Moroccan Jewish affairs. Haim's daughter Gladys graduated from Columbia University and in 1947 married Jules Braunschvig, who later become president of the AIU. These wealthy and well-connected people formed Benatar's American circle of support.[21]

In preparation for the meeting, Benatar wrote an agenda and submitted it to the Residency. She proposed an eleven-point program that included giving Jews equal standing in Muslim courts, ensuring their representation on government councils, and granting official recognition to Moroccan Zionist organizations. Each of these points directly challenged long-standing colonial policy.[22] Her agenda had an explosive effect. The Residency was shocked that the Moroccan delegation would put such "local" issues on the table at a meeting of international Jewry. According to one colonial official, it would be like "washing our dirty linen in public."

At the instigation of the Residency, WJC operatives were summoned from Algiers to bring the Moroccans "back into line." The Algerian WJC representative Benjamin Heler arrived in Casablanca in a matter of days, accompanied by the chief rabbi of Algeria, Maurice Eisenbeth. Both men held high offices in French-sponsored Jewish institutions in Algeria.[23] Predictably, the Moroccans did not welcome them with open arms. Over the following days, Heler and Benatar entered into fiery verbal combat, with Benatar leading the charge. She reacted "violently" (her word) to Heler's high-handed manner. Heler's ignorance of local codes of behavior had uncorked Benatar's famous effervescence.

The spectacle of Jews fighting with one another was not a new one, yet it was unnerving. The Algerians complained that the Moroccans were naïve and inexperienced; the Moroccans considered the Algerians arrogant and overbearing. Some Moroccans even thought Heler was actually "Heller," an Ashkenazi Jewish name. The Moroccans refused to stand down and the wrangling went on for days. Finally, at the end of March, the makeup of the delegation was settled by popular vote. Benatar and Lévy were once again selected as delegates, with Lévy as head of the delegation. But the rancor never really went away.

Nelly Benatar never attended the WJC meeting in Atlantic City. Records show she applied for an entry visa to the United States in March, but months passed with no answer.[24] She asked her Quaker friends in Philadelphia to make inquiries. Word came back that the application had been denied by the US State Department because, in 1940, Benatar had applied for a permanent visa to the United States. That request was blocking the temporary visa request. Benatar renounced the permanent visa application, hoping that would speed up the process.[25] But other obstacles came up, derailing the application. The State Department claimed that Benatar was disqualified because she had family in the hands of the Nazis, which was not true. Objection piled upon objection. By the end of October, when other members of the delegation had their visas in hand, Benatar still had not received hers.

Why this fiasco? Diplomats in Washington were ready to approve Benatar's application, but organizers at the WJC were not. Friends at the AFSC tried to sort out the mess: "[Benatar] was definitely not regarded as important enough to risk the special effort which [the WJC] felt should only be exerted on behalf of very important figures. . . . [I]t may well be that the services she has so capably rendered to other groups figure in this reaction," was one explanation.[26] Benatar's relationship with the JDC, a political rival of the WJC, did not work in her favor. The Quakers also reported that there was "derogatory information" in Benatar's file, with no specific explanation. Did her public feud with Heler brand her as an annoying troublemaker? Were her ties to the JDC a hindrance? Was her period as a *resistante* held against her? The archives are silent. Her pain and embarrassment must have been profound.[27]

The Moroccan delegation at the WJC prepared to meet the wider Jewish world. Prosper Cohen, a young teacher from Meknes, took Benatar's place, and Menahem Murciano, a merchant from the provincial town of Safi, represented the "countryside." With S. D. Lévy at its head, and Pinto and Toledano joining in New York—Thurscz's name had been removed from the list—the official group was five. Preparatory work was assigned to Lévy, including writing an overview of the situation of Moroccan Jewry, and to Cohen, who would report on the problem of education.[28]

Prosper Cohen kept a journal of his stay in Atlantic City. The atmosphere at the meeting was highly charged. The motto was "everything that is Jewish is ours." Cohen was especially moved by the soaring oratory of Rabbi Stephen Wise, president of the World Jewish Congress. Overcome with emotion, Cohen struggled to express his thoughts. He felt like a "novice" and decided to listen rather than speak. "A spark was lit inside me," he wrote, and "it needed a breath of air to catch on fire."[29]

In their presentation to the plenary, the Moroccans focused on the situation at home. Lévy argued that while Moroccan Jews supported the idea of a Jewish state, their contribution to "the immense effort of post-war reconstruction" would be one of self-rehabilitation.[30] His speech initiated European delegates into the unfamiliar world of Moroccan Jewry. He spoke about how France, for all its love of justice, had inflicted a deep wound on Moroccan Jews, keeping them in an inferior status, not recognizing their basic human rights. He talked about schools and education—only 50 percent of Moroccan

FIGURE 7.1 The North African delegation to the World Jewish Congress's emergency meeting, Atlantic City, New Jersey, November 1944. Rabbi Stephen Wise is seated third from left, S. D. Lévy is seated second from right, and Prosper Cohen is in the back row, fourth from right.

Jewish children were receiving a modern education. He touched on social conditions and the fact that most of the Jewish population lived "in a sordid and shameful promiscuity," sparing none of the ugly details. Weaving his way across an unfamiliar landscape, he demystified the situation of Moroccan Jews by revealing some uncomfortable truths.[31]

The conference offered numerous opportunities for the Moroccans to make their case. In private conversation with Maurice Perlzweig, head of the WJC's Political Office, the delegation clarified its position on the matter of Jewish legal rights. Lévy told Perlzweig that in Morocco "There are no laws, no legal code, no rights" pertaining to Jews. Lévy asked Perlzweig to petition the CRIF (Conseil Représentatif des Institutions Juives de France, the Representative Committee of the Jews of France) to lobby the French government to put pressure on Sultan Mohammed V to address the legal status of Moroccan Jews. Lévy believed that the sultan was the only one with the prestige and authority to reform the laws that kept Moroccan Jews in a subordinate position.[32] Lévy was not asking for individual protections for Moroccan Jews. He wanted reforms that would confer on Jews as a collectivity rights equal to Muslims. With France in charge, this radical proposal was both fanciful and impractical; yet, like a fisherman casting his line into an unfamiliar pond, Lévy gave it a try. Preoccupied with European matters, Perlzweig listened politely to the Moroccans, but could do nothing for them. Lévy's proposal went nowhere. The demand to reform Jewish legal status within the French Protectorate regime would continue to haunt the postwar years, until the final French departure from Morocco in 1956.[33]

Most of the delegates were not in the mood to hear about troubles in North Africa. Their attention was focused elsewhere. During the war, American Jewish opinion had veered sharply toward a territorial solution for the "Jewish problem." Mainstream Zionists believed that the rapid removal of survivors to Palestine should be their immediate goal.[34] Lévy did not see the territorial option as suitable for his own people, who were not ready to emigrate in large numbers. Instead, his strategy was to gain concessions from France to improve conditions at home. This approach was one that the rest of the Jewish world, following the Nazi experience, considered fruitless. The Moroccans found themselves woefully out of step with world Jewish opinion.

Nonetheless, and despite their political awkwardness, the Moroccans made a good showing at the World Jewish Congress of 1944. They met Jews from other parts, and they learned about vocational training, health and sanitation practices, credit cooperatives, and other modern programs for community development. They placed their mark on the map of world Jewry.[35] The delegation returned home to a tumultuous greeting. Prosper Cohen joked that people thought they carried in their suitcases certificates of emigration to Palestine. Public meetings were organized in all the big cities. Cohen spoke to packed halls about the horrific dimensions of the slaughter in Europe, news that his listeners greeted with disbelief. He read out loud the resolution to create a Jewish commonwealth in Palestine. The crowd asked him to read the text again and again. "It was as if there were nothing more to do," he said, "other than grab a ticket, pack a bag, and leave for the Holy Land."

Enthusiasm for the Zionist cause was infectious. After his return, Cohen left his teaching post and joined the newly formed Central Committee of the World Zionist Federation in Casablanca. Membership in this organization—75 people when he started out—mushroomed to 475 paying members in less than three months. In Morocco, the Zionist spark had finally caught fire.[36]

The war was not yet over, and Jewish statehood was still only an aspiration. In Morocco, the refugee situation had finally stabilized. Most refugees were managing on their own, having found employment, a place to live, and for some, even a new family. Benatar's client base was a tenth of what it used to be. She was looking for ways to be useful elsewhere.

The UNRRA camp at Philippeville, Algeria, was about to open.[37] Ned Campbell, the director, heard about Benatar and invited her to join his staff. On October 30, 1944, Benatar packed up her daughter Myriam (designating the nineteen-year old as her "secretary") and flew to Algiers. From there, she took the train to Philippeville. Benatar's first assignment was to take a census of all the camp's residents.[38] Aid workers from around the world were joining UNRRA in a mad dash to fill its staffing needs. Some new recruits—there were those who said far too many—were Jews, and Zionists to boot. The British in particular were put off by the Jewish flavor of the UNRRA organization, remembering that its head, Governor Herbert Lehman of New York, was also Jewish. British newspapers made the false claim that 80 percent of UNRRA workers were Jews. Barely disguising their intent, they described UNRRA as too "cosmopolitan," and not at all charity-based.[39]

Those who signed up ignored the negative publicity and were impatient to get to work. The American Sonnia Levine was one of the first medical workers to arrive at Philippeville. A trained biomedical researcher who specialized in infectious diseases, Levine originally joined a medical unit of Hadassah, the American women's Zionist organization, but she was in a hurry to get to the field, so she switched to UNRRA. Not long after her arrival in Philippeville, she corresponded with her friend Louis Sobel, who worked for the JDC in New York. She wrote to him on the thin blue paper of a US government aerogram. The letter eventually found its way into the archives of the JDC:

> I am actually in the UNRRA business now, except it is not in the welfare part—rather in the medical division. . . . I have had the privilege of meeting and having long talks with Madame Benatar from [Casablanca]. She is an amazing person,

small in stature, plump, with lively black eyes. She spent five days with us and worked with the refugees from morning until 10–12 o'clock at night. On only two nights were we able to get her to talk to us. Her purpose in coming here was to get full information on all the people in order to work out their repatriation to their own countries or to be sent to others. We were delighted to hear from her that the majority of people here have a good chance of being repatriated.

You, no doubt, have heard about or from her. I understand that the JDC has made her their representative in North Africa. You have made a happy choice. Although a successful advocate by profession, she is the most humane and understanding welfare worker—a step above the theoretical and scientific social worker. She seems to be giving all of her energy and most of her time to refugee problems. The sincerity of her deep interest is quite evident. She must be a most useful liaison officer for you with the French authorities in North Africa. Her accounts of refugee problems and refugee camps since 1940 would make interesting reading. It has been a real privilege to know her.[40]

Philippeville would be the setting for the last chapter of Nelly Benatar's war. Once again, she was deep into the business of refugees. Her foray into the world of international Jewish politics in 1944 had been a disappointing one. Perhaps she understood, as Levine noted, that her strength was as "the most humane and understanding welfare worker." But for Benatar, that was not enough. She believed that "the abstract nakedness of being nothing other than human," in Hannah Arendt's words, was not just inadequate—for refugees, it was positively dangerous. By restoring their legal status, she was not simply "rescuing" them; she was building a protective wall against the sort of inhuman savagery that stalked Europe in the last days of the war.[41]

1945

The Shock of Recognition

ON NOVEMBER 27, 1944, the second day of the emergency meeting of the World Jewish Congress in Atlantic City, Leon Kubowitzki, head of the WJC's Political Department, told the stunned delegates that 5.5 million Jews had already been killed by the Nazis. Offering a shred of hope, he said that the WJC was persisting in its rescue efforts, seeking the status of "civilian prisoners of war" for Jews still left in the Nazi camps in order to distribute life-saving food packages. But even this sounded hollow, more like wishful thinking than a realistic plan. Central Europe was an unfathomable black hole that no one could enter. As the war entered its final and most frenetic phase, the mood among Jews on the outside was fatalistic beyond words.[1]

On January 27, 1945, Soviet troops reached the main camp at Auschwitz and found it still smoldering and emptied of all life. The blackened ruins were not the final act in the mass slaughter begun in 1942, only an intensification of it. Over the following weeks, the outlying Nazi extermination camps were systematically vacated. Hundreds of thousands of prisoners were moved—by train, by boat, and eventually on foot—away from the front and into the heartland of the Reich. In the East, the Soviet advance crashed through the German lines, crossed the Oder, and took the road to Berlin. Now millions of Germans were in flight, and the chaos was indescribable. Looking squarely into the face of defeat, the Nazi response was not to surrender but to increase the tempo of killing. At Buchenwald, bloated with inmates transferred from other camps, the SS recorded more deaths in the first three months of 1945 than during all of 1943 and 1944 combined.[2]

Relief organizations peered frantically into the cauldron, having lost sight of the nearly 715,000 people supposedly still alive in the Nazi gulag as of January 1945. Keeping up appearances, they filled their public announcements with vain hopes and deliberate obfuscations. A JDC report of March 15, 1945, promised relief to the "destitute Jews in Poland" and offered the possibility of delivering food to "civilian internees who do not have the protection of the Geneva Convention." The report also promised that "efforts will be made to evacuate as many of the Jewish internees from the camps as soon as possible to Switzerland," suggesting that such an operation was even possible at this apocalyptic moment.[3]

The idea of prisoner releases was not a complete illusion, but the time for them had passed. On December 6, 1944, a group of 1,368 Jews from the Bergen-Belsen concentration camp in central Germany crossed over the Swiss border to safety, following weeks of intense negotiations between Saly Mayer, the JDC representative in Geneva, and Nazi representatives taking orders directly from Reichsführer-SS Himmler. A German-born Orthodox Jew, Mayer's strict ways and prickly personality did not endear him to everyone. As a Swiss citizen, Mayer was permitted to negotiate with the Nazis, something that the Americans and British were not allowed to do. In mid-1944, the Germans seemed ready to "make deals," and as distasteful as it was to interact with them, Mayer entered into negotiations with the SS, hoping to save as many Jews as he could. Behind the scenes was the War Refugee Board, keeping a low profile but encouraging negotiators to complete the exchange.[4]

Mayer warned the Nazis about the price of their coming defeat and suggested that their actions "now" might mitigate the inevitable judgment against them. His alarms worked, at least in the short run. On January 30, 1945, another 826 persons arrived in Switzerland from Bergen-Belsen, holders of so-called protective papers. A week later, on February 7, a third group of 1,210 former prisoners crossed into Switzerland. This release was the last one, bringing the total number to about 3,400. Widely reported in the Swiss press, this crossing generated so much publicity that Hitler personally ordered an end to all future prisoner releases.[5]

Some of these ex-prisoners eventually reached the Jeanne d'Arc Center at Philippeville. Benatar and her daughter Myriam were present when a group of Bergen-Belsen survivors arrived in late February. Never before had Benatar witnessed at close hand the brutality of the Nazi concentration camps. Twenty-one people arrived on stretchers, too weak to walk: "All were malnourished, with skin and bones for limbs . . . bloated stomachs, haggard faces . . . scars from beatings."[6] For Ned Campbell, it was a revelation: "I am now ready to believe the propaganda published about the treatment Germany affords people in its concentration camps," he confessed.[7] For Benatar, the meeting with the Bergen-Belsen survivors was also a shock. For the first time, she felt the depths of the tragedy that had befallen the Jews of Europe. She did not write about her feelings, but her daughter Myriam did. They come to us through the voice of Serge Lapidus:

> Seeing a young Dutch boy, about fourteen years old, his body covered with scars, Nelly was completely shaken and questioned his mother, Madame Sarfaty, about it. Smothering a sob, [the mother] revealed yet another Nazi "stunt" at Bergen-Belsen. Every morning, the [guards] gathered the children in the center of a ring, while their mothers formed a circle around them. Then they exuberantly whipped their innocent victims until they bled. If a mother had the misfortune to move or cry out, the child-martyr was immediately dispatched with a pistol shot. The horrible scars of this young boy were proof of the "playful" sadism of these "ordinary" perpetrators.[8]

This firsthand encounter with the horror of the Nazi camps changed Benatar's relationship to her work. Hearing Madame Sarfaty's story and the stories of other former inmates, she engaged in a form of "witnessing," that is, participating in the event without actually having being there. Exchanges such as this must have happened regularly, bringing welfare workers and survivors together into a single universe of shared experience.

During her six months at the Jeanne d'Arc Center, Benatar came to understand that liberation was not the goal, but only the beginning of a long process of readjustment for those who had survived. As one ex-prisoner put it, "there was no ecstasy, no joy at our liberation. We had lost our families, our homes. . . . Nobody was waiting for us anywhere. We had been liberated from death and the fear of death, but not from the fear of life."[9] The plight of the "Jewish remnant" after the war, nearly a million and a quarter survivors, eventually drew the attention of world leaders. But in that winter of 1944–1945, with the war still raging, people like Benatar focused on the here and now.[10]

Nelly Benatar's mission at the Jeanne d'Arc Center in October 1944 was a return to the familiar. Like Fedala, it was located close to the sea. The residents' quarters consisted of barracks, hospital, administrative buildings, kitchen and dining hall, recreation hall, and a school. From any point in the camp, one could look out over the blue-green waters of the Mediterranean.

But the settled appearance of the camp was misleading. Almost as soon as the Jeanne d'Arc Center opened, its future was in doubt. The camp was designed to serve up to forty thousand residents; at its peak, it housed only about eight hundred people, and then for only a short time. It was also too isolated. Constantine, the nearest train station, was thirty miles away, and Algiers, the hub of transportation, another two hundred miles distant. Winter brought fierce winds and Mediterranean storms. Visitors to the camp came away with a depressing sense of stifled expectations, underused facilities, and an atmosphere of endless waiting.[11]

Not only that, the organization of the camp was anomalous: partly under military administration, partly run by civilian workers, its command structure was always in a state of flux. A dedicated staff complained about the confusion but soldiered on, while the higher-ups dispatched reports to Washington, advising that the camp should be closed down. Army officers controlled distribution of food, transport, and housing, dispensing resources with strict military efficiency.[12] Private philanthropies like the JDC found themselves at a disadvantage, unable to set policies, yet expected to carry out the orders of people they considered newcomers to the field of social welfare. The atmosphere was fraught with competition over exactly who was in charge.

All the squabbling was a minor distraction to Nelly Benatar. Her days were packed with activity. Because of the shortage of trained case workers, Benatar, by then called a "welfare officer," was in charge of interviewing residents on arrival, as well as sorting, processing, and eventually resettling them.[13] She was the most experienced staff person in sight.

The purpose of the interview was to establish a baseline for repatriation, allowing the individual to receive an official identity card. Benatar's knowledge of legal limits, her command of languages, her deep familiarity with geographies, histories, and mentalities of the refugee population—all made her absolutely indispensable. "She is giving a month of her time free," one coworker wrote, "they simply have no one with the time, interest or knowledge to do such jobs."[14]

Many of the refugees arriving from Bergen-Belsen already had entry visas to countries in the Western Hemisphere such as Haiti, Paraguay, Uruguay, Peru, Ecuador, Honduras, and Bolivia, acquired before their imprisonment. Benatar set to work contacting the relevant embassies and consulates to clear the way to their resettlement. Melvin Goldstein, who worked for the JDC in its Lisbon office, visited Philippeville and filed a report on Benatar's activities: "Mme. Benatar has set up complete records for the residents of the Center and is doing everything possible so that the transmigration of these people will be realized. She is in constant touch with the appropriate representatives of various governments . . . and in accordance with information gathered she has made applications for repatriation or emigration of refugees."[15]

Much of Benatar's work at Philippeville was devoted to dealing with officials in the French ministries in charge of repatriating refugees. The Jeanne d'Arc Center was officially under the direction of the French Ministry of Refugees and Deportees in Paris, working under strict orders from de Gaulle to speed up the process of return. Eligible expatriates fell into three broad categories: those who wanted to return to France, those who had the right to return but wished to go elsewhere, and those who wanted to emigrate to Palestine. Two further subheadings separated "escapees" (*évadés*) from "civilians." For political reasons, until February 1945, the ministry permitted only *évadés*—mainly ex-soldiers—to return to the metropole. After that date, civilians, too, were allowed to go home.

Benatar saw an opportunity to repatriate a large number of UNRRA residents to France under these new rules. After "numerous interviews" with the head of military security in Algiers, she received assurances that even stateless refugees—the majority of her clients—who wanted to return to France could be repatriated, but only after sixty thousand French citizens still in North Africa had gone home. She calculated that at this rate, for all her clients to return, it could take up to two years. The problem was lack of transport, for only three small ships had been designated by the French government to carry refugees from North Africa to the metropole. Benatar's solution was to go directly to the Ministry of the Interior in Paris, where she demanded a group visa for all the Jeanne d'Arc internees seeking repatriation. Armed with this document, she then asked the American military to make airborne troop carriers available to fly her clients home. Amazingly, the Americans agreed, and by mid-August 1945, most of the residents seeking repatriation to France had left the center.[16]

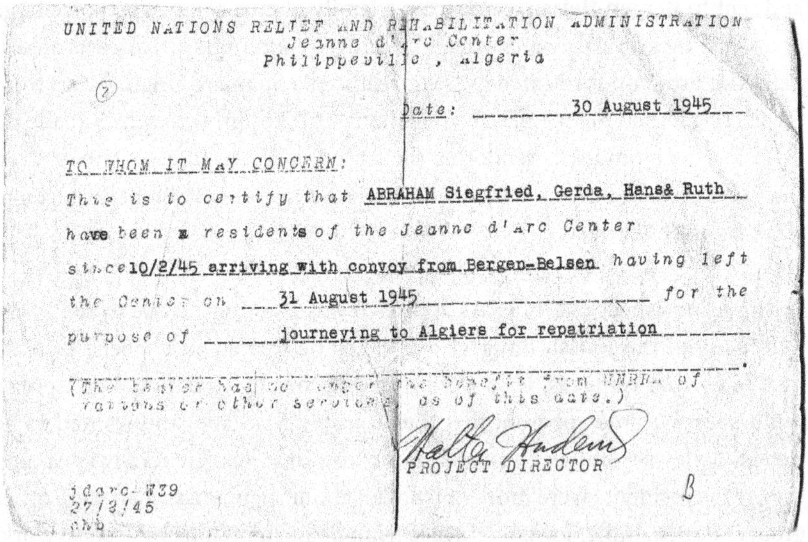

UNITED NATIONS RELIEF AND REHABILITATION ADMINISTRATION
Jeanne d'Arc Center
Philippeville , Algeria

Date: 30 August 1945

TO WHOM IT MAY CONCERN:

This is to certify that ABRAHAM Siegfried, Gerda, Hans& Ruth have been residents of the Jeanne d'Arc Center since 10/2/45 arriving with convoy from Bergen-Belsen having left the Center on 31 August 1945 for the purpose of journeying to Algiers for repatriation.

(The bearer has no longer the benefit from UNRRA of rations or other services, as of this date.)

PROJECT DIRECTOR

jdarc-W39
27/8/45
chb

FIGURE 8.1 "Resident's identity card," belonging to Gerda Abraham, survivor of Bergen-Belsen. Gerda arrived at Jeanne d'Arc Center in February 1945.

While waiting for the bureaucratic gears to turn, life at the center was busy. On arrival, new residents, most of them former concentration camp inmates, received a letter from the director that greeted them as a "dear friend." The letter had a cheerful, breezy tone:

> The period of time which you will spend at this Center is not known. We join you in hoping that it will be a short time only and that you find the homes you want. However, no matter how short or long a time you will be here, it is only reasonable that we should all join to make it as pleasant and as comfortable a stay as possible. To accomplish this, it is necessary that we all assume responsibility for the camp, its maintenance and security, and to work in whatever way we can to make it the kind of place we want it to be.[17]

During the day, the residents were free to go to town, walk on the seashore, or visit a café, but they were obliged to return by midday. At night there were entertainments—musicals, cards, checkers, ping-pong, singing. Engeline Lessing Van Leer, a Dutch Jewish resistance fighter captured by the Gestapo and sent to Bergen-Belsen, came from a family of musicians. She took charge of organizing musical events where the refugees' internationalism was on display. The program for March 25, 1945, featured a Spaniard singing arias from *Pagliacci*, a Dutch pianist playing selections by Chopin, and a choir made up of Yugoslav communists rendering their version of "An Ode to Tito."[18] Even the ex-inmates of Bergen-Belsen who arrived in such a pitiable state began to show signs of recovery.

A surprising aspect of UNRRA's approach was its initial failure to recognize that many of the Jewish refugees wanted to be treated as a special case. At first, like other refugees, Jews were sorted according to national groupings, but it soon became apparent that they rejected that label and wanted to be treated as Jews—not as Germans, Austrians, or Poles. Generally speaking, the Jewish residents were more outspoken about their needs than were other groups. For example, Jewish refugees from Spanish prisons refused to work. Their exceptionalism was explained in behavioral terms: "They are primarily of the commercial class," the Quaker representative Willis Weatherford wrote, "and their long period of idleness in Spain caused them to lose their initiative."[19] Naïve assumptions associated with the "normal" were applied to people whose life situation was completely outside of the "normal."

Some Jews at Philippeville, especially the more religious, wanted to be housed separately, fed separately, and counseled separately, asserting at every opportunity their solidarity as a group. Orthodox Jewish leaders in America chimed in with letters complaining that the observant Jews at the center were not getting kosher food. Confounded by what he considered an unreasonable demand, the camp director at first refused to make exceptions. But he finally relented, making provisions for Sabbath services, prayer books, Jewish newspapers, and other tokens of empathy. The gradual process of recognizing Jewish survivors as "paradigmatic victims" entitled to special treatment—most often associated with the displaced persons camps in Germany in the postwar years—is evident at Philippeville in 1945.[20] Jewish residents were already setting themselves apart, feeling comfortable in their exceptionality, recognizing that their experience of suffering was unique. The "ideological nature of their victimization" placed them in a category of their own, according to the historian G. Daniel Cohen, transforming them into a collectivity "on the brink of becoming 'national.'"[21]

Benatar's relationship with the JDC was the subtext to her work at the camp. Developments at the center were closely monitored by the JDC's Lisbon office. The role of the JDC was vital to all aspects of the migration process, including chartering ships and paying for the migrant's passage.[22] UNRRA fed and clothed the refugees, but the JDC footed the bill for almost everything else. That included the mountain of overseas cables necessary for arranging visas, as well as Benatar's frequent trips to embassies and consulates in Algiers, and even her trips to Paris to negotiate with officials at the various ministries.[23] Many refugees had visas to somewhere and were ready to leave as soon as transport became available.

Some Jewish residents at Jeanne d'Arc refused repatriation to their home countries and wanted to go to Palestine. UNRRA officials, eager to reduce the camp's population, were complicit, naïvely thinking that these "Zionists" could be quietly transferred inside the UNRRA system directly to Palestine. But obstacles stood in the way. In March 1945, a group of residents who held certificates to emigrate to Palestine were told a ship would soon dock in Algiers. The ship arrived on March 15, but it tied up only for a day—not long enough to get the Philippeville residents to Algiers. The ship left the port with sixty empty berths.

Arranging transport to Palestine proved to be one of the most difficult problems Benatar would face. The Lisbon office of the JDC took the lead in chartering boats, and Benatar took on the job of getting certificate holders to collection points on the coast. The SS *Lima*, a Portuguese ship chartered by the JDC and headed to Palestine in August 1945, made stops in Casablanca, Algiers, and Tunis. Thirty-eight residents of Philippeville were on the list of prospective passengers, their emigration arranged by Benatar.[24]

V-E Day, May 8, 1945, found Nelly and Myriam Benatar at Philippeville. By early June, Nelly was back in Casablanca, attending to her son Marc, who had fallen ill. Thus ended her "apostolate" with UNRRA. During her time at the Jeanne d'Arc Center, she had cared for hundreds of refugees, helping to put them back on the road to life. For each unresolved case, she left behind a carefully documented dossier. The Jeanne d'Arc camp closed in August 1945 as UNRRA's focus turned to Central Europe, where hundreds of thousands of displaced people were living in conditions not much better than the prison camps they had left behind.

Benatar's "retirement" from refugee work was not an extended one. The JDC was drowning in a tide of refugees, and Joe Schwartz, head of European operations for the JDC, now relocated to Paris, desperately needed her help.[25] In August, Benatar, along with Myriam, still in medical school, and Marc, enrolled in the prestigious Lycée Louis-le-Grand, along with her faithful housekeeper Tchatcha, boarded a US Army Air Force Superfortress and flew to Marseille. From there, they took a train crowded with returning refugees and headed to Paris.

The Glorious Years were over. Nelly Benatar did not even have time to pen an epitaph, but immediately jumped into a new life. The heart-pounding excitement, the paralyzing fear, the danger and anxiety of the war years were behind her, replaced by a daily grind of arranging visas, filling voids, finding lost relatives. She had no further reflections and left no self-evaluations about why and what she had done. She did not look back. She simply put all her notes, letters, memos, documents, and photographs into boxes, shuttered her apartment, and left.

That was all, that was enough.

CHAPTER 9

AFTER THE WAR

PARIS, JUNE 1946. Unleashing her deliciously mordant wit, the *New Yorker* writer Janet Flanner announced that the nightmare of six years of war was finally over. Austerity was in retreat and items once thought extinct were reappearing in Parisian shops, along with other signs of revival: armloads of newborns, swarms of shiny taxis filling the *grands boulevards*, and metro stations—some of them closed for years—once again put to their proper use. And for everyone, the reopening of cabarets and music halls, featuring an "eye-popping new show" at the venerable Folies-Bergère, where scantily clad demoiselles kicked up their heels in the brilliant footlights.[1]

It is unlikely that Nelly Benatar took part in any of these entertainments. She was working feverishly for the JDC, dealing with the problem of hundreds of thousands of homeless Jews languishing in European refugee camps. In mid-1946, these survivors were augmented by new migrations of desperate Jews fleeing westward, away from a rash of violent anti-Semitic attacks in Poland and other parts of Eastern Europe.[2] Crowded into already-bursting reception centers in the American zone of occupied Germany, they joined a restless population who needed to go somewhere, and quickly. Repatriation to their former homelands was out of the question, and resettlement the only reasonable option.[3]

The swelling numbers of refugees caught international relief organizations like the JDC off guard. By late 1945, UNRRA, the chief Allied relief agency, was shutting down its operations, making way for the new UN-sponsored International Refugee Organization. For the moment, the weight of resettling Jewish refugees in Europe fell on private organizations like the JDC. Its Emigration Department on rue Tehéran in the north of Paris, where Nelly Benatar was associate director, was the hub for processing Jewish displaced persons from all over Europe. The daunting task of arranging visas, providing identity cards, granting certificates of good health, and purchasing tickets for refugees in transit fell on her hastily assembled staff, many of them refugees themselves, with no experience with this sort of work.[4]

Seduced by Joe Schwartz's plea for help, Benatar had uprooted her children and brought them to Paris, but she rarely saw them. She wrote a friend that she was so preoccupied, "I really do not have a moment for myself."[5] Her first address in Paris was a small hotel in St. Germain-des-Près, requisitioned for refugees. After an exhaustive search, Benatar found an apartment at 2, rue du Cygne, near Les Halles, the great Parisian food emporium. The reason for its availability soon became apparent. The apartment shook day and night from the incessant rumbling of lorries delivering produce to the nearby markets. Furthermore, the round-the-clock activity made the neighborhood a magnet for prostitutes. A family story told how a night worker took up a post at the entryway to Benatar's building and served as an informal concierge. When Nelly came home from work late at night, her voluntary doorkeeper would announce: "Madame, your daughter has already arrived!"[6]

Humor was scarce in those days, and Benatar's two years in Paris working for the JDC were among the bleakest of her career. During the war, she had relied on her friend and assistant, Célia Bengio, who understood Benatar's hastily scribbled marginal notes and acted on them to perfection. She now found herself alone, in charge of a cumbersome staff that struggled to handle the heavy workload. Benatar took on the more difficult cases herself, but she hardly made a dent. In her work for UNRRA, her success had hinged on her ability to treat each refugee individually, but the sheer number of clients postwar made this method impossible. Benatar was plainly out of her element.[7]

Most of her "protégés," as she called them, had no papers, or if they did, they were false and had to be replaced. Survivors, almost all of them stateless, were at a loss to prove their place of birth or the nationality of their parents, who, in any case, were no longer alive. The gold standard was a state-issued passport, but most refugees had to settle for lesser forms of validation, such as a displaced persons card issued by the Allied military, or an International Red Cross certificate, or at the very least, a numbered entry card issued by UNRRA. With this meager documentation, Benatar would try to construct for each refugee a convincing profile, useful for justifying a claim for assistance.[8] For Benatar, a refugee's loss of nationality was problematic but not fatal. To her lawyerly mind, statelessness was a condition that could be overcome given the right evidence and a persuasive argument.

The question of statelessness was, at that moment, a compelling one, engaging distinguished international lawyers as well as people on the front lines of refugee relief. Debates around the question of national belonging were heated, as the memory of the failure of the League of Nations to protect the multitudes of Europeans who had lost their citizenship in the interwar period haunted experts in international law.

In her powerful essay "The Stateless People," the refugee-philosopher Hannah Arendt was unsparing in her critique of recent European history, when "one nation after the other drove whole groups of its population over its borders—the saddest product . . . of the disintegration of European national states."[9] Arendt's view of the situation in Europe in 1945 was a dark one. It used to be the case, she mused, that stateless people, or *apatrides*, could claim the "right of asylum," an unwritten but "sacred" law of long standing that would provide a modicum of protection. But that was no longer the case. The current war had produced a "new breed of humanity"—stateless people with no national identification, no claim to basic rights, and little hope of retrieving them. The effort to distinguish between refugees who had fled their homes and were unable to return and stateless people deliberately stripped of their rights as citizens was a futile one, according to Arendt, because "all refugees are practically stateless, and nearly all the stateless are refugees."[10]

Arendt was one of the first political theorists to recognize that the condition of "statelessness" also had its benefits. It was certainly true in the case of ex-German Jews, who were "fighting desperately" to have their statelessness recognized to avoid the stigma of being labeled as Germans, a clear liability in the postwar era.[11] Like Benatar, Arendt understood that citizenship and nationality were not immutable concepts but could be manipulated by making reference to a refugee's past record and present intentions. Benatar in the refugee camps and Arendt in New York simultaneously made the discovery that refugees lived in highly fluid life situations. Recognizing the subjective dimensions of a refugee's profile—intentions, loyalties, aspirations, communal ties—was just as important in establishing a person's rights as the fixed categories of legal documentation.

This observation took on special meaning when applied to Jewish refugees. Jews were the quintessential example of "a people . . . without a state and a territory [who] still retain a national identity," according to Arendt. This reality was not lost on Allied decision makers, who had the power to restore to refugees their "inalienable" rights.[12] In the UNRRA refugee camps in 1944 and 1945, Benatar witnessed firsthand how Jewish residents had exercised their individuality, creating new profiles for themselves and asserting their rights as Jews for permanent resettlement into majoritarian Jewish settings.

Once international opinion had gathered sufficient momentum behind the concept of a Jewish nation-state and made it a reality, the territorial option became the preferred solution to the problem of Jewish statelessness. More than three hundred thousand Holocaust survivors, motivated by emotional contingencies as well as economic necessity, emigrated to Israel between 1948 and 1952, largely under the auspices of international aid agencies like the JDC. Benatar's idea of a *foyer d'élection*, a "home of choice," vaguely construed in 1944, would by 1948 become a principle of resettlement, as hundreds of thousands of stateless Jewish refugees regained their national identity by taking up residence in the new State of Israel.[13]

Benatar's position on this fundamental transition is an unambiguous one. After years of working with refugees, she understood the malleability of refugee lives, the possibilities inherent in them, how to remake them for the better. Razor-sharp in her opinions, confident in her power to persuade, she believed in the plasticity of the human condition and in her skills as an advocate—an inventor of convincing stories from disparate facts—to make people whole. Her desk piled high with dossiers, Benatar went about the job of assigning new futures to her refugee clients, returning to them what she believed were their "inalienable" rights.

The mountain of problems in JDC's emigration bureau made the work climate toxic. Benatar's nemesis was the new director, who locked horns with her almost as soon as he arrived in early 1946. Stubborn and ambitious, Irwin Rosen was obsessed with creating a disciplined Emigration Department that operated with industrial efficiency—hardly Nelly's style. He accused her of undermining his efforts at reorganization: "She was always getting down into the case work assigned [to others], disrupting their routines, and taking away from them cases . . . which in her judgment were being improperly handled." Her intensity and attention to detail were not, in his eyes, a virtue. But the real rub was that "she never really accepted my authority as director."[14] Benatar kept her morale up by making frequent trips home to Casablanca, which irritated Rosen even more.[15]

She disliked her American boss for another reason. He was prejudiced and condescending. He regarded refugees from Poland as "primitive" and demanding; German Jewish refugees, on the other hand, had "kept their good prewar manners" and were "grateful for any assistance."[16] As a Moroccan Jew, Benatar must have wondered where she stood in his hierarchy of nations and peoples. The two clashed so often that Rosen decided to make her position superfluous.

Her response to these threats gives us a rare look into a troubled soul, exhausted by overwork, filled with self-doubt. In fluent English, she summarized for her superiors the source of her chagrin: "At no moment did I consider the persons protected by us as material for calculations and statistics, but always took care of their needs, regarding them as human beings and persecuted persons with the right to all care and attention from our department. [Rosen's actions were] a hideous maneuver to do me out of a work to which I have been devoting myself for these seven years. It is a moral prejudice for me when facing my friends, my collaborators and even my own children."[17]

Benatar was anxious to leave. After two years of living in Paris, she was homesick for Casablanca and emotionally exhausted. It was important to help survivors, "but we must not forget the hundreds of thousands of Jews who are living a precarious existence in North Africa," she wrote to Joe Schwartz. Not wishing to lose her, he created a new position: "representative of the JDC in North Africa," a post she held until 1951. Her assignment was to seek out opportunities to expand JDC programs across the North African region.[18] To help her, the JDC increased funding for its North African programs—$150,000 a year for Morocco alone.[19]

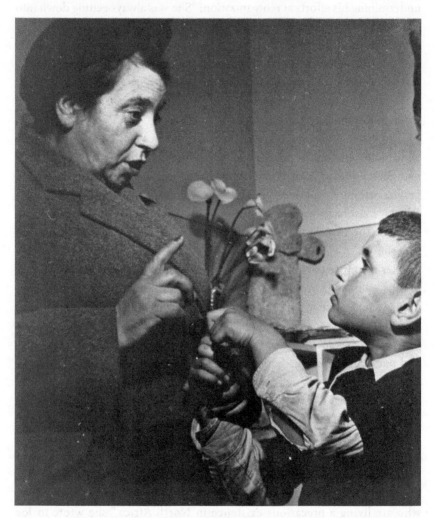

FIGURE 9.1 JDC representative Benatar visiting a children's orphanage,
Casablanca, 1950.

* * *

The JDC's renewed interest in North African Jews came at a critical time. It was a moment of churning events and lightening changes in the Maghrib. Independence movements were on the rise across the region. Moroccan nationalists had established political networks in Egypt and the Levant, in Europe, and at the United Nations, where they lobbied for self-rule.[20] In 1947, Sultan Mohammed V threw in his lot with the nationalist movement, lending it a new layer of legitimacy. None of this augured well for Morocco's Jews, who were politically divided, geographically dispersed, and lacking a unified voice. Moreover, the situation in Palestine was worsening, with repercussions for Jews elsewhere in the Middle East. On May 14, 1948, the State of Israel was declared, setting off a reaction around the globe.

In Morocco, attacks on Jews had been escalating throughout the spring of 1948. The sultan publicly warned his Jewish subjects against supporting the Zionist cause, predicting that it would lead to disaster. In a matter of days, his words took on a fearsome reality. On June 7, 1948, in the eastern Moroccan city of Oujda, a Muslim mob attacked unsuspecting Jews and killed four; they then went to the nearby mining town of Djerada and slaughtered forty more, including the local rabbi and his entire family. These brutal murders sent shock waves across the country. Benatar was asked by the JDC to launch an inquiry and traveled to Oujda to investigate. Her report on the incident was both provocative and prescient; after presenting the facts, she predicted that Morocco was no longer "safe for Jews."[21] Over the following six months, more than nine thousand Jews left the country, marking the start of a multi-year emigration that would eventually reduce Morocco's Jewish population to the near-vanishing point. Benatar continued in her position as the JDC's North African representative, but by 1951, she had enough. The JDC and Benatar parted ways, and Benatar returned to her private legal practice in Casablanca.[22]

In 1953 and 1954, Benatar made several trips to the United States under the auspices of the United Jewish Appeal (UJA), the parent organization of the JDC. The UJA was the biggest and most influential of the American Jewish donor agencies, and at the time it was headed by her old friend Joe Schwartz. Stylishly coifed, her dowdy dresses left at home, an updated Nelly Benatar became the international public figure she always wanted to be.[23]

FIGURE 9.2 Nelly Benatar surrounded by community leaders and JDC officials, Casablanca, January 1953.

Flyers advertising her public talks described her as a "heroine of the French underground, lawyer, and authority on the Jews of the Muslim world" whose experiences "sound like material for a thriller."[24]

She crisscrossed the United States in the early months of 1953, visiting New York, Miami, New Orleans, Los Angeles, and places in between, speaking to packed houses, spreading the word about the Jews of North Africa, reminding American Jewish audiences—weary of incessant appeals to their pocketbooks to help Israel—that Jewish philanthropy could be directed to Jews in other places.[25] On her return home, a radiant Nelly Benatar was greeted at Casablanca airport by the leaders of the local Jewish community. During her mission abroad, she had rubbed shoulders with the great and the near great: Eleanor Roosevelt, Henry Morgenthau Jr., the French ambassador to the United States, and at a stopover in Princeton, New Jersey, Albert Einstein—surely an apotheotic moment.[26]

In 1956, Morocco achieved independence, triggering yet another wave of Jewish departures. This time the exiles included all of Benatar's immediate family, her daughter Myriam and son-in-law, Serge, her brothers and sister and all their children. Nelly was determined to remain in Casablanca, and it continued to be her home for six more years. Finally, the Arabization of the legal profession determined her fate. The requirement that lawyers use Arabic in the courtroom forced her to cease practicing law. In 1962, she left for Paris, taking up residence at 78, rue du Cardinal Lemoine, in the shadow of the Panthéon. At the age of sixty-four, she passed the French bar for a second time and resumed her law practice.

FIGURE 9.3   Nelly Benatar, far right, meeting with Eleanor Roosevelt at the United Nations, 1953.

In those last years in Paris, Benatar tried repeatedly to win recognition for her war work and her role in the Resistance, but without success. To her chagrin, the coveted Médaille de la Résistance, awarded to more than fifty thousand others, passed her by.[27] She kept her disappointment to herself, but the evidence in her archive is painful to read—dossiers fruitlessly compiled, letters sent, testimonies transcribed, all to no avail. She stood by while others collected medals, accolades, and honors. Joe Schwartz received the Legion d'Honneur in 1946 for his wartime work, and Benatar congratulated him warmly but surely not without a dose of envy. Finally, in 1969, a modest breakthrough: she was awarded a medal by the British-French Friendship Association for "services rendered to the Allied cause, to liberty, and for peace." Small compensation, and not from her beloved France, but any recognition was better than none.

On July 7, 1979, Benatar's daughter Myriam telephoned her mother, her usual end-of-the-day call. At the age of eighty, Nelly was still living on her own. There was no answer. She had died sometime during the night. On July 11, her family gathered in the sprawling Cimetière de Pantin, on the northern edge of Paris, in a section set aside for Sephardic Jews who ended their days in France. There Nelly Benatar was laid to rest, and a year later, following Jewish tradition, her children placed a headstone on her grave with an epitaph etched in gold:

À notre Mére, Femme légendaire, qui secourut toutes les détresses.

"For our Mother, a heroic Woman, who comforted so many in distress."

TO WHAT EXTENT can a single life illuminate an entire era? Like every story, this one is a transaction between the testimony of the witness, and the more complex motives of the biographer. How do historians access the spirit of a time if they do not give voice to those who were actually there? Benatar was the quintessential truth teller; she gathered her papers, she suspended judgment, and she left the rest to those who would come after her.

In 1936, the philosopher and essayist Walter Benjamin wrote "The Storyteller," a meditation on the narrative qualities of the nonfiction story and its relevance to his own life. Benjamin, by nature a pessimist, concluded that the age of factual storytelling was past, that authentic tales were out of reach, and

FIGURE 9.4 Nelly Benatar's gravesite, Cimetière Pantin, Paris, 2019.

that "truth was dying out."[28] The spirit of the times nurtured such thinking. Hitler was on the rise, liberalism was in retreat, and intolerance, especially against Jews, was rampant. Soon Benjamin himself was on the run, fleeing Nazi-occupied Paris with a briefcase full of papers. In September 1940, he reached the Spanish border but was turned back because he lacked the necessary exit visa. Desperate and exhausted, he took his own life.

Benjamin's thoughts about storytelling come to mind when thinking about Nelly Benatar's archive and the narratives that emerge from it. How easy it would be to resort to ingenuity and weave a rich tale of fantasy based on her war experiences. We recall the publicity for her lecture series in 1953, when American audiences were told that her life read "like a thriller." Yet even when the melodrama is set aside, her story still commands our attention, because it is embedded in actual experience—what Benjamin calls a "chain of tradition"—that magically gains strength as it unfolds.

Why is this so? One reason may be that the themes reverberating through Nelly Benatar's war are universal ones—loyalty, trust, love, duty, human frailty, a commitment to truth. Unlike others who hid behind closed doors, Benatar rejected passivity and seized the moment. She called the war years her *années glorieuses*, her glorious years. Why "glorious" when European Jews were being slaughtered by the millions, when entire peoples, landscapes, civilizations, were being reduced to ash? She was not insensitive to the suffering of others—her actions are proof enough of that. So what did she mean by *glorieuse*? Perhaps she saw the war as a personal test, a chance to prove her worth. During those six years, she lived life to the fullest, with more intensity than most of us feel in a lifetime.

The aftermath was of lesser grandeur. The postwar period began on a high note, with the declaration of the State of Israel in 1948 reviving pride in one's Jewish identity, for Benatar and many others. But how quickly everything dissolved into chaos. In 1965, fifty-five thousand Jews were left in Morocco, less than one-third of the number in 1947. The Six-Day War (1967) unleashed yet another hemorrhage. By the time of Benatar's death in 1979, the Jewish community in Morocco was less than one-tenth of its former size, reduced to twenty thousand people from a 1947 high of more than a quarter million.[29] Today, less than two thousand Jews live permanently in Morocco, most of them in Casablanca, custodians by default of a shrinking patrimony.

How should we understand the wartime refugee crisis in Morocco over the *longue durée*? What was the effect of the arrival of so many foreign refugees on Moroccan soil, what did it mean for Moroccan Jews, and for Moroccans more broadly, and to what extent did wartime events promote the massive outflow of indigenous Jews in the decades that followed? No doubt the effects of the Holocaust on North Africa were very different from their impact on Europe. Morocco was on Europe's periphery, both geographically and conceptually, and its Jews cannot be considered "survivors" in the same sense that European Jews were. Yet Moroccan Jews were deeply marked by their encounter with fascism and with the Vichy regime. The war was an especially turbulent moment of transition along the long road that began with their isolation in premodern Morocco and ended with their imperfect integration into empire. Over time, it became clear that the promise of equality and personal freedom made to Jews and endorsed by republican France was an empty one. According to the historian Daniel Rivet, "It would be fair to say that the Jews considered themselves as the step-children of the Protectorate."[30]

It was not long before signs of rebellion emerged, mainly among the educated Jewish elite, the *alliancistes* of the AIU schools. Young people like Nelly and Moyses Benatar abhorred the status quo and sought paths to reform their community as well as their relationship to the state. Their goal was not to reject France altogether but to follow the Algerian model by establishing legal parity with the colonizer and becoming full citizens of the Republic. Under Vichy, behind a false façade of French "national revival," a profoundly anti-Semitic system of governance took hold that thwarted their ambitions. More than ever, Jews were the outcasts of empire. The injustices of the Vichy period were not sui generis; rather, they were an exaggerated outcome of a long history of oppression within the colonial context.

The world at war brought unprecedented threats to Moroccan Jews, such as loss of education, loss of property, loss of self-respect. But it also ignited aspirations to move forward. The influx of thousands of European Jewish refugees helped to awaken local Jews to their place in the world. Refugees were agents of modernity, and the ferment of ideas, people, and opportunities raised in the context of refugee politics fundamentally transformed the attitude of Moroccan Jews toward their own futures. Helping agencies like the JDC came with deep pockets, far-flung networks, and exceptional ideas,

among them the concept of Moroccan Jewish rebirth through democratic reform and self-improvement.

Yet in the space of a just few years, a majority of Moroccan Jews were on
the road to somewhere else. They took many different directions, given their
extreme diversity in terms of culture, politics, and economic status. Latent
schisms became manifest: differences between rich and poor, Francophone
and Arabophone, urban and rural, professionals and peasants, religious and
secular, and every shade in between. Moreover, these schisms were marked
by temporalities: first the very poor left, and only later, the bourgeoisie. The
historian Orit Bashkin has observed that scholarship has moved beyond such
categories as "the Jews of Islam," or "Oriental Jews" that elide identities and
erase differences.[31] Along the way, generalities based on notions of a single
community of "Moroccan Jews" have also been exposed as misleading and in
need of further explanation.

As their community dwindled, Moroccan Jews wrestled with the question of
memory, and how to preserve aspects of their culture and history for future
generations. What that legacy should consist of, and for whom it should be
preserved, was the pressing issue. Should it be a factual, written history, or a
sampling of material culture in museums? Should synagogues and cemeteries
be restored, only to remain empty or twice abandoned, or should this rich
heritage be preserved as the diaphanous stuff of personal memory? Should it
be targeted to Moroccan Jews, Moroccan Muslims, or should it become the
property of the Jewish people as a whole? These questions have become the
subject of public debate, with the small number of Jews still living in Morocco
at its epicenter, compelled to triangulate their own fraught perspectives, the
opinions of a scattered diaspora, and in more recent years, the interventions
of a Moroccan state thoroughly attuned to the deafening silence left behind
by its absent Jews.

The French historian Pierre Nora tells us that memory "is in permanent
evolution, open to the dialectic of remembering and forgetting . . . vulnerable
to manipulation and appropriation," while history is "reconstruction, always
problematic and incomplete."[32] In other words, the soft clay of memory is
easily reshaped, but the hard facts of history, far more difficult to remodel,
are more resistant to loss. Among Moroccan Jews, it has been said, there is
a dearth of both memory and history. Memorialists have shunned the facts,

replacing them with a sentimentality that has little connection to reality.[33] Yet historians agree that both history and memory are necessary for a recall that embraces a diversity of participants and a multiplicity of experiences.

The historian Denis Peschanski has written eloquently about the Holocaust in France. He claims that without a consensus on collective memory, people have difficulty in connecting with one another and with larger themes in world history.[34] The outcome is a fractured identity and incessant infighting about how to interpret the past. In France, a plethora of contradictory narratives about the war and Vichy, complicated by the failure of successive governments to define a clear path toward memorialization, created deep divisions within French society that have taken decades to heal.[35]

In Morocco, the problem is equally as complicated. Moroccan Jews demonstrate similar patterns of confusion about how to remember World War II and its aftermath. Individuals have vivid recall, but they lack the shared memories that contribute to collective awareness and communal solidarity. Instead, Moroccan Jews have been bequeathed European-inspired narratives of the Holocaust that specifically exclude them, complicating their understanding of where they fit in the central drama of the Shoah, which stands at the heart of Jewish self-identity today. History has become a zone of contestation rather than a platform for reconciliation that could bring all parts of this now-diffuse diaspora together.

The politics of the postwar universally demanded a shift in epistemes, away from the microhistories of the dispossessed and toward narratives of the resurgent nation-state. As a result, the subject of European refugees and their Moroccan interlude during World War II lost its place in time. But now, thanks to a new generation of scholarship, we have compelling stories based on facts to fill the void. In this moment of revisionism, the war years—*les années glorieuses*—deserve a place of honor, so that figures like Nelly Benatar, who meandered for decades looking for a place in Walter Benjamin's great "chain of tradition," may finally find a home.

Acknowledgments

Although I have been a student of Moroccan history for decades, this book is my first foray into the history of the World War II and its impact in North Africa. Writing it has taken me to many new places and into the heart of countless new topics. Choosing the genre of biography to tell the story was also a departure from my previous work. It required learning new techniques of conceptualizing and writing history, a challenge all its own. It was my privilege to meet many talented and inspiring people as I went along who shared my enthusiasm for telling this story, and to them, I owe my deepest gratitude.

My inquiries began in 2011 in Rabat, where Professor Jamaa Baïda, director of the National Archives of Morocco, directed me to the Archives of the French Protectorate. To him and to Professor Mohammed Kenbib, of Mohamed V University of Rabat, pioneers in the study of contemporary Moroccan history, I owe a great debt. They lit the way forward for me. Other Moroccan historians who have shaped my perspective are Mohammed Hatimi, Khalid Bensrhir, Maati Monjib, Ahmed Toufiq, and Mohamed Mezzine, who sadly passed on just as this book was going to press. Also among Moroccan friends, I want to thank André Gomel of Rabat for his enthusiasm and support; Sonia Cohen-Azagury of Tangier, who taught me almost everything I know about Sephardic Moroccan culture; and Hicham Alaoui, world citizen and all-around good friend.

Vanessa Paloma El Baz's invitation to meet with the Jewish community of Casablanca in 2018 was a watershed moment. The staff of Casamémoire introduced me to the city, and Victor Mamane was my charming guide. Serge Berdugo, head of the Jewish community of Casablanca and his wife, Arlette, were welcoming. Vanessa introduced me to the extraordinary Abderrahim Kassou, master architect and Moroccan human rights activist, who suggested the bold idea of visiting the sites of the Saharan forced-labor camps. David Miller completed the party, and on Sunday, September 4, 2018, the three of us set off from Rabat to eastern Morocco, following Nelly Benatar's itinerary of sixty-five years earlier.

We covered hundreds of kilometers in Kassou's mighty BMW, crossing mountains and stony deserts to the Algerian border, always under the watchful eye of the local gendarmerie. Often questioned but never detained, we were protected by a letter of blanket permission from the National Council of Human Rights, signed by its former president, the lawyer and human rights activist Driss El Yazami. In each place, we were greeted by members of the local branch of the council who led us to prison sites, graveyards, ruined houses, and work sites. Our guides introduced us to local informants, often of an advanced age, yet eager to share their memories with us. It was a memorable phase of my research. We met with Lahcen Ghali (Djerada); Abdelilah Mouatabit (Oued Zem); Allal al-Basraoui (Beni Mellal); Mohammed Armati (Oujda); Mohammed Kouchen (Bou Arfa); Milou Belhaloum (born in 1916), and his son Moustafa Belhaloum (Bou Arfa); Mohamed Bin Ali (Figuig); Mohammed Zrigui, Lahcen Sekhmane, Ahmed Bouha, Hassan Lamrabet, and Mohammed Algiz (Bou Denib); and Mohammed Chafik (Missour). My thanks to all these brave men; without their participation it would have been impossible to understand the isolation and the vastness of the Vichy camps system.

In the course of my research, I visited many archives. Thanks to the Norman Raab Foundation Fellowship at the Jack, Joseph, and Morton Mandel Center for Advanced Holocaust Studies, I spent four months in Washington, DC, in 2014 at the United States Holocaust Memorial Museum. The archivists Megan Lewis, Ron Coleman, and Vincent Slatt guided me through the museum's endless reserves and hardly ever lost patience with me. The historian Rebecca (Becky) Embelding, fellow researcher, was generous with advice. The staff scholars Betsy Anthony, Suzanne Brown-Fleming, Leah

Wolfson, and Kierra Crago-Schneider shared their knowledge of the archives with me. Kierra Crago-Schneider was especially kind, going far out her way to help. My carrel mate, Corry Guttstadt, scholar of the Holocaust in Turkey, was a delightful new friend.

In New York, the archives of the American Joint Distribution Committee were another source of enlightenment. Thanks to a Fred and Ellen Lewis Fellowship in 2012, I was introduced to the historical records of this exceptional organization. I owe warmest thanks to Linda Levi, director of global archives at the JDC, and Isabelle Rohr, manager of academic programs and outreach, as well as researchers Misha Meisel and Claus Hirsch. At the archives of the Center for Jewish History in New York City, Gunnar Berg, YIVO archivist, and Herman Teifer, archivist for the Leo Baeck Institute, directed me to the HICEM collection as well as to US Army chaplains' reports. The American Jewish Archives in Cincinnati contained the complete records of the World Jewish Congress meeting of 1944; Dana Herman, director of research and collections, made a special effort to allow me access them in the midst of the COVID-19 epidemic. My warmest thanks to her.

My visit to the JDC Archives in Jerusalem was also rewarding, thanks to Ori Kraischer, archivist, and Anat Kutner, director. Also in Jerusalem, I used the archives of the Ben Zvi Institute, especially the personal collection of Moroccan Jewish publicist Raphael Benazeraf. Prof. Haim Saadoun, Moti Ben-Ari, Haya Brown, and Shay Lavi were my guides to the print and photograph collections there. Other friends and associates in Israel are Yaron Tsur, Orit Yekutieli, Samir Ben-Layashi, Aviad Moreno, and Michal Ben Ya'akov. Anwar and Waeem Jayosi of Ramallah, both involved in Palestinian human rights work, extended to me the warm hospitality of their home.

France was another stop on my archival odyssey. The Centre des Archives Diplomatiques at Nantes was an especially rich source for material on refugees. My thanks to the archivists Gervaise Delaunay, Maryannick Kervily, and Raphael Froment for their kind assistance. In Paris, at the Alliance Israélite Universelle Library, the director Jean-Claude Kuperminc led me to the personal archives of Jonathan Thurscz. The Centre de Documentation Juive Contemporaine at the Musée de la Shoah has an expansive collection of North African material available on microfilm.

In Paris, I found new pathways to understanding Nelly Benatar and her times when I had the good fortune of meeting members of her immediate family. Her grandson, Michel Lapidus, distinguished professor of mathematics at UC Riverside, introduced me to his equally brilliant father, Dr. Serge Lapidus, who was a treasure house of information. Now in his late nineties, Serge lent me many photographs and two unpublished manuscripts he wrote dedicated to Nelly's work and life. Other informants in Paris include Joel and Sylvie-Anne Haroche, and Patricia Lévy, director of the Galerie Gérard Lévy, who preserves the joyful aura of her unforgettable father. Friends Isi Beller and Ruth Zilkha provided impeccable hospitality. Also in Paris, I met for the first time (after a long correspondence) the inimitable Peggy Frankston, whose many contributions to the world of Holocaust research deserve a prize. I am especially grateful to Nadia Blumenfeld Charbit, curator of the estate of Erwin Blumenfeld, for her permission to use the photographs of wartime Morocco taken by her grandfather Erwin Blumenfeld. Nadia's husband Jean-Louis Charbit, Casablancan by birth, introduced me to his remarkable mother, Odette Charbit, friend of the Benatar family, now in her upper nineties.

Others who shared their wartime experiences with me are Lilli Joseph of Palm Springs, Dr. Clark Blatteis of Memphis, Dr. Sophie Freud of Concord, Massachusetts, and Henry Sibony of San Francisco; my deepest thanks to one and all. Hilary Applebaum led me to the Herbert and Cora Goold papers. Marina Pinto Kaufman filled me in on her uncle, Jack Pinto, and David Braunschvig told me many interesting things about Tangier and his grandfather, Haim Toledano. Dorrie Slutsker introduced me to the Haroche family, descendants of the Doctors Roublev. The response of perfect strangers enthused by the idea of a book on Nelly Benatar was wonderfully affirmative.

Closer to home, special gratitude goes to my beloved friends and colleagues, whose work has influenced my own beyond measure: Professors Emily Gottreich, Jessica Marglin, Alma Heckman, Chris Silver, Ethan Katz, Daniel Schroeter, Sarah Stein, Susan Slyomovics, David Stenner, and Aomar Boum have transformed the field of contemporary North African studies, as well as my own thinking on the topic. My thanks to UC Davis History Department colleagues David Biale and Sally McKee for reading and commenting on early versions of the manuscript. Omnia El Shakry, Edward Dickinson, Diana Davis, Ali Anooshar, Baki Tezcan, and Suad Joseph have given me rock-solid support from my first days at Davis. My thanks also to Samia Errazouki, Sam Ribakoff, Logan Clendenning, John Zandler,

Elizabeth Kurtz, and Laurie McGeoghegan for their invaluable research assistance. Marion Kaplan and Reeva Simon have both explored aspects of my topic and offered sage advice. Yaëlle Azagury, Susan Kahn, Mark Dowie, Bill Granara, and Doris Ober encouraged me at crucial moments. Special thanks to my Davis Bookies, who have shaped my reading tastes and introduced me to the pleasures of feminist biography. And to the nameless and faceless heroes of the Widener Library Scan and Deliver Service, a big shoutout of thanks.

I had the opportunity to speak about my work-in-progress at numerous conferences, workshops and other presentations at UC Davis, UC Berkeley, UCLA, UC San Diego, and the University of Southern California; at Camilo Gómez Rivas's workshop on the Maghrib at UC Santa Cruz; as well as at the Académie Royale in Rabat, al-Akhawayn University in Ifrane, the JDC in New York, the Van Leer Institute in Jerusalem, the Hebrew University, the US Holocaust Memorial Museum in Washington, DC, the CNRS-GDRI -SAJ conference in Lausanne on the social anthropology of contemporary Judaism, and the Jewish Theological Seminary in Berkeley. My thanks to the organizers of these gatherings for allowing me to express my incomplete ideas. The international symposium "Morocco from World War II to Independence," held at the University of Cambridge in May 2013, cosponsored by the Wolff Institute for the Study of Interfaith Relations and the Prince Alwaleed Bin Talal Center for Islamic Studies and organized by Dr. Shana Cohen, was the incubator for everything that followed. My thanks also to the editors of the *Journal of North African Studies* for publishing the proceedings of this seminal meeting in volume 19, number 4, in 2014.

The team at Stanford University Press was led by the gracious, wise, and amazing Kate Wahl, editor-in-chief and publishing director, who led me down the path of clear and expressive writing and gently redlined verbal excess. This book is far better because of her. Caroline McKusick, assistant editor, a fine scholar and happy addition to the publishing world, gently pushed me along the track. Senior production editor Susan Karani and copy editor Katherine Faydash kept me on time and pruned my prose with care. I want to express my appreciation to the Susan Groag Bell Publication Fund in Women's History at the Stanford University Press for its welcome support toward the publication of this book. Also my thanks to the anonymous reviewers whose comments were as generous as they were insightful.

Finally, I want celebrate my family—Daphne, Sam, Philip, and the next generation, Arlen, Emet, and Max—for their all-around loving support; and above all, my dearest David, who spent countless hours as my companion of the road, my sounding board, my patient muse, taking time away from his own important work of expanding opportunities for grassroots economic development for men and women around the world. I dedicate this book to him.

Image Credits

1.1 Private collection, Dr. Serge Lapidus, Paris, courtesy of Prof. Michel Lapidus.

1.2 Private collection, Dr. Serge Lapidus, Paris, courtesy of Prof. Michel Lapidus.

1.3 Private collection, Dr. Serge Lapidus, Paris, courtesy of Prof. Michel Lapidus.

1.4 Collection Galerie Gérard Lévy, Paris, courtesy of Patricia Lévy.

1.5 Private collection, Dr. Serge Lapidus, Paris, courtesy of Prof. Michel Lapidus.

2.1 Collection Galerie Gérard Lévy, Paris, courtesy of Patricia Lévy.

2.2 Photograph by Sophie Freud, US Holocaust Memorial Museum, #54630, courtesy of Sophie Freud.

2.3 Photo reproduced from Laredo, *Memorias de un viejo Tangerino* (1935).

3.1 US Holocaust Memorial Museum, #KE 76650/50, Collection Jacques Wiesel.

3.2 Photo reproduced from *Le Petit Marocain*, February 23, 1940.

3.3 Private Collection, Dr. Serge Lapidus, Paris, courtesy of Prof. Michel Lapidus.

4.1 Photograph by Erwin Blumenfeld, © The Estate of Erwin Blumenfeld, APH 1642-61, courtesy of Nadia Blumenfeld Charbit.

4.2 Photograph by Erwin Blumenfeld, © The Estate of Erwin Blumenfeld #P1011083, courtesy of Nadia Blumenfeld Charbit.

4.3 Photograph by Erwin Blumenfeld, © The Estate of Erwin Blumenfeld APH-1643-62, courtesy of Nadia Blumenfeld Charbit.

4.4 NY_03636, courtesy of the JDC Archives, New York.

5.1 NY_06958, courtesy of the JDC Archives, New York.

5.2 Collection of Daniel Abraham.

5.3 Photographer anonymous, Collection of Eugenez (Zenka) Siedlecki, Wikipedia Commons, https://en.wikipedia.org/wiki/Trans-Saharan_ Railway.

5.4 United States Holocaust Memorial Museum, #50722, courtesy of Sami Dorra.

5.5 United States Holocaust Memorial Museum, #50721, courtesy of Sami Dorra.

7.1 United States Holocaust Memorial Museum, #05436, courtesy of Mathilde Tagger.

8.1 United States Holocaust Memorial Museum, #75431, courtesy of Hildegard Abraham.

9.1 Photographer Al Taylor, NY_08354, courtesy of the JDC Archives, New York.

9.2 NY_16862, courtesy of the JDC Archives, New York.

9.3 Private Collection, Dr. Serge Lapidus, Paris, courtesy of Prof. Michel Lapidus.

9.4 Private collection of the author.

Notes

INTRODUCTION

1. The script of *Casablanca*, written by Julius and Philip Epstein, is available online at http://mckeestory.com/wp-content/uploads/Digital-CASABLANCA.pdf. On the making of the film, N. Isenberg, *We'll Always Have Casablanca: The Life, Legend, and Afterlife of Hollywood's Most Beloved Movie* (New York: W. W. Norton, 2017); A. Harmetz, *Round Up the Usual Suspects: The Making of Casablanca—Bogart, Bergman, and World War II* (New York: Hyperion, 2002).

2. Refugee rights is a burgeoning field of historical study. Recent works include S. Moyn, "Two Regimes of Memory," *American Historical Review* 103, no. 4 (October 1998): 1182–86; G. D. Cohen, *In War's Wake* (New York: Oxford University Press, 2011) and "The Politics of Recognition: Jewish Refugees in Relief Policies and Human Rights Debates, 1945–1950," *Immigrants and Minorities* 24 (July 2006): 125–43; E. Borgwardt, *A New Deal for the World: America's Vision for Human Rights* (Cambridge, MA: Harvard University Press, 2005); J. Loeffler, *Rooted Cosmopolitans: Jews and Human Rights in the Twentieth Century* (New Haven, CT: Yale University Press, 2018); and relevant articles in E. Fiddian-Qasmiyeh, G. Loescher, K. Long, and N. Sigona, *The Oxford Handbook of Refugee and Forced Migration Studies* (Oxford: Oxford University Press, 2014).

3. V. Woolf, *A Room of One's Own* (1929; New York: Harcourt, Brace, Jovanovich, 1981), 89.

4. A. Tartakower and K. R. Grossman, *The Jewish Refugee* (New York: Institute of Jewish Affairs of the American Jewish Congress and World Jewish Congress, 1944), 422–27.

5. "Private Collection Hélène Benatar, P129," Central Archives for the History of the Jewish People (CAHJP), Hebrew University, Givat Ram, Jerusalem. The collection was digitized by the US Holocaust Memorial Museum (USHMM) in Washington, DC, as RG 68.115M, "Private Collection Hélène Benatar, 1936–1953." Dr. Serge Lapidus, of Paris, husband of Benatar's daughter, Myriam, wrote two memoirs about his mother-in-law: *Nelly Benathar; une femme de tête, de coeur et de courage*, n.d., and *Tanger & Gibraltar, Les colonnes d'Hercule, berceaux des ancestres de Myriam*, also undated. My heartfelt thanks to Dr. Lapidus for sharing with me this unpublished material.

6. S. Bar-Asher, "Jewish Refugees from Nazi Europe in North Africa: A Document from the Archive of Cazes Ben-Attar" [in Hebrew], *Pe'amim: Studies in Oriental Jewry* 114–15 (2008): 257.

7. M. Ben Ya'akov, "European Jewish Refugees in Morocco during World War II," *Avotaynu* 31, no. 2 (2015): 41–45; and "Hélène Cazes Benatar et ses activités en faveur des réfugiés juifs au Maroc, 1940–1943," in *Les juifs d'Afrique du Nord face à l'Allemagne nazie*, ed. H. Saadoun and D. Michman (Paris: Perrin, 2018), 177–98; Y. Gershon, "L'aide aux réfugiés juifs du Maroc pendant la Seconde Guerre mondiale," *Revue d'Histoire de la Shoah* 2 (2016): 413–46. See also two recent publications that mention Benatar and her wartime activities: M. Hindley, *Destination Casablanca: Exile, Espionage, and the Battle for North Africa in World War II* (New York: Public Affairs Press, 2017); R. S. Simon, *The Jews of the Middle East and North Africa: The Impact of World War II* (Abingdon, UK: Routledge, 2020).

8. A. Farge, *The Allure of the Archives* (New Haven, CT: Yale University Press, 2013), 32.

CHAPTER 1

1. J.-L. Miège, *Le Maroc et l'Europe* (Rabat: Ed. La Porte, 1989), 2:560–80; Miège, *Chronique de Tanger, 1820–1830, Journal de Bendelac* (Rabat: Ed. La Porte, 1995), 9–42; Miège, "Chronique de Tanger," *Revue Maroc Europe* 1 (1991): 15–25.

2. S. Lévy, *Essais d'histoire et de civilisation judéo-marocaines* (Rabat: Centre Tarik Ibn Zyad, 2001), 15; Y. Azagury, "Choosing Which Language to Live In," *Lilith* 41, no. 1 (2016): 36–39; A. Chouraqui, *Les juifs d'Afrique du Nord* (Paris: Presses Universitaires de France, 1952), 268–76.

3. A. I. Laredo, *Les noms des juifs du Maroc: Essai d'onomastique judéo-marocaine*, Consejo Superior de Investigaciones Científicas Series E3 (Madrid: Instituto B. Arias Montano, 1978), 1036–40; S. Lapidus, *Tanger & Gibraltar*, 35.

4. Abraham Laredo, historian of Jewish Tangier, treated this topic with discretion, saying that Amram Cazes "lent important services to the authorities, especially during the First World War." Laredo, *Les noms des juifs*, 1039.

5. D. J. Schroeter, "Vichy in Morocco: The Residency, Mohammed V, and His

Indigenous Jewish Subjects," in *Colonialism and the Jews*, ed. L. Leff, E. Katz, and M. Mandel (Bloomington: Indiana University Press, 2017), 218.

6. I. Laredo, *Memorias de un viejo tangerino* (1935; reprint, Rabat: Éditions de la Porte, 1994), 18–19.

7. Lapidus, *Nelly Benathar*, 5–11.

8. V. Paloma, "Judeo-Spanish in Morocco: Language, Identity, Separation, or Integration?" in *La bienvenue et l'adieu: Migrants juifs et musulmans au Maghreb (XVe–XXe siècle), Temps et espaces, Actes du colloque d'Essaouira*, ed. F. Abecassis and K. Dirèche (Casablanca: La Croisé des Chemins, 2012), 1:103–12.

9. Words in quotation marks are from a private communication from Dr. Yaëlle Azagury, August 10, 2020.

10. A. Rodrigue, *French Jews, Turkish Jews: The Alliance Israélite Universelle and the Politics of Jewish Schooling in Turkey, 1860–1925* (Bloomington: Indiana University Press, 1990): M. Laskier, *The Alliance Israélite Universelle and the Jewish Communities of Morocco, 1862–1962* (Albany: State University of New York Press, 1983).

11. D. J. Schroeter and J. Chetrit, "Emancipation and Its Discontents: Jews at the Formative Period of Colonial Rule in Morocco," *Jewish Social Studies* 13, no. 1 (2006): 170–74.

12. M. Twain, *The Innocents Abroad; or, The New Pilgrims' Progress; Being Some Account of the Steamship Quaker City's Pleasure Excursion to Europe and the Holy Land; with Descriptions of Countries, Nations, Incidents and Adventures, as They Appeared to the Author* (New York: Random House, 2003), 50.

13. A. Adam, *Casablanca: Essai sur la transformation de la société marocaine au contact de l' Occident* (Paris: Centre Nationale de la Recherche Scientifique, 1968), 1:28.

14. S. G. Miller, "Kippur on the Amazon: Jewish Emigration from Northern Morocco in the Late Nineteenth Century," in *Sephardi and Middle Eastern Jewries: History and Culture in the Modern Era*, ed. H. Goldberg (Bloomington: Indiana University Press, 1996), 190–209; A. Moreno, "Moroccan Jewish Emigration to Latin America: The State of Research and New Directions," *Hespéris-Tamuda* 51, no. 2 (2016): 123–40.

15. Lapidus, *Tanger & Gibraltar*, 52.

16. The "Tazi building" where the Benatars resided still stands at the intersection of Boulevard de Paris and rue Idriss Lahrizi, formerly rue Gallieni. It was built in 1930 after plans drawn by the architects Louis-Paul and Félix Joseph Pertuzio. G. Wright, *The Politics of Design in French Colonial Urbanism* (Chicago: University of Chicago Press, 1991), 95. The magisterial work on interwar architecture in Casablanca is J.-L. Cohen and M. Eleb, *Casablanca: Mythes et figures d'une aventure urbaine* (Paris: Hazan, 1998).

17. A. R. Heckman, *The Sultan's Communists: Moroccan Jews and the Politics of Belonging* (Stanford, CA: Stanford University Press, 2020), 28–29, 45, 53, 55–56.

18. J. M. Marglin, *Across Legal Lines: Jews and Muslims in Modern Morocco* (New Haven, CT: Yale University Press, 2016), 192–94; Schroeter and Chetrit, "Emancipation and Its Discontents," 193–95.

19. M. Kenbib, *Juifs et musulmans au Maroc (1859–1948)* (Rabat: Université Mohammed V, Faculté des Lettres, 1994), 551; and "Juifs et musulmans au Maroc à l'époque du Front populaire, 1936–1938," *Hespéris-Tamuda* 24–25 (1987): 169–89; M. Abitbol, "Zionist Activity in North Africa up to the End of the Second World War," in *Pe'amim: Studies in Oriental Jewry* 2 (1979): 65–91; for a biographical sketch of Samuel Lévy, see M. Kenbib, "Samuel-Daniel Lévy," in *Encyclopedia of Jews in the Islamic World* (Leiden: Brill, 2010).

20. The Crémieux Decree of 1870 granted French citizenship to most Algerian Jews—about thirty-five thousand people—during the Franco-Prussian War. It was named after the Jewish statesman Adolphe Crémieux (1796–1880), twice France's minister of justice, a defender of Jewish rights, and among the founders of the AIU. D. Rivet, *Lyautey et l'institution du Protectorat français au Maroc* (Paris: L'Harmattan, 1988), 2:264–68; Z. Yehuda, "The Place of Aliyah in Moroccan Jewry's Conception of Zionism," *Studies in Zionism* 6, no. 2 (1983): 202.

21. A. R. Heckman, "Multivariable Casablanca: Vichy Law, Jewish Diversity, and the Moroccan Communist Party," *Hespéris-Tamuda* 51, no. 3 (2016): 18–19.

22. *L'Avenir Illustré* can be read online at https://web.nli.org.il/sites/JPress/English/Pages/default.aspx, the website of the Historical Jewish Press.

23. Nelly Benatar, "La 'WIZO' devant les evenements d'Eretz-Israel," *L'Avenir Illustré*, February 29, 1937.

24. M. Mazower, *No Enchanted Palace: The End of Empire and the Ideological Origins of the United Nations* (Princeton, NJ: Princeton University Press, 2008), 106–7; M. Marrus, *The Unwanted: European Refugees from the First World War through the Cold War* (Philadelphia: Temple University Press, 2002), 166–89.

25. W. Hoisington, *The Casablanca Connection: French Colonial Policy, 1936–1943* (Chapel Hill: University of North Carolina Press, 1984), 13–18, 26–28.

26. M. Benatar, *Plan de réorganisation de la communauté israélite de Casablanca* (Casablanca: Impriméries réunies de *La Vigie Marocaine* et du *Petit Marocain*, 1939). The library of the Ben Zvi Institute in Jerusalem has a copy.

CHAPTER 2

1. "Moses Benatar n'est plus," *L'Avenir Illustré* 13, no. 279 (December 31, 1938–January 15, 1939).

2. Lapidus, *Nelly Benathar*, 19–20. Serge Lapidus wrote that his wife, Myriam, suffered for years because of her mother's despondency. She was forbidden to wear any color other than black and was not allowed to "go out" with other young

people or enjoy any entertainment until she was eighteen, "leading her to the edge of suicide."

3. USHMM RG 68.115, R1/F29; Benatar later lowered her estimate of enlistees to 1,200. USHMM, RG 68.115/R1/F31, November 14, 1941.

4. *Le Petit Marocain*, August 2 and 3, 1939.

5. USHMM, RG 43.154/R3, "Project for the Organization of a Jewish Legion," October 13, 1939. See also A. [*sic*] Montagne, "Étude sur l'utilisation à la guerre des Israélites marocains," October 17, 1939, Ben Zvi Institute, Raphael Benazeraf Collection, P59.9, F6.1–F6.12.

6. In 1943, after the American landing in North Africa, Moroccan Jewish youth joined the pro-Gaullist Free French in numbers, serving in the Italian campaign and the liberation of France.

7. For a summary of Nazi emigration policies before the war, see M. Marrus, *The Unwanted: European Refugees from the First World War through the Cold War* (Philadelphia: Temple University Press, 2002), chap. 4.

8. J. M. Palmier and D. Fernbach, *Weimar in Exile: The Antifascist Emigration in Europe and America* (London: Verso, 2006), 185–87, 434–36.

9. J. Jackson, *France: The Dark Years, 1940–1944* (New York: Oxford University Press, 2001), 104.

10. A. Tartakower and K. R. Grossmann, *The Jewish Refugee* (New York: Institute of Jewish Affairs, 1944), 134–36; D. Peschanski, "Communistes, juifs, collabos, la France des camps," *L'Histoire* 264 (April 2002): 74.

11. J. Flanner, *Paris Was Yesterday, 1925–1939* (New York: Viking, 1972), 203.

12. Z. Szajkowski, "The Soldiers That France Forgot," *Contemporary Jewish Record* 5 (1942): 590.

13. B. Bernadac and P. Gallocher, *Histoire de la compagnie de navigation Paquet et des relations France-Maroc-Levant-Sénégal de 1863 à nos jours* (Marseille: Tacussel, 1991), 111–70.

14. "Jewish Emigration from Reich Ceases," *New York Times*, September 8, 1939; "U.S. Refugee Ships Are for Americans," *New York Times*, September 28, 1939; "Exile Haven Here Rivals Palestine," *New York Times*, October 29, 1939. See also R. Breitman and A. M. Kraut, *American Refugee Policy and European Jewry, 1933–1945* (Bloomington: Indiana University Press, 1987), chap. 5; and Y. Bauer, *American Jewry and the Holocaust: The American Jewish Joint Distribution Committee, 1939–1945* (Detroit: Wayne State University Press, 1981), chap. 1.

15. J. L. Cohen and M. Eleb, "The Whiteness of the Surf: Casablanca," *ANY: Architecture New York* 16 (January 1996): 16–19.

16. M. Eisenbeth, *Les juifs de l'Afrique du Nord: Démographie & onomastique* (Algiers: Imprimerie du Lycée, 1936), 21. M. Bernard, "La communauté juive de

Casablanca au temps du Protectorat," *Mémoire de Maitrise, Université de Paris I, Panthéon-Sorbonne* (1998), 35; A. Adam, *Casablanca: Essai sur la transformation de la société marocaine au contact de l'occident*, 2 vols. (Paris: Centre Nationale de la Recherche Scientifique, 1968), 1:184.

17. M. Kenbib, *Juifs et musulmans au Maroc, 1859–1948* (Rabat: Université Mohammed V, 1994), 509–10.

18. I. Laredo, *Memorias de un viejo tangerino* (Madrid: C. Bermejo, 1935).

19. C. de Nesry, *Le juif de Tanger et le Maroc* (Tangier: Eds. Internationales, 1956), 32. Isaac Laredo's writing practices were described to the author by Jack Laredo, nephew of Don Isaac, in Madrid in 1999.

20. On ties between northern Moroccan Jews and the Hispanophone world, see E. Calderwood, "Moroccan Jews and the Spanish Colonial Imaginary, 1903–1951," *Journal of North African Studies* 24, no. 1 (2019): 86–110.

21. Laredo, *Memorias*, 450.

22. CJH 245.5/Series 2, France 1/190, 1/192, February 19, 1939.

23. USHMM RG 68.115/R8/F504, Garzon to Lévy, February 28, 1939.

24. CJH 245.5/Series 2, France 1/190, Garzon to HICEM Paris, June 20, 1939.

25. CJH 245.5/Series 2 France 1/189, "Rapport sur les activités du mois de juillet 1939."

26. CJH 245.5/Series 2, France 1/190, Garzon to HICEM Paris, August 8, 1939.

27. Dr. Augusto d'Esaguy was Garzon's counterpart in Lisbon, serving as chair of the Comissão Portuguesa de Assistência aos Judeus Refugiados, or the Portuguese Commission for Assistance to Jewish Refugees. My thanks to Prof. Marion Kaplan for sharing this information.

28. De Nesry, *Le juif de Tanger*, 40–47; CJH 245.5/Series 2, France 1/1613/192, Kohn to HICEM, October 19, 1938.

29. A. Kaspi et al., eds., *Histoire de l'Alliance Israélite Universelle de 1860 à nos jours* (Paris: Armand Colin, 2010), 353–55; A. Michel, *Jules Braunschvig, juif humanist; l'homme et l'Alliance* (Paris: AIU/Nadir, 2006).

30. CJH 245.5/Series 2, France 1/192, Braunschvig to JDC Paris, August 14, 1939; CJH 245.5/Series 2, France 1/190, January 15, 1939, German refugees to Dijour; CJH 245.5/Series 2, France 1/192, Tangier, February 19, 1939; Dijour to AAE-AIU; Y. Bauer, *American Jewry and the Holocaust: The American Jewish Joint Distribution Committee, 1939–1945* (Detroit: Wayne State University Press, 1981), 21–35; Tartakower and Grossmann, *Jewish Refugee*, chap. 14.

31. Y. Bauer, *American Jewry and the Holocaust*, 21–35; Tartakower and Grossmann, *The Jewish Refugee*, chap. 14; A. Patt, A. Grossmann, L. Levi, and M. Mandel, *The JDC at 100: A Century of Humanitarianism* (Detroit: Wayne State University Press, 2019), 10–11.

32. CJH 245.5/Series 2, France 1/192, Braunschvig to Troper, August 11, 1939.

33. JDC-NY 33-44/363/87, Memorandum of meeting," June 4, 1939; JDC-NY 33-44/378/261, Memorandum of meeting, June 5, 1939; CJH 245.5/France 1, Series 2/192, d'Esaguy to (?), August 15, 1939.

CHAPTER 3

1. R. Barthes, *Camera Lucida: Reflections on Photography*, trans. R. Howard (New York: Hill and Wang, 1981), 4–7.

2. A symbol of selfless humanitarianism during World War I, in this war, the International Committee of the Red Cross was neither neutral or humanitarian. Yielding to Nazism's campaign against the Jews, the organization accepted Germany's definition of Jews as "detained civilians," criminalizing them and placing them beyond help. It is not surprising that in the postwar era, Benatar was mute about her connection to the International Red Cross. Lapidus, *Nelly Benathar*, 22–23; see also J.-P. Le Crom, "La Croix-Rouge française pendant la seconde guerre mondiale: La neutralité en question," *Vingtième Siècle* 101, no. 1 (2009): 149–62; M. N. Penkower, "The World Jewish Congress Confronts the International Red Cross during the Holocaust," *Jewish Social Studies* 41, nos. 3–4 (1979): 231; USHMM RG 68.115/R1/F29 is a fragment of Benatar's curriculum vitae noting her wartime service to this organization. The photo of Benatar as a nurse in training is from *Le Petit Marocain*, February 23, 1940.

3. R. Murphy, *Diplomat among Warriors* (New York: Doubleday, 1964), 49.

4. Reporting on the public mood, see *Le Petit Marocain* of July 5, 6, and 9, 1940, and especially "Casablanca, été 1940," July 15, 1940.

5. USHMM RG 43.154/11 MA 900/847/F494–95, "Questions à examiner en ce que concerne les convois français," June 22,1940.

6. USHMM RG 43.154/11 MA 900/847/F241–43, Contard to Political Section, July 2, 1940.

7. The figure of two thousand detainees at Aïn Chock appears in a memo from Benatar to the chief of municipal services in January 1941, complaining about the delay in receiving relief promised by the municipality. AIU/AP 24/Thurscz, January 13, 1941.

8. USHMM RG 43.154/11 MA 900/847/F419, Port Police to Public Security, June 30, 1940.

9. Lapidus, *Nelly Benathar*, 28. See also JDC-NY 33–44/745/709, Kelber to Troper et al., July 6, 1940.

10. Lapidus, *Nelly Benathar*, 27; USHMM RG 68.115/R1/F53–54, Nelly Benatar, "Curriculum Vitae, 1939–1962."

11. USHMM RG 43.154, 11 MA 900/847/F212-214. Contard to Benatar, July 16, 1940.

12. AIU/AP 24/Benatar to Bouquet, January 13, 1941. In Casablanca, the going exchange rate in April 1940 was forty-five francs to the dollar; in Tangier it was ninety to ninety-five francs to the dollar. Goold Family Papers, Cora Goold to Felix Smith, April 19, 1941.

13. USHMM RG 43.154/11 MA 900/847/F316; USHMM RG 43.154/11 MA 900/847/F285, Herviot to Contard, July 24, 1940;USHMM RG 43.154, 11 MA 900/847/F282–84.

14. USHMM RG 43.154/11 MA 900/847/F281.

15. USHMM RG 43.154/11 MA 900/847/F1364, "Police report," August 27, 1940; in the same dossier, F1459–60, Contard to Herviot, August 28, 1940. The stolen bicycle is in *Le Petit Marocain*, "Un réfugié volait des bicyclettes," March 5, 1941. On medical issues, see USHMM RG 43.154/11 MA 900/847/F865.

16. Goold Family Archive, Cora Goold to her brother Felix, November 25, 1940. NARA, Personnel Records/Goold/Murphy to Hall, January 17, 1941; and "Memo of conversation," Goold and Eberhardt, April 1, 1941.

17. The group included 107 children, 406 men between the ages of seventeen and fifty, 47 men older than fifty, and 253 women. At least half of the refugees were "indigent" and incapable of contributing to the cost of their ongoing journey. Of the 813 refugees, 736 were Jews and 77 were non-Jews. JDC-NY 33-44/745/F723–25, Benatar to JDC, September 17, 1940.

18. USHMM RG 43.154/11 MA 900/847/F234, July 26, 1940, lists the declarations of capital, including gems, brought into Morocco by refugees.

19. USHMM RG 43.154/11 MA 900/847/F122–23, Benatar to Contrôleur en Chef de la Region civile, September 2, 1940.

20. Thurscz's personal archive, including material relating to his years in Casablanca, is found in the collections of the Alliance Israélite Universelle in Paris, "Fonds Jonathan Thurscz," AP 24. My thanks to the conservator Jean-Claude Kuperminc for directing me to this source.

21. In 1942, Thurscz was accused by a former refugee of favoritism and even of "collusion" with Vichy officials while he was working for the Casablanca Refugee Committee. The World Jewish Congress took up the matter and put Thurscz "on trial," using as evidence testimony from former refugees. The inquiry ended with an acquittal, but Thurscz never worked for a Jewish aid organization again. After the war, he joined the US State Department. He was suspended in 1953, as a "security risk" during the McCarthy era, then cleared and reinstated in 1956. Thurscz died in 1976 in Baltimore at the age of eighty-one. "Zionist Jonathan Thurscz Dies," *Jerusalem Post*, May 7, 1976.

22. JDC-NY 33–44/745/F713. Schwartz to Troper, July 12, 1940.

23. JDC-NY 33–44/745, Schwartz to New York, July 27, 1940; AIU/AP24/Commission to JDC Lisbon, July 22, 1940.

24. JDC-NY 33–44/745/Schwartz to NY, July 27, 1940.

25. O. Wieviorka, *The French Resistance*, trans. J. M. Todd (Cambridge, MA: Harvard University Press, 2016), chap. 15. R. O. Paxton offers a different view in "The Truth about the Resistance," *New York Review of Books*, February 25, 2016. On foreigners in the resistance, see D. Peschanski, *Des étrangers dans la Résistance* (Paris: Atelier, 2002).

26. Lapidus, *Nelly Benathar*, 34.

27. Notes in USHMM RG 68.115/R8/F382–92, written in the 1970s, report on Nelly Benatar's work in the underground. Her account is corroborated by the testimony of Albert El Koubbi, "Notes sur l'action et la formation du reseau 'Schumann-Mengin à Casablanca,'" CAHJP/RP 117, also written after the fact.

28. USHMM RG 68.115/R8/F383.

29. USHMM RG 68.115/R8/F393.

30. AIU/AP 24, Benatar to Zagury, September 10, 1940; USHMM RG 43.154/11 MA 900/847/F882, DAP to Contrôleur civil, Casablanca, September 21, 1940; USHMM RG 43.154/11 MA 900/847/F917, Czech consulate, Casablanca, to?, June 28, 1940; USHMM RG 68.115/R8/F493, Region civile to Benatar, September 9, 1940. For Benatar's list of her collaborators, see USHMM RG 68–115/R8/F392.

31. NAUK/SOE/HS 9/1020/2, "Rapport du s. lieutenant Mercier," Gibraltar, August 14, 1942. Mercier was one of Mengin's aliases. To confuse matters even more, Mengin's name was often misspelled; Benatar made the mistake of writing it as "Mangin." Information about Mengin is taken from his dossier in the British archives cited above.

32. Ibid.

33. Maurice Schumann became famous during the war for his radio program *Honneur et Patrie* (Honor and Country), beamed from BBC London to occupied France. Maurice had an illustrious political career after the war; his brother Robert disappeared from view. Born to a Jewish father and a Roman Catholic mother, the Schumann brothers traced their ancestry to the Jews of Alsace. Maurice converted to Catholicism in 1937, but there is no evidence that Robert did the same. He is not to be confused with another Robert Schumann, French statesman and an architect of the European Union, who served in the Vichy regime in 1940–1942.

34. David King figures extensively in M. Hindley, *Destination Casablanca: Exile, Espionage and the Battle for North Africa in World War II* (New York: Public Affairs, 2017), chap. 17. See also E. B. Litsky, "The Murphy-Weygand Agreement: The United States and French North Africa (1940–1942)" (PhD diss., Fordham University, 1986), 150–60.

35. Service Historique de la Defense (SHAT), Château de Vincennes, dossier #GR 16 P 410655, a very brief and uninformative report of Mengin's war record.

36. NAUK/HS 9/1020/2. "Report of R. H. Osborne," n.d.

37. El Koubbi, CAHJP/P117, "Notes."

38. Ibid.

39. According to Serge Lapidus, it was Colombo, not El Koubbi, who recruited Nelly Benatar to join the Schumann-Mengin organization. Lapidus incorrectly names the head of the network as "Mangin." Lapidus, *Nelly Benathar*, 43.

40. During World War II, the journalistic landscape in Morocco was bleak. The nationalist press was shut down in 1937, and in 1940, leftist newspapers suffered the same fate. Still circulating were newspapers of the right-wing Mas group (*Le Petit Marocain, La Vigie Marocaine, Le Courrier du Maroc*) and an Arabic newspaper, *Es-saada*, the mouthpiece of the Residency. People who owned radio sets tuned in to BBC London for news. My thanks to Prof. Jamaa Baïda for this information.

41. El Koubbi, CAHJP/P117, "Notes." The subsequent narrative of El Koubbi's arrest and torture is taken from this source.

42. CADN/11 MA 900/31bis, "El Koubbi affair," July 6, 1942.

43. USHMM RG 43.144/F84–87, El Koubbi to Frenay, July 2, 1944.

44. NAUK HS 9-1010-2/F29. R. Mengin, "Impressions sur l'Afrique du Nord," August 15, 1942. Historians have noted that the Vichy-sponsored race laws of 1940 did not produce a counterattack from the French resistance; rather, the decrees were seen as the result of the general mistrust that Jews as a group inspired. When word spread of the mass deportations of Jews from France beginning in July 1942, "the resistance [in France] remained silent even as genocide on an unprecedented scale was being perpetuated," according to Olivier Wieviorka, *French Resistance*, 220.

45. Wieviorka, *French Resistance*, 403.

46. C. R. Browning, "Who Resisted the Nazis?" *New York Review of Books*, July 2, 2020, 24–25.

CHAPTER 4

1. A. Seghers, *Transit* (New York: New York Review of Books, 2013), vii, 35, 55, 78. Anna Seghers (1900–1983), a German Jew, fled to France in 1933. With the help of Varian Fry, she sailed to Mexico on the same boat as André Breton, Victor Serge, and Claude Lévi-Strauss in 1941. A devoted communist, she returned East Berlin after the war. In 2018, her book became a movie by the same name. "'Transit' Review: An Existential Puzzler with Jackboots and Terror," *New York Times*, February 28, 2019, https://www.nytimes.com/2019/02/28/movies/transit-review.html.

2. V. Fry, *Surrender on Demand* (New York: Random House, 1945), 13, 96. Two thousand is the number usually given for those whom he rescued.

3. C. Schine, "It Had to Be Her," *New York Review of Books*, January 16, 2020.

4. V. Fry, "Our Consuls at Work," *The Nation*, May 2, 1942, 507–9. Fry depicts

US consular officials as vacuous toadies standing in the way of getting people out of Europe.

5. Since his death, Fry has been the subject of museum displays, a potboiler film, and various academic symposia, as well as the posthumous recipient of the Chevalier de la Legion d'Honneur from the French government. The most recent addition to Fry iconography is a fanciful novel based on his life—*The Flight Portfolio: A Novel*, by J. Orringer (New York: Knopf, 2019). The most factual account of his wartime activities was authored by his colleague Daniel Bénédite, *La filière marseillaise: Un chemin vers la liberté sous l'occupation* (Paris: Clancier Guénaud, 1984).

6. E. Jennings, "Last Exit from Vichy France: The Martinique Escape Route and the Ambiguities of Emigration," *Journal of Modern History* 74, no. 2 (June 2002): 289–324; and Jennings, "The Best Avenue of Escape: The French Caribbean Route as Expulsion, Rescue, Trial, and Encounter," *French Politics, Culture & Society* 30, no. 2 (2012): 33–52.

7. R. Dray-Bensousan, "Les filières d'émigration juive de 1940 à 1942," in *Varian Fry, du refuge à l'exil, Actes du Colloque du 20 Mars 1999* (Aix-en-Provence, France: Actes-Sud, 2000), 15–33; M. Gottschalk, "The Jewish Emigrant—1941," *Contemporary Jewish Record* 4 (1941): 261–68.

8. S. Freud, *Living in the Shadow of the Freud Family*, ed. E. D. Freud (Westport, CT: Praeger Publishers, 2007), 262.

9. Fry, *Surrender on Demand*, 188–89.

10. Between October 1940 and May 1941, all twelve boats that took the Marseille to Martinique route stopped at Casablanca, according to E. Jennings, *Best Avenue*, 37.

11. Fonds Lapidus, Benatar to Madame Courtin, head of the "Fratérnité de Guerre," August 14, 1940.

12. C. Noguès, *Le Procés du Général Noguès devant la Haute cour de Justice* (Paris: Ministère Public, 1956), CRL Electronic Resource, https://dds.crl.edu/crldelivery/24479.

13. Ibid. Benatar's testimony is in fasc. 2,"Depositions des Temoins (suite)," 116–20. Benatar claimed that more than ten thousand Spanish political refugees were being held in Moroccan internment camps as of May 1941 (118).

14. E. B. Litsky, "The Murphy-Weygand Agreement: The United States and French North Africa (1940–1942)" (PhD diss., Fordham University, 1986).

15. R. O. Paxton, *Parades and Politics at Vichy: The French Officer Corps under Marshal Pétain.* (Princeton, NJ: Princeton University Press, 1966), 221–26; *Haute Cour, Audience du 26 octobre 1956; Plaiderie de Me Vienot*, 23.

16. On Noguès's efforts to isolate the Germans, see *Haute cour*, fasc. 3, 45. See also CADN/1MA/200/96, "L'effort de Resistance du Maroc de juin 1940 à novembre 1942 et la préparation à la réprise de la lutte contre l'Allemagne," n.d. Pierre Voizard,

secretary-general of the Protectorate in 1941 and one of Noguès's closest aides, testi-
fied at Noguès's second trial in 1956 that the resident-general did everything he could
to thwart the German Armistice Commission, employing a policy of "silence and
withdrawal." According to Voizard, Noguès and his wife "never received a German
at their table."

17. Hoover Institute, Murphy Papers, B46/F10, Auer to Murphy, January 2, 1941.

18. Goold refused to accept another post and left the Foreign Service before the
age of retirement. Goold Family Papers, Cora Goold to Felix Smith, May 9, 1941, and
May 15, 1941; NARA, Personnel Records, Herbert Goold: Murphy to Hall, January
17, 1941, and Memo of conversation, Goold and Eberhardt, April 1, 1941; Noguès to
Vichy, February 17, 1941; Chief, Division of Foreign Service Personnel (name illeg-
ible) to Board of Foreign Service Personnel, August 6, 1942. For background, see
E. Litsky, "The Murphy-Weygand Agreement," 137–39. Another perspective is J. R.
Childs, *Operation 'Torch,' an Object Lesson in Diplomacy*, 1950s [date unknown], J.
Rives Childs Collection, University of Virginia Library, 42–46.

Herbert Goold was not the only foreign service officer to be punished for de-
fying US State Department policy in that era. Hiram Bingham, consul in Marseille,
worked closely with Varian Fry to obtain US visas for Fry's protégés. Admonished by
Washington for being too liberal in issuing visas, Bingham was also recalled and sent
to South America. He, too, requested early retirement. On Hiram Bingham IV, see
https://en.wikipedia.org/wiki/Hiram_Bingham_IV, accessed on July 3, 2018.

19. CADN/11 MA 900/31bis, n.d..

20. USHMM, RG 68.115/R8/F383–85, Benatar, "Demande de carte de combat-
tant volontaire," 1939–1945, n.d. AIU/AP24/Thurscz/F463–67, Benatar to Noguès,
June 24, 1941. The threat to imprison Benatar is at USHMM RG 68.115/R10/F351.

21. Lapidus, *Nelly Benathar*, 43; USHMM RG 68.115/R8/F384–85; RG 68.115/R1/
F54.

22. *Le Procés du Général Noguès*, fasc. 2, "Depositions des Temoins (suite)," 118.

23. USHMM RG 68.115/R8/F390.

24. Lapidus, *Nelly Benathar*, 45.

25. H. Blumenfeld, *Autobiography*, unpublished manuscript, n.d., 122. My thanks
to Nadia Blumenfeld Chabrit for sharing this document with me.

26. Jennings, *Best Avenue of Escape*, 40 and n36.

27. USHMM RG 43.006–3/R 16, Vichy-Maroc, Note to Direction politique, unsigned, June 16, 1941.

28. USHMM RG 43.006/R6/Fry to Ministry of Foreign Affairs, Vichy, June 25,
1941; Bénédite, *Filiére marseillaise*, 191, 227; on the *Alsina*, see USHMM RG 43.006,
unsigned to Weygand, July 1, 1941. USHMM RG 43.006-3 R16/95–96, Fry to Minister
of Foreign Affairs at Vichy, June 23, 1941.

29. AIU/AP24 Thurscz/F246/June 24, 1941.

30. Documents on the *Wyoming* are scattered throughout the Benatar archive. See RG 68.115/R 16/F982/F12, F14; RG 68.115/R10/F361; also Andover Harvard Theological Seminary (AHTL), Records of the Universalist Unitarian Service Committee, bMS 16007/20 (3)/F18–21, "List of Refugees from the Centre Américain de Secours who have migrated," [May 1942?].

31. Le Vernet was an internment camp for foreign Jews located in the French Pyrenees; in 1942, inmates from Le Vernet were deported to Nazi extermination camps with the help of French police. E. Blumenfeld, *Eye to I: The Autobiography of a Photographer* (London: Thames and Hudson, 1999), 324–26. Rabbi Abraham Moul El Nis is a Moroccan Jewish *tsaddiq*, or saint, whose tomb is located in a cave outside of the town of Azemmour.

32. H. Blumenfeld, *Autobiography*, 125–26. See also USHMM Oral History Project, RG 50.030, *0623, 2011, interview with Henry Blumenfeld by Peggy Frankston. Henry joined the US Army after arriving in the United States and spent the rest of the war years with a medical unit in the European theater. After the war, he finished his degree at Harvard and earned a doctorate in physics at Columbia

33. USC Shoah Foundation, Visual History Archive, Interview #11913. Lilli Joseph, February 9, 1996. Author's interview with Lilli Joseph, Palm Springs, CA, December 15, 2017.

34. USHMM RG 50.163.0012, interview with Hans Julius Cahnmann, 1989.

35. JDC-NY/33–44/387/767. "118 Refugees Arrive off Serpa Pinto, Escape Aided by Joint Distribution Committee." Undated press release, probably December 26, 1941. USHMM, RG 68.115/R1/F156–66.

36. USHMM RG 68.115/R8/F488, Benatar, "Note to the file," n.d.

37. A detailed study of the impact of the Vichy anti-Semitic legislation in Morocco is yet to be written. See USHMM RG 81.001: Bibliothèque Nationale, Royaume du Maroc, Archives of the Protectorate, 18 reels for the Protectorate documentation. M. Laskier, "Between Vichy Antisemitism and German Harassment: The Jews of North Africa during the Early 1940s," *Modern Judaism* 11, no. 3 (1991): 343–60; M. Abitbol, *The Jews of North Africa during the Second World War* (Detroit: Wayne State University Press, 1989), 74–83; M. Kenbib, *Juifs et Musulmans*, 596–638. For historical debates over the impact of the race laws, see D. J. Schroeter, "Vichy in Morocco: The Residency, Mohammed V, and His Indigenous Jewish Subjects," in *Colonialism and the Jews*, ed. L. Leff, E. Katz, and M. Mandel (Bloomington: Indiana University Press, 2017), 215–50, esp. 216–17. A related controversy that reflects more about current politics than past history is the search for "good" Muslims who may have helped North African Jews during the war. An example of this genre is R. Satloff, *Among the Righteous: Lost Stories From the Holocaust's Long Reach into Arab Lands* (New York:

Public Affairs, 2007). A response to Satloff is S. Wagenhofer, "Contested Narratives: Contemporary Debates on Mohammed V and the Moroccan Jews under the Vichy Regime," in *Quest: Issues in Contemporary Jewish History, Journal of Fondazione CDEC* 4 (November 2012): 145–64. A Moroccan point of view is J. Baïda, "Sidi Mohamed V et les lois antijuives," *Zamane* (May 2013): 42–45.

38. USHMM RG 81.001/R2/F16; RG 81.001/R2/F319–20; *Le Petit Marocain*, August 16, 1941; *La Vigie Marocaine*, August 20, 1941; CJDC LXXX-16, Darlan to Vallat. On Vallat's role in managing Jewish affairs, see Paxton, *Vichy France: Old Guard and New Order, 1940–1944* (New York: Knopf, 1972), 177–79; V. Caron, *Uneasy Asylum: France and the Jewish Refugee Crisis, 1933–1942* (Stanford, CA: Stanford University Press, 1999), 328–30; D. Schroeter, "Vichy in Morocco," 225, is an effort to clarify some of the confusion surrounding this topic.

39. "Règlement au Maroc," *La Vigie Marocaine*, September 29, 1941; USHMM, RG 81.001/R7/F282.

40. USHMM RG 43.070/R1/LIV25, "Dossier of 18 August 1941," February 2, 1942.

41. The social science literature on patron-client relations in Morocco is extensive: J. Waterbury, *The Commander of the Faithful; the Moroccan Political Elite—A Study in Segmented Politics* (New York: Columbia University Press, 1970) is the classic work; A. Hammoudi, *Master and Disciple: The Cultural Foundations of Moroccan Authoritarianism* (Chicago: University of Chicago Press, 1997), explores the sociological roots of clientelism. For a Jewish perspective, see L. Rosen, *Two Arabs, a Berber, and a Jew: Entangled Lives in Morocco* (Chicago: University of Chicago Press, 2016).

42. W. Hoisington, *The Casablanca Connection: French Colonial Policy, 1936–1943* (Chapel Hill: University of North Carolina Press, 1984), 191–93. Noguès ordered a substantial military buildup in Morocco outside of Vichy control. See CADN 1 MA/200/96, "L'effort de resistance du Maroc de juin 1940 à novembre 1942 et la préparation à la reprise de la lutte contre l'Allemagne," n.d.

43. J. Dahan, *Regard d'un juif marocain sur l'histoire contemporaine de son pays* (Paris: L'Harmattan, 1995), 33.

44. R. Cadet testimony, *Haute cour*, fasc. 3, October 25, 1956, 16–17.

CHAPTER 5

1. H. Arendt, "We Refugees," *Menorah Journal* 31, no. 1 (1943): 69–77.

2. When she wrote this, in "We Refugees," Arendt may have been thinking of her friend, German Jewish philosopher Walter Benjamin, who committed suicide on the border of France and Spain in 1940 after being denied entry into Spain.

3. L. Stonebridge, *The Judicial Imagination: Writing after Nuremberg* (Edinburgh, UK: Edinburgh University Press, 2011), chap. 4.

4. On writing refugee lives, see M. Fawaz, A. Gharbieh, M. Harb, D. Salamé, "Refugees as City Makers," *Jadaliyya*, October 1, 2018, www.jadaliyya.com/Details /38034.

5. J.-L. Cohen, "Henri Prost & Casablanca; The Art of Making Successful Cities," *The New City: "Modern Cities"* 3 (1996): 107.

6. On Lyautey's plan for Casablanca, see J.-L. Cohen and M. Eleb, "The Whiteness of the Surf: Casablanca" *ANY—Architecture New York* 16 (1996): 16–19. For Prost's own thoughts, see "Le plan de Casablanca," *France-Maroc* 1, no. 8 (August 1917): 7–12. P. Rabinow, *French Modern: Norms and Forms of the Social Environment* (Chicago: University of Chicago Press, 1995), chap. 9.

7. *La Vigie Marocaine*, April 10, 1942, and April 17, 1942.

8. M. Eleb, "Apartment Buildings in Casablanca," *The New City: "Modern Cities"* 3 (1996): 95–106; J.-L. Cohen and M. Eleb, *Casablanca: Mythes et figures d'une aventure urbaine* (Paris: Hazan, 1998), 167–68.

9. "Logements," *La Vigie Marocaine*, April 2, 1942.

10. USHMM RG 68.115/R10/Fr284, "A List of ex-EVDGs and their places of residence."

11. Telephone interview with Dr. Clark Blatteis, December 17, 2014.

12. USHMM RG 67.008/B1/F25/Fr27, "General Conditions in Large Towns in Maroc [*sic*]: Summary," August 25, 1942; "La carte de consommation familial va être établie au Maroc," *Le Petit Marocain*, July 14, 1940; "La hausse du prix de la vie au Maroc doit être arrêté," *Le Petit Marocain*, March 1, 1941; "Ravitaillement de la population européenne," *La Vigie Marocaine*, January 5, 1942. J. Berque, *French North Africa: The Maghrib between Two World Wars* (New York: Praeger, 1967), 302.

13. *La Vigie Marocaine*, April 27, 1942.

14. Mazower, *Hitler's Empire: How the Nazis Ruled Europe* (New York: Penguin, 2008), 262; JDC NY 33–44/F745/Fr770–76, "Sheldon Report," November 4, 1941.

15. C. Blatteis interview, December 17, 2014.

16. J. Dahan, *Regard d'un juif marocain sur l'histoire contemporaine de son pays: de l'avènement de Sa Majestè le Sultan Sidi Mohammed ben Youssef, au dénouement du complot d'Oufkir (1927–1972)* (Paris: L'Harmattan, 1995), 31.

17. D. Rivet, "La récrudescence des épidémies au Maroc durant la Deuxième guerre mondiale: Essai de mesure et d'interpretation" *Hespéris-Tamuda* 30, no. 1 (1992): 98–99; Rivet, "Hygiénisme colonial et médicalisation de la société marocaine," in *Santé, médicine et société dans le Monde arabe*, ed. E. Longuenesse (Paris: L'Harmattan, 1995), 105–28. JDC NY 33–44/F745/Fr770–76, "Statement of Health Conditions in French Morocco," by Dr. W. H. Sheldon. November 4, 1941.

18. V. Roublev, *Le grand escalier*, ed. Joel Harroche (n.p.: n.d), 86. My thanks to Joel Haroche for sharing this unpublished family memoir with me.

19. USHMM RG 68.115/R6/F358. Benatar to Director General Grud, June 10, 194[?].

20. Most notably, Dr. Leon Benzaquen, a well-known Casablanca doctor who later became the personal doctor of King Mohamed V and the first Moroccan Jew to serve as a minister in the independent Moroccan state. Benzaquen's consultations were made "on a purely gratis basis." USHMM RG 68.115 R8/F438–39.

21. Email communication from Joel Haroche, Paris, January 31, 2016; Roublev, *Le grand escalier*, 116–21. In 1941, Vala Roublev married Albert Haroche, a Moroccan Jewish lawyer from Marrakech. Albert Haroche was an associate of Benatar's during the war and completed an apprenticeship in her law office. The Haroches had four sons; Serge Haroche, born in Casablanca in 1944; Joel, born in 1947, was followed by two more brothers. The Roublev-Haroches migrated to France in 1956. Serge Haroche became a physicist and won the 2012 Nobel Prize for his work on quantum mechanics. Joel, a writer and editor, married Sylvie-Anne, an Argentinian Jew. Their son, Raphaël, born in 1975, is a well-known French singer and songwriter. Vala's parents, Sacha and Sofa, left Morocco in 1943 and migrated to the United States, returning to Morocco in 1946. Shortly thereafter, their marriage ended. Sacha returned to America, where he died in 1976; Sofa went to Palestine, where she became the medical doctor of Kfar Szold. The Roublev-Haroches collectively represent a family odyssey having its roots in wartime Morocco.

22. D. Dwork, "Rescuers," in *Oxford Handbook of Holocaust Studies*, ed. P. Hayes and J. K. K. Roth (Oxford: Oxford University Press, 2010), 181.

23. USHMM RG 67.008/B5/F97/Fr4–5, Kimberland to McCollum, April 23, 1942.

24. USHMM RG 68.115/R4/Fr779.

25. USHMM RG 68.115/R9/Fr398, Benatar to JDC Lisbon, May 30, 1942. JDC 33–44/F366/Fr1022, "List of Boats Sailed from Europe," n.d.; CJH 245.5/France II/137, [unknown] to Lisbon, CJH 245.5, France 17.9/II 150, Oettinger to Spanien, March 26, 1942; JDC 33–44/F366/Fr1185, "Monthly Breakdown of Visa Approvals and rejections received in the JDC Office from State Department Between February 23 through December 31, 1942"; M. Marrus, *The Unwanted: European Refugees from the First World War through the Cold War* (Philadelphia: Temple University Press, 2002), 258–68. On Lisbon's role in the wartime refugee crisis, see M. Kaplan, *Hitler's Jewish Refugees: Hope and Anxiety in Portugal* (New Haven, CT: Yale University Press, 2020).

26. A. I. Laredo, *Les noms des juifs du Maroc* (Instituto Arias Montano, 1978), 1002–3.

27. USHMM RG 67.008/B5/F82/Fr119, Heath to Philadelphia, September 2, 1943.

28. USHMM RG 68.115/R8/Fr700, Schwartz to Benatar, March 17, 1941; RG 68.115/R8/Fr798, Benatar to Schwartz, November 3, 1941.

29. JDC NY 33–44/745/Fr736, Katz to Kahn, February 10, 1941; JDC NY 33–44/745/Fr735, Schwartz to Kahn, March 7, 1941.

30. USHMM RG 68.115/R9/Fr460–61, Benatar to Cysner, March 17, 1941.

31. H. Pol, "Vichy's Slave Battalions," *The Nation* 152, no. 18 (May 3, 1941): 527–29; "Sahara Slavery Denied by French," *New York Times*, July 25, 1941; JDC NY 33–44/745/Fr744, "Memorandum," Desick to Slobodin, May 27, 1941.

32. USHMM, RG 68.115/R8/Fr798–99, Benatar to JDC Lisbon, November 3, 41.

33. Paxton, *Vichy France*, 136–39.

34. P. Gaida, *Camps de travail sous Vichy: les "groupes de travailleurs étrangers" (GTE) en France et en Afrique du Nord, 1940–1944* (Paris: ANRT, 2008), 220–78. On the delivery of goods to Germany, see Paxton, *Vichy France*, 143–45.

35. R. Selke, "Trans-Saharan Inferno," *Free World* (February 1942), 60. A protégé of Varian Fry, Selke transited Morocco in 1941.

36. USHMM RG 67.008/B6/F104/Fr59–69, "Testimony from Camp Inmates," January 30, 1943. USHMM RG 67.008, "American Friends Service Committee Records Relating to Humanitarian Work in North Africa, 1942–1945," has important material on the Vichy prison camps. C. Levisse-Touzé, "Les camps d'internement d'Afrique du Nord: Politiques répressives et populations," in *L'Empire colonial sous Vichy*, ed. E. Jennings and J. Cantier (Paris: O. Jacob, 2004), 177–94; J. Baïda, "Les 'réfugiés' juifs européens au Maroc pendant la seconde guerre mondiale," in *La bienvenue et l'adieu: Migrants juifs et musulmans au Maghreb XVe-XXe siècles*, vol. 2, *Ruptures et recompositions, Actes du colloque d'Essaouira*, ed. K. Dirèche, R Aouad, and F. Abécassis (Paris: Karthala, 2012), 57–66; Z. Szajkowski, *Jews and the French Foreign Legion* (New York: Ktav Publishing House, 1975); J. Oliel, *Les camps de Vichy, Maghreb-Sahara, 1939–1944* (Montreal: Eds. du Lys, 2005); A. Boum, "Eyewitness Djelfa: Daily Life in a Saharan Vichy Labor Camp," in *The Holocaust and North Africa*, eds. A. Boum and S. Stein (Stanford, CA: Stanford University Press, 2018), 149–67. For a comprehensive overview, see G. P. Megargee and J. R. White, eds., "Vichy Africa" in *The United States Holocaust Memorial Museum Encyclopedia of Camps and Ghettos* (Bloomington: Indiana University Press, 2018), 240–300.

37. Gaida, *Camps de travail*, 253–54.

38. CADN/1MA/200/Fr133, Contrôleur Civil, Casablanca to Directeur des Affaires Politiques (DAP) Rabat, November 9, 1941.

39. Author's visit to Boudenib camp on September 30, 2018. My gratitude to members of the local chapter of the National Council of Human Rights who served as my guides.

40. P. Jalée, *L'ancre dans L'Avenir: Mémoires d'un militant heureux* (Paris: Karthala, 1981), 59.

41. USHMM, RG 67.008/B3/F34/Fr15–18, "Liste nominative des étrangers," n.d.

42. Paxton, *Vichy France*, 144.

43. Ibid., xiii.

44. O. Ouaknine-Yekutieli, "Corporatism as a Contested Sphere: Trade Organization in Morocco under the Vichy Regime," *Journal of the Economic and Social History of the Orient* 58, no. 4 (2015): 453–89, esp. 467–69. Prominent Moroccan families involved in the corporate scheme included the Benkirane, al-Hajawi, Mekouar, Gessous, Berrada, and Benjelloun. The stated goal was to control trade for the "benefit of the Moroccan worker"; the unstated goal was to take advantage of Vichy's policy of "Aryanization" that eliminated Jewish competition and created monopolies that reaped huge profits. After 1942, the US government continued exporting strategic materials from Morocco to Britain: NARA, RG 169, Foreign Economic Administration Research Reports, RR 26, B18, "French North Africa as a Source of Supply for Nazi Germany," n.d. See also P. Morgan, *Hitler's Collaborators: Choosing between Bad and Worse in Nazi-Occupied Western Europe* (Oxford: Oxford University Press, 2018).

45. P. Voizard testimony, *Haute cour*, October 25, 1956 (*soir*), fasc. 4, 46–47.

46. C. Metzger, "L'empire colonial français dans la stratégie du troisième Reich (1936–1945)," *Relations internationales* 101 (Spring 2000): 51; C. Lévisse-Touzé, *L'Afrique du Nord dans la guerre, 1939–1945* (Paris: A. Michel, 1998), 103–4, 111–12.

47. *Encyclopédie coloniale et maritime, Le Maroc*, 3rd ed. (Paris: 1941), 247, 319; B. Thomas, "The Railways of French North Africa," *Economic Geography* 29, no. 2 (April 1953): 95–106.

48. R. Ginio, "La propagande impériale de Vichy," in *L'Empire colonial*, ed. Jennings and Cantier, 118. On the importance of Kenadza, see J. Oliel, *Les Camps du Vichy*, 83, and references cited therein.

49. "M. Berthelot à inauguré le premier tronçon du Méditerranée-Niger de Bou Arfa à Kenadza, " *Le Petit Marocain*, December 9, 1941.

50. Author's interviews with Mohammed Amarti, university professor, Oujda; Mohammed Kouchen, retired postal worker, Bou Arfa; Miloud Bel Haloumi (age one hundred) and his son Mustafa, Bou Arfa, Morocco, September 6–8, 2018.

51. JDC NY 33–44/437/Fr708–9, Schwartz to Gozlan, July 11, 1942.

52. Morice Tondowski, USC VHA Interview #34664.

53. USHMM, RG 67.008M/B1/F15, "Wyss-Dunant Report, 1942."

54. USHMM RG 67.008, B1/F33/Fr33–35, Leslie Heath, "Camps in North Africa," November 7, 1942.

55. USHMM RG 68.115, R5/Fr384, 390–93, 397, 404.

56. USHMM RG 68.115/R5/F399–403, R6/Fr121, 255, 258.

57. USHMM RG 68.115/R5/Fr408, Bernard Leska to Benatar, September 9, 1942.

58. USHMM RG 68–115 R5/Fr317, Max Brakl to Benatar, February 3, 1942.

59. USHMM RG 68.115/R5/Fr305–7, Felix Ohrbach to Benatar, November 29, 1942.

60. USHMM RG 68.115/R5/Fr467, Baum to Benatar, November 9, 1941.

61. USHMM RG 67.008/B2/F28/Fr8, December 29, 1942.

62. USHMM RG 68.115/R14/Fr189–93.

63. Arendt, "We Refugees," 373.

64. USHMM RG 68.115/R4/Fr873–74, Weingarten to Benatar, November 19, 1941.

65. USHMM RG 68.115/R4/Fr263, Benatar to Wiesel, January 1, 1943.

66. USHMM RG 68.115 R5//Fr232–33, Benatar to Pack, June 15, 1943.

67. USHMM RG 68.115/R8/Fr1083, Benatar to the Director of Industrial Production, August 7, 1942.

68. USHMM RG 68.115/R8/Fr949–92, Fr987, 989. Jeanne Martin's mother, Juliet Bougerol, was the cook for the Hormel family of Austin, Minnesota, owners of Hormel Foods.

69. USHMM RG 68.115/R4/Fr277–301.

70. USHMM RG 68.115 R8/Fr568–69, Benatar to Selkowitsch, February 18, 1943.

71. Hoisington, Casablanca Connection, 231.

72. Lapidus, Nelly Benathar, 51.

73. USHMM RG 67.008/B1/Fr29/FR 42–45,"Letter from Leslie Heath," November 22, 1942. For a Jewish point of view, see JDC NY 33–44/434/242–47, "Violences juives après le debarquement americain au Maroc," n.d.

74. A. Hardy, Sidi El Hakem: Mémoires d'un contrôleur civil au Maroc, 1931–1956 (Rabat: Éditions La Porte, 2003), 114–16.

75. "I have requested the liberation of all persons in Northern Africa who had been imprisoned because they opposed the efforts of the Nazis to dominate the world, and I have asked for the abrogation of all laws and decrees inspired by Nazi Governments or Nazi ideologies. Reports indicate that the French of North Africa are subordinating all political questions to the formation of a common front against the common enemy." "F. D. Roosevelt's Statement on North African Policy," Department of State Bulletin, vol. 7, November 17, 1942; JDC NY 33/44/745/Fr841, Leavitt to Schwartz, November 19, 1942; JDC NY 33/44/745/Fr838, Schwartz to Leavitt, November 18, 1942.

CHAPTER 6

1. See the map of Benatar's Camps' tour of 1943 on page 95. See the map of Benatar's Camps' tour of 1943 on page 95. A copy of the laissez-passer is found at USHMM

RG 68.115/R1/F43, February 19, 1943; the letter from Industrial Production is in USHMM/RG 43.122/R2/Fr306, February 8, 1943.

2. Vanikoff's autobiography, *Le temps de la honte: De Rethondes à l'isle de Yeu* (Paris: Creator, 1952), gives more detail on his human rights activities before and after the war. His personal papers are in the National Archives of France. Excerpts are found at USHMM, RG 43.122. Vanikoff, a striking personality, deserves a separate study of his own.

3. Lapidus, *Nelly Benathar*, 54–55; Benatar to Dr. Lévy-Lebhar, USHMM RG 68.115/R4/Fr159, May 3, 1941.

4. "Les Routes," in *Le Maroc*, ed. Guernier (Paris: Encyclopédie Coloniale et Maritime, 1941), 305–13.

5. JDC NY 33–44/F435/Fr644–45, "Memorandum on Situation of Refugees in North Africa," December 24, 1942.

6. J. Rives Childs, *Operation "Torch," an Object Lesson in Diplomacy*, unpublished manuscript, Special Collections, University of Virginia Library, 180; C. Levisse-Touzé, *L'Afrique du Nord dans la guerre, 1939–1945* (Paris: A. Michel, 1998), 268.

7. J. Jackson, *De Gaulle* (Cambridge, MA: Harvard University Press, 2018), 251; Levisse-Touzé, *L'Afrique du Nord*, 279; USHMM RG 81.001/R3/Fr238–39, Giraud to Noguès, January 6, 1943.

8. D. Middleton, "Disbelief in Allies Found in Morocco," *New York Times*, January 28, 1943.

9. USHMM RG 67.008/B1/F14/Fr4, Wyss-Dunant to Heath, November 24, 1942; USHMM RG 67.008/B1/F31/Fr3–4, Chapman, "Memorandum of a Conversation," December 24, 1942; USHMM RG 67.008/B1/F33/Fr32, Schnek to Zaga, November 22, 1942.

10. The estimate was 3,357, including 1,333 Spanish inmates. USHMM RG 67.008/B6/F104/Fr33. In March 1943, the number went down to 1,977, a statistic that included civilian political prisoners being held in *residence forcée*. USHMM RG 67.008/B3/F55/Fr66, April 13, 1943. At the end of April 1943, the figure had dropped to 565, but many in this group were already in transition to another status, with only 150 men still left in limbo. USHMM RG 67.008/B3/F31/Fr24, "Report for Inter-Allied Commission, May 8, 1943.

11. USHMM RG 67.008/B6/F123, "AFSC Activities in North Africa, September 10, 1942–August 1, 1943," 4.

12. USHMM RG 68.115/R8/F1075, Benatar to Pugh, December 15, 1942.

13. USHMM RG 68.115/R 8, Fr933–34, 1075–76; RG 67.008/B1/F18/Fr24–25; JDC NY 33–44/F435/Fr383 is an English translation of RG 68.115/R8/Fr1075–76.

14. The Sidi El Ayachi release took place on January 25, 1943. USHMM RG 67.008/B3/F54/Fr3, Heath to Murphy, January 25, 1943.

15. USHMM RG 67.008/B6/F1010/Fr4–6, Benatar to the Director of Political Affairs, January 11, 1943.

16. R. Erbelding, *Rescue Board: The Untold Story of America's Efforts to Save the Jews of Europe* (New York: Doubleday, 2018), 30.

17. "Hopeful Hint Ends Bermuda Sessions," *New York Times*, April 30, 1943; "To 5,000,000 Jews in the Nazi Death-Trap, Bermuda was a 'Cruel Mockery,'" *New York Times*, May 4, 1943.

18. R. Breitman and A. Kraut, *American Refugee Policy and European Jewry, 1933–1945* (Bloomington: Indiana University Press, 1987), 176.

19. USHMM RG 67.008/B6/F105/Fr26–27, Hull to US Consulate Algiers, February 10, 1943. US officials consistently underestimated the number of Jews held in the work camps, deliberately including them in the category of "ex-Axis" to hide their actual numbers. USHMM RG 67.008/B6/F105/Fr48–49, Doolittle to Murphy, March 12, 1943; see also the report to Col. Saltzmann, Fifth Army headquarters, who requested statistics on Jewish camp inmates from French sources, USHMM RG 67.008/B6/F105/Fr50–54, March 6, 1943. This report lists 1,563 men left in the Moroccan camps, of which only 114 were Jews, a dubious statistic. American sources acknowledged that the French continued to be "somewhat evasive" on the subject of political internees as late as May 1943. RG 67.008/B6/F105/Fr66–67, Doolittle to Murphy, May 3, 1943.

20. USHMM RG 43.122, R2/Fr27–41, "Rapport sur la visite des camps de travailleurs étrangers au Maroc," unsigned, February–March 1943. Benatar was most likely the author.

21. USHMM RG 68.007/B3/F54/Fr11, Murphy to Heath, February 8, 1943; USHMM RG 67.008/B6/F104/Fr27–32, "Report of Col. Younger," British representative on the Allied Joint Commission; USHMM RG 67.008/B3/F31/Fr11, April 7, 1943. The American representative on the Allied Joint Commission was Major Donald Coster. USHMM Accession #2016.394.1, "Donald Coster Collection."

22. USHMM RG 68.115/R8/Fr212, Benatar to Barrard, April 21, 1943.

23. JDC NY 33–44/435, Benatar to Voizard, March 9, 1943.

24. RG 68.115/R8/Fr562, Benatar to Heath, March 29, 1943.

25. JDC NY 33–44/F434/Fr150, Hartley to AFSC, May 8, 1943.

26. JDC NY 33–44/F435/F145, Johnson to "Loom," May 14, 1943.

27. USHMM RG 67.008/B5/F82/Fr150, Johnson to Heath, October 29, 1943.

28. USHMM RG 67.008/B2/F11/Fr3–4, Johnson to Katzki, April 3, 1943.

29. USHMM, RG 68.066, R38/F7, Selected Records from the American Jewish Joint Distribution Committee (AJDC) Archives, Jerusalem, 1937–1966 (1940–1950), "Report on Moroccan Trip of Inspection," n.d.

30. USHMM RG 81.001/R1/Fr43–44, Benatar to Noguès, March 5, 1943; RG 81.001/R1/Fr192, Voizard to Benatar, March 9, 1943.

31. USHMM RG 68.115/R10/Fr932, Benatar to Contrôleur Civil, July 9, 1943; USHMM RG 68.115/R10/Fr992, Benatar to President of the French branch of the International Committee of the Red Cross, Casablanca, August 2, 1943.

32. USHMM RG 67.008/B2/F19/Fr2, Pugh to Benatar, 1–1943. This correspondence contains references to Col. John Ratay of US Army Intelligence and his need for qualified informants.

33. CJH/I-337/Veterans' Affairs—Subgroup III/Series B, Chaplaincy/Subseries I/B70/F33, various documents relating to Rabbi Samuel Kaufman's chaplaincy in Morocco in 1943. French sources estimated that six thousand "Anglo-Saxon" Jewish soldiers arrived in Morocco with the Allied landings. E. Coidan, *Le Sionisme au Maroc*, unpublished manuscript, Ben Zvi Institute (Rabat, 1946), 5. My thanks to Dr. Samir Ben Layashi for transmitting to me a copy of this manuscript.

34. USHMM RG 68.115/R7/F691, [unknown] to Benatar, April 16-1943.

35. The multipage inventory of skills of ex-EVDGs in Casablanca looking for work is found at USHMM RG 68.115/R1/F257–323; among them were architects, hairdressers, furriers, doctors, metal workers, leather workers, painters, plumbers, and tailors.

36. Schwartz's file is found at USHMM RG 68.115/R6/Fr289–95. Statistics on Jewish labor are found in USHMM RG 67.008/B5/F90/Fr8, "Memorandum" signed KGK, dated May 2, 1943.

37. JDC NY/33–44/F434/Hartley to Frawley, April 24, 1943; JDC NY/33–44/F475, Kimberland to McCollum, June 30, 1943; USHMM RG 67.008/B6/F101/Fr18–19, Benatar to Kimberland, June 29, 1943.

38. USHMM RG 67.008/B2/F19/Fr33,34, Benatar to Johnson, September 27, 1943.

39. USHMM RG 67.008/B6/F101/Fr33, Benatar to the Director of Civil Affairs, October 1, 1943; RG 68.115/R10/F1041, Johnson to Benatar, November 16, 1943; USHMM RG 68.115/R10/Fr392, n.d.

40. UNRRA's mandate was to "plan, coordinate, [and] administer" aid to victims of war . . . through the provision of "food, fuel, clothing, shelter, and other basic necessities." The United States contributed most of its operating funds, but fundamental to UNRRA's work was coordination with other nations. Over its four-year life span, the agency distributed about $4 billion worth of goods, food, and medicine. The literature on UNRRA is extensive. Recent studies include D. Tananbaum, *Herbert H. Lehman: A Political Biography* (Albany: State University of New York Press, 2016); S. Gemie et al., *Outcast Europe: Refugees and Relief Workers in an Era of Total War, 1936–48* (London: Continuum, 2012); J. Reinisch, "We Shall Rebuild Anew a Powerful Nation': UNRRA, Internationalism and National Reconstruction in Poland," *Journal of Contemporary*

History 43, no. 3 (2008): 451–76; and Reinisch, "Internationalism in Relief: The Birth (and Death) of UNRRA," *Past and Present* 210, no. 6 (2011): 258–89.

41. Paxton, *Vichy France*, 286.

42. Ibid., 329.

43. R. Aron, *Histoire de l'épuration* (Paris: Fayard, 1967), 135–40.

44. USHMM RG 68–115/R7/Fr418. "Liberation des apatrides actuellement au camp Sidi El Ayachi," Benatar note to the archive, n.d.

45. USHMM RG 68.115/R7/Fr423, Coen to Benatar, August 31, 1943.

46. USHMM RG 68.115/R7/Fr419, "Oncles de Coen Enrico," n.d.

47. Léon Marchal was one of five members of the French embassy staff in Washington, DC, to resign in protest against Vichy policy April 1942. In 1943, Marchal joined de Gaulle in Algiers.

48. P. Flamand, *Diaspora en terre d'Islam: Les communautés israélites du sud marocain* (Casablanca: n.p., 1959?), 97–98; D. J. Schroeter, "The Shifting Boundaries of Moroccan Jewish Identities," *Jewish Social Studies* 15, no. 1 (Fall 2008): 145–64.

49. USHMM RG 43.122/R2/Fr142–147, Schumann to Marchal, February 5, 1944; RG 43.122/R2/Fr135 Schumann to Benazeraf, May 6, 1944; RG 43.122/R2/Fr139, Schumann to "cher ami," May 6, 1944. JDC 33–44/F745/Fr973–75, Jews of Tineghir to Resident-General Puaux; USHMM RG 43.112/R2/Fr210, November 29, 1943.

CHAPTER 7

1. Joe Schwartz estimated in April 1943 that eight thousand Jewish escapees waiting in Spain were ready to move to more permanent sites. Refugees were still crossing the frontier from France into Spain at the rate of 100 to 150 per day. JDC NY 33–44/434/167–68, Joseph Schwartz, April 19, 1943; JDC NY 33–44/434/172, news release, February 8, 1943.

2. Y. Bauer, *American Jewry*, 212; M. Abitbol, "L'Afrique du Nord et le sauvetage des réfugiés juifs pendant la Seconde guerre mondiale: L'échec de la solution du camp de Fédala," in *Présence juive au Maghreb: Hommage à Haïm Zafrani*, ed. N. Serfaty and J. Tedghi (St. Denis, France: Bouchene, 2004), 37–49.

3. R. Erbelding, *Rescue Board: The Untold Story of America's Efforts to Save the Jews of Europe* (New York: Doubleday, 2018).

4. Ibid., 78.

5. Ibid., 79–80; JDC NY 33–44/F434/108–11, "Refugee Situation in North Africa," July 18, 1943; JDC NY 33–44/F434/"Evacuation from Spain to North Africa," August 27, 1943.

6. Papers of the Greene Family, Schlesinger Library on the History of Women, Radcliffe Institute, Harvard University, Kate Greene, carton 202, April 2, 1944. Katrine Rosalind Copley Greene (1912–1966) was a graduate of Radcliffe College who, like

many others, joined UNRRA for the adventure. Her letters home offer a close look at the encounter between a privileged American aid worker and her refugee clients.

7. JDC-NY 33–44/F434/272–81, "Report on Visit to UNRRA "North African Refugee Center (NARC)," M. Kessler, July 1944.

8. USHMM RG 50.030*0515, Oral interview with Nick Levi. M. Rozen, "Jews and Greeks Remember Their Past: The Political Career of Tzevi Koretz," *Jewish Social Studies* 12, no. 1 (Fall 2005): 111–66; I. Dijour, "The Refugee Problem," *American Jewish Yearbook* 46 (1944–1945): 311. In December 1944, when the Fedala camp was finally closed, the Salonicans were dispersed to other camps within the UNRRA system. Some returned to Greece, and others went to a transit camp in Gaza. From there they were infiltrated into Palestine. Y. Gershon, "L'aide aux réfugiés juifs du Maroc pendant la Seconde guerre mondiale," *Revue d'Histoire de la Shoah* 205 (2016): 413–46.

9. JDC NY 33–44/F434/272–81, "Report."

10. USHMM RG 68.115/R7/F247–48, Benatar to Sequera, May 20, 1943; See also USHMM RG 68.115/R1/F406–7, "Liste des personnes en Espagne dont nous demande le transfert à Casablanca," August 1, 1943; RG 68.115/R7/Fr261, 264, 266.

11. Eugene Kulischer (1881–1956) was born in Kiev, studied law in St. Petersburg, and returned to Kiev after the Russian Revolution. In 1920, following pogroms in Soviet Ukraine, he fled with his family to Berlin. In 1941, he arrived in the United States and began working for the Office of Strategic Services. For the rest of his life, he was employed by various US government agencies until his death in 1956.

12. Kulischer, *Jewish Migrations: Past Experiences and Post-War Prospects*" (New York: American Jewish Committee, 1943). Another work of Kulischer's published at the same time, *The Displacement of Population in Europe* (Montreal: International Labour Office, King & Staples, 1943), documents, on a country-by-country basis, the various kinds of transfer the Jews of Europe had undergone since the war began. "These uprooted people are living a precarious life under the constant threat of further transfers . . . all their moorings have been cut, and they can rely on no one to protect them" (116).

13. On changing norms in postwar refugee relief, see G. D. Cohen, *In War's Wake* (Oxford: Oxford University Press, 2011), chaps. 2 and 3.

14. Not all UNRRA workers agreed with Benatar. Kate Greene was critical of those who had not "moved on" to jobs that were "tough and sensible," and instead, stayed dependent on UNRRA, "dear little UNRRA [that] will give them back their shops, their stock, and their money, all of which Hitler has used up long since . . . some of these creatures have far less notion of what's been going on than [a] Republican club woman you can meet on Beacon Street." This barb may have been directed

at the Salonican Jewish refugees, who refused to be repatriated. Kate Greene, Green Papers, carton 202, n.d.

15. E. Borgwardt, *New Deal for the World*, 53.

16. USHMM RG 67.008/B7/F11/Fr16–17, Kessler to Pilpel, July 5, 1944; USHMM RG 67.008/B7/F11/Fr7, "Possibilities de travail à Casablanca," most likely authored by Benatar, June 1944.

17. USHMM RG 67.008/B7/F8/Fr70, 10–44.

18. When the residents of Fedala camp were finally dispersed, they scattered everywhere: 147 Libyan Jews were sent home to Tripoli; 348 European Jews went to Palestine; 22 joined the British Pioneer corps; 30 joined the Yugoslav army; 8 returned to Russia; 35 remained in Morocco, awaiting repatriation to France; an Italian was returned home to Italy; a British subject went to an unknown destination; 4 went to work for the US Army; 2 were mentally ill; 2 went to a "French camp"; 3 were in the hospital; 3 joined the Foreign Legion; and 238 went to Philippeville—a total of 845 redistributed and supposedly "repatriated," although most had not yet reached their final destination. USHMM RG 68.066/R 110/"General Letter," November 30, 1944.

19. D. Rivet, "Des reformes portées par des réformistes? La parenthèse de 1944–1947 dans le Protectorat français au Maroc," *Hespéris-Tamuda* 39, no. 2 (2001): 195–213; M. Kenbib, "Les années de guerre de Robert Montagne (1939–1944)," in *La sociologie musulmane de Robert Montagne, actes du colloque EHESS & College de France, Paris, 5–7 Juin 1997*, ed. F. Pouillon and D. Rivet (Paris: Maisonneuve & Larose, 2000), 185–209.

20. J. M. Marglin, *Across Legal Lines*, chap. 7; D. J. Schroeter and J. Chetrit, "Emancipation and Its Discontents," 170–206; S. Lévy, "La communauté juive dans le contexte de l'histoire du Maroc," *Essais d'histoire et de civilisation judéo-marocaines* (Rabat: Centre Tarik Ibn Zyad, 2001), 95–145. Alma R. Heckman's impressive study, *The Sultan's Communists: Moroccan Jews and the Politics of Belonging* (Stanford, CA: Stanford University Press, 2020), takes a close look at radical Jewish involvement in Morocco's nationalist project.

21. Personal communication from David Braunschvig, September 8, 2019.

22. USHMM RG 81.001/R20/Fr163–64, Lemaire to Directeur des Affaires Politiques, February 24, 1944.

23. R. Assaraf, *Une certaine histoire des juifs du Maroc* (Paris: Gawsewitch, 2005), 477–78. Heler was a member of the Consistoire Central of France. Francophile and Zionist at the same time, he promoted Jewish emigration to Palestine from Algeria after the war. According to Sophie Roberts, Algerian Jewish leaders were reluctant to attend the WJC meeting, fearing it would stir up a hornet's nest of anti-Semitism.

S. Roberts, *Citizenship and Antisemitism in French Colonial Algeria, 1870–1962* (Cambridge: Cambridge University Pres, 2017), 329, 332.

24. USHMM RG 68.115/R10/Fr1098, Calamaro to Benatar, August 23, 1944.

25. USHMM RG 2002.296, AFSC Refugee Assistance Case Files, "Benatar," Weatherford to Schauffler, September 16, 1944.

26. USHMM RG 2002.296, AFSC Refugee Assistance Case Files, "Benatar," Schauffler to Weatherford, October 20, 1944.

27. Erbelding, *Rescue Board*, 76; USHMM RG 50.030.0189, interviews with Gerhart Riegner, April 28, 1991, and May 11, 1992.

28. P. Cohen, *La grande aventure: Fragments autobiographiques* (Jerusalem: Graphit Press, 1993), 43. According to Cohen, in the late 1930s he "never heard anyone speak of Zionism or the Zionist idea, much less of the Zionist movement." It was only after the war that Moroccan Jews experienced a "national awakening" (31).

29. Ibid., 44–45.

30. Bernard, *Casablanca*, 90–91.

31. CDJC/CCCLXXXXV-6, "Rapport d'Ensemble sur la Situation des Juifs au Maroc," n.d.

32. YBZ, Benazeraf Collection, P59/F12, December 12, 1944.

33. A. Chouraqui, *La condition juridique de l'israélite marocain* (Paris: Presses du Livre Français, 1950).

34. Mazower, *No Enchanted Palace*, chap. 3; *Resolutions: War Emergency Conference of the World Jewish Congress, Atlantic City, New Jersey, November 26–30, 1944* (New York: World Jewish Congress, 1944).

35. Only two women were official delegates, one from Argentina and the other from Britain. The official delegation of the American Jewish Committee included a number of women. *Resolutions*, 7–10. See also JDC-NY 33–44/F745/Fr1017, "Situation in Algiers and Morocco," November 28, 1944.

36. Cohen, *Grande Aventure*, 46–47.

37. USHMM RG 67.008/B10/F65/Fr34, Kimberland to Blickenstaff, October 4, 1944; USHMM RG 67.008/B9/F60/Fr106, Kimberland to Judkyn, September 25, 1944. Lapidus, *Nelly Benathar*, 57–61.

38. USHMM RG 68.115/R1/Fr47, "Ordre de Mission, Myriam Cazes-Benatar," October 14, 1944.

39. Gemie et al., *Outcast Europe*, 144.

40. JDC NY 33–44/435/Fr532, Levine to Sobel, November 28, 1944.

41. H. Arendt, "'The Rights of Man': What Are They?" *Modern Review* 3, no. 1 (1949): 31.

CHAPTER 8

1. "Effective Agency to Aid Jews Urged," *New York Times*, November 27, 1944.

2. N. Wachsmann, *KL: A History of the Nazi Concentration Camps* (New York: Farrar, Straus & Giroux, 2015), 561.

3. US HMM RG 68.066/R110, "Report of the Secretary to the Executive Committee of the JDC," March 21, 1945.

4. JDC NY AR 45–54/4/241–42. The War Refugee Board was in the process of being phased out early in 1945. JDC funds played an undisclosed role in securing the prisoners' release.

5. Y. Bauer, *Jews for Sale? Nazi-Jewish Negotiations, 1933–1945* (New Haven, CT: Yale University Press, 1994), 218–41, for an account based on Saly Mayer's personal papers. A firsthand account of the releases is E. W. [*sic*], "The Last Phase of the War in Europe: A Personal Impression from Switzerland," *World Today* 1, no. 3 (September 1945): 126–35. Details of the bargain that Swiss negotiators struck with the Nazis are unclear, although it is certain that thousands of US dollars exchanged hands. A number of organizations were involved, including the JDC, the International Red Cross, Orthodox Jewish groups, representatives of the War Refugee Board, and the Swiss government. See Erbelding, *Rescue Board*, 236–40.

6. USHMM RG 67.008/B12/F44/Fr45–47, Weatherford to Jessup, February 20, 1945.

7. USHMM RG 67.053/S-1242-0000-0044-0015-0016, Campbell to Keeny, February 15, 1945.

8. Lapidus, *Nelly Benathar*, 60. Joost Sarfaty, the boy in question, was interviewed by the USC Shoah Foundation at his home in Sydney, Australia, in 1995. Joost made no mention of these incidents at the Bergen-Belsen camp. In fact, he said that the Dutch group received "preferential treatment" for most of their stay, until food ran out in late 1944. Joost's children, also interviewed, said that for many years, their father refused to talk about his wartime experiences. Joost Sarfaty, interview #4761, Visual History Archive, USC Shoah Foundation Institute, November 13, 2019.

9. Hadassa Rosensaft, in R. Torricelli and A. Carroll, *In Our Own Words: Extraordinary Speeches of the American Century* (New York: Kodansha International, 1999), 159.

10. G. D. Cohen, *In War's Wake*, chap. 1; B. Shephard, *The Long Road Home: The Aftermath of the Second World War* (New York: Anchor, 2012), chaps. 3 and 4.

11. JDC NY AR 45–54/4/221, Goldstein to Lisbon, April 26, 1945.

12. Shephard, *Long Road Home*, 44–45; Lapidus, *Nelly Benathar*, 59.

13. An International Red Cross directive in the archives of the AFSC suggests that an international tracing system was already in place at Fedala camp. See USHMM

RG 67.008/B8/F41/Fr4, "Note technique concernant le fichier central des failles dispersées, crée par le Comité international de la Croix-rouge," January 1944.

14. USHMM RG 67.053, S-12420000-0044-0072 "UNRRA General Bulletin No. 71," September 1, 1944.

15. JDC NY AR 45–54/4/221, Goldstein to Lisbon, April 26, 1945.

16. JDC NY AR 45–54/3/1296, "Report" by Mme. Benatar on the repatriation of refugees [from] the UNRRA Center Jeanne d'Arc [to] France," March 12, 1945. The original French version is JDC NY AR 45–54/3/1303.

17. USHMM, Lessing Family Papers, accession no. 2017.642.16, Engeline Lessing, Jeanne d'Arc Refugee Camp, 1945.

18. Ibid.

19. USHMM 67.008/B12/F43/Fr60–62, Weatherford to Jessup, "Trip to Gibraltar and Spain," June 18, 1945.

20. G. D. Cohen, "The Politics of Recognition," 129–31.

21. Ibid., 133.

22. USHMM JDC Geneva, 45–54/F38/Fr650, Fr639.

23. JDC NY AR45–54/4/221, Goldstein to Lisbon, April 26, 1945; USHMM 68.066, JDC Geneva, R38-2, Trobe (JDC) to Lindner, April 27, 1945.

24. USHMM RG 68.115/R7/Fr836, August 14, 1945. Included on the list of the Casablanca émigrés are the names of Haim Zafrani, who later became a professor of Hebrew at the Sorbonne, and Simon Lévy. who never migrated from Morocco; Lévy, a professor of Hispanic studies at Mohammed V University, was also a lifelong leftist. USHMM RG 68.115/R10/Fr291, August 16, 1945. On Jewish emigration from Morocco, see J. Baïda, "The Emigration of Moroccan Jews, 1948–1956," in *Jewish Culture and Society in North Africa*, ed. E. Benichou Gottreich and D. J. Schroeter (Bloomington: Indiana University Press, 2011), 321–33 and references cited therein.

25. A. Patt and K. Crago-Schneider, "Years of Survival: The JDC in Postwar Germany, 1945–1957," in *The JDC at 100*, 361–420.

CHAPTER 9

1. "Letter from Paris," *New Yorker*, June 1, 1946, 69.

2. Most notably, the Kielce, Poland, pogrom of July 4, 1946.

3. USHMM RG 68.066/R110, Is 4/2 (JDC-NY News Releases), "Report on Europe," by Dr. J. J. Schwartz, October 4, 1946.

4. HICEM was decommissioned in 1945, its functions returned to HIAS (Hebrew Immigrant Aid Society). The International Refugee Organization (IRO), chartered in 1946, did not really begin operations until 1948.

5. USHMM RG 68.115/R11/Fr323, Benatar to Aurore Benchimol, November 30, 1945.

6. S. Lapidus, *Nelly Benathar*, 62.

7. JDC-NY, General Files, J. J. Schwartz Personnel File, "Report of the European Chairman Dr. J. J. Schwartz to the Executive Committee Meeting of the JDC, June 20, 1945."

8. JDC Geneva (Jerusalem) G45–54/SM 7/H. C. Benatar, "Rapport sur les conditions d'obtention d'un passeport en France par les réfugiés de nationalité étrangère et les personnes déplacées," June 1946.

9. H. Arendt, "The Stateless People," *Contemporary Jewish Record* 8 (April 1945): M. Siegelberg, *Statelessness: A Modern History* (Cambridge, MA: Harvard University Press, 2020), especially chaps. 5 and 6; on Jewish international lawyers and their thinking on this topic, see J. Loeffler and M. Paz, *The Law of Strangers: Jewish Lawyers and International Law in the Twentieth Century* (Cambridge: Cambridge University Press, 2019).

10. Arendt, "Stateless People," 140.

11. Ibid., 143–44.

12. Ibid., 151, 153.

13. G. D. Cohen, "The Politics of Recognition," 137.

14. JDC-Geneva G45–54, Fr037/0070, Rosen to JDC, n.d.

15. USHMM RG 68.115/R3/F261 for data on refugees remaining in Casablanca postwar.

16. JDC-Geneva G45–54, F037/0070.

17. JDC-Geneva G45–54, F007R/0841, Benatar to Schwartz and Beckelman, April 19, 1947.

18. In a letter to local Moroccan officials, the JDC gave Benatar a different title— "Consultant at AJDC European headquarters in Paris for North African problems." The letter made it clear that Benatar would not be the director of the JDC's Casablanca office. Rather, an "American citizen" would "in all probability" take on the role. See JDC Geneva G45–54/NA4/281, Beckelman to Pasquier, April 18, 1949.

19. JDC-NY/AR 45–54/2/294, Benatar, "Report," July 24, 1947; JDC NY/Oral History, Herbert Katzki, OH 4/2, p. 24. JDC-NY AR 45–54/2/269, "Budget Proposals for 1948," Benatar to Beckelman, November 2, 1947.

20. D. Stenner, *Globalizing Morocco: Transnational Activism and the Postcolonial State* (Stanford, CA: Stanford University Press, 2019).

21. On the events in Oujda-Djerada, see M. Kenbib, *Juifs et musulmans au Maroc*, 677–87; also Y. Katan, *Oujda: Une ville frontière du Maroc (1907–1956); Musulmans, juifs et chrètiens en milieu colonial* (Paris: L'Harmattan, 1990); 599–644, for an account based on the diplomatic archives at Nantes. Benatar's report is found at JDC NY 45–54/F45 "Enquête sur les evenements d'Oujda et de Djerada" July 12, 1948. Y. Tsur, *Kehilah keru'ah: Yehude Maroko veha-le'umiyut 1943–1954* [A torn community: The Jews

of Morocco and nationalism, 1943–1954; in Hebrew] (Tel Aviv: Am Oved, 2001), 84–91. My thanks to Prof. Tsur for directing me to this source.

22. Lapidus, *Nelly Benathar*, 70.

23. On Benatar's American tour, see JDC Geneva G45–54, ADM 7/873–74, "Extract from the minutes of the Executive Committee, April 29, 1953.

24. "French Heroine to Talk at Life Saver's Luncheon," *Miami News*, March 16, 1953.

25. JDC Oral History Archives, Interview with Herbert Katzki by Menachem Kaufman, March 30, 1976, 42–43; See also USHMM RG 68.115/R1/F41, "Mme. Hélène Benatar."

26. "Mme. Hélène C. Benatar rentre d'une tournée de conférences aux U.S.A," *Maroc Presse*, May 20, 1953; Lapidus, *Nelly Benathar*, 76–77.

27. USHMM R-G 68.115/R8/282–93, "Demande de carte de combattante volontaire," with an accompanying note by Benatar that her efforts ended when her son Marc died suddenly at the age of thirty-nine.

28. The essay was first published in *Orient and Okzident* in 1936. Its full title is "The Storyteller: Reflections on the Works of Nicolai Leskov." It was reprinted in a collection of Benjamin's writings entitled *Illuminations*, trans. and ed. H. Zohn, introduced by H. Arendt (New York: Harcourt Brace Jovanovich, 1968), 83–109.

29. Y. Bin-Nun, "The Contribution of World Jewish Organizations to the Establishment of Rights for Jews in Morocco (1956–1961)," *Journal of Modern Jewish Studies* 9, no. 2 (July 2010): 253–54.

30. D. Rivet, *Le Maroc de Lyautey à Mohammed V*, 414; quoted in D. Schroeter, "From Dhimmis to Colonized Subjects: Moroccan Jews and the Sharifian and French Colonial State," in *Studies in Contemporary Jewry, Jews and the State: Dangerous Alliances and the Perils of Privilege,* ed. E. Mendelsohn (Oxford: Oxford University Press, 2004), 113.

31. O. Bashkin, *Impossible Exodus: Iraqi Jews in Israel* (Stanford, CA: Stanford University Press, 2017), 13.

32. P. Nora, "Between Memory and History: Les lieux de mémoire," *Representations* 26 (Spring 1989): 8.

33. The portrait of the "Sultan-savior" who saved Moroccan Jews from the worst offenses of the Vichy regime is considered inauthentic by many contemporary historians. Even Moroccan historians now question it and have had the temerity to publish their views in the popular press. They argue that the Sultan was under French "protection" and had no real independent power, certainly not enough to veto the edicts of Vichy. "Comment le Maroc s'est vidé de ses juifs," *Zamane*, November 2010, 8. See also the more definitive statement of D. J. Schroeter, "Vichy in Morocco: The Residency, Mohammed V, and His Indigenous Jewish Subjects," in *Colonialism and*

the Jews, ed. L. Leff, E. Katz, and M. Mandel (Bloomington: Indiana University Press, 2017), 215–50.

34. B. Cyrulnik, "Entretien avec Denis Peschanski," *Mémoire et traumatisme: L'individu et la fabrique des grands récits* (Bry-sur-Marne, France: Eds. INA, 2012).

35. O. Wieviorka, *Divided Memory: French Recollections of World War II from the Liberation to the Present* (Stanford, CA: Stanford University Press, 2012); H. Rousso, *The Vichy Syndrome: History and Memory in France since 1944* (Cambridge, MA.: Harvard University Press, 1991).

Bibliography

ARCHIVES

In the notes to this book, the citations to these archives use an abbreviation system, where RG = record group, B = box, R = reel, F = folder, and Fr = frame.

Alliance Israélite Universelle, Paris (AIU)
　　Fonds Jonathan Thurscz AP 24
American Jewish Archives, Cincinnati, Ohio (AJA)
　　World Jewish Congress Records, M361
American Joint Distribution Committee, New York (JDC-NY)
　　Records of the New York Office, 1933–1944
　　Records of the Geneva Office, 1945–1954
　　Records of the Jerusalem Office, 1944–1952
　　New York, Oral Histories File
Ben Zvi Institute, Jerusalem (YBZ)
　　Raphael Benazeraf Collection, P 59
Center for Jewish History, New York (CJH)
　　HIAS-HICEM Europe Collection, RG 245.5
　　National Jewish Welfare Board Military Chaplaincy Records, I 337
Central Archives for the History of the Jewish People Jerusalem (CAHJP)
　　Hélène Benatar Private Collection P129
　　Albert Alkoubi Collection P117
Contemporary Jewish Documentation Centre, Musée de la Shoah, Paris (CJDC)
Fonds Serge Lapidus, Paris (Private Collection)

Hoover Institution Archives, Stanford University, Stanford, California
Robert Daniel Murphy Papers, 1913–1978
Ministère des Affaires Étrangères, Centre des Archives Diplomatiques de Nantes
(CADN)
"Protectorat français au Maroc"
Ministère de la Defense, Service Historique de l'Armée de Terre, Château de
Vincennes (SHAT)
Dossier "Roger Mengin"
National Archives of Morocco, Rabat (NAM)
Archives of the Protectorate
National Archives of the United Kingdom, Kew (NAUK)
Special Operations Executive: Personnel Files HS9/1020/2
National Archives, Washington, DC (NARA)
RG 84: Casablanca General Records, 1940–1945; US Legation Tangier, General
Files, 1940–1945
RG 169: Records of the Foreign Economic Administration, Board of Economic
Welfare, 1941–1943
Schlesinger Library on the History of Women in America, Radcliffe Institute for
Advanced Study, Harvard University
Green Family Collection, Papers of Katrine R. C. Greene (1912–1966)
US Holocaust Museum and Archives (USHMM)
RG 43 (FRANCE)
RG 43.006M "Vichy-Maroc"
RG 43.048M International Refugee Organization (IRO)
RG 43.070M Centre de Documentation Juive Contemporaine (CDJC) Collec-
tion LIV, Morocco
RG 43.122M Vanikoff Collection (Vanikoff)
RG 43.154M Ministère des Affaires Étrangères, Centre des Archives Diploma-
tiques de Nantes (CADN); "Protectorat français au Maroc"
RG 43.144M World Jewish Congress (WJC) Afrique du Nord, Maroc

AMERICAN FRIENDS SERVICE COMMITTEE
RG 67.008 American Friends Service Committee (AFSC) Records Relating to
Humanitarian Work in North Africa, 1942–1945
RG 2002.296 Refugee Assistance Case Files, Philadelphia and Casablanca

OTHER COLLECTIONS

RG 67.046M Selected UNRRA Records, 1943–1949 (UNRRA)

RG 67.053M Selected UNRRA Records, 1943–1949 (UNRRA)

RG 68.045M World Jewish Congress Geneva Office Records, 1936–1986 (WJC Geneva)

RG 68.066M Selected Records from the American Jewish Joint Distribution Committee Archives, Jerusalem (1937–1966) (JDC-Jerusalem)

RG 68.115M Private Collection Hélène Benatar, 1936–1953

RG 81.001M Selected records from the National Library of Morocco, 1864–1999

PUBLISHED SOURCES

Abécassis, Armand. *Rue des synagogues*. Paris: Robert Laffont, 2008.

Abitbol, Michel. "L'Afrique du Nord et le sauvetage des réfugiés juifs pendant la Seconde Guerre Mondiale; l'échec de la solution du camp de Fédala." In *Présence juive au Maghreb: Hommage à Haïm Zafrani*, edited by N. Serfaty and J. Tedghi, 37–49. St. Denis, France: Bouchene, 2004: 37–49.

———. *The Jews of North Africa during the Second World War*. Detroit: Wayne State University Press, 1989.

———. "Zionist Activity in North Africa up to the End of the Second World War." *Pe'amim: Studies in Oriental Jewry* 2 (1979): 65–91.

———. "Zionist Activity in the Maghreb." *Jerusalem Quarterly* 21 (1981): 61–84.

Abouker, J. "Temoignage, Alger, 8 novembre 1942." *Le Monde juif* 50 (1994): 146–53.

Adam, André. *Casablanca: Essai sur la transformation de la société marocaine au contact de l' Occident*. 2 vols. Paris: Centre Nationale de la Recherche Scientifique, 1968.

Albo, Michal Meyer. "Solidarité du judaïsme marocain envers les juifs réfugiés d'Europe durant la Seconde Guerre mondial." *Pardès* 17–18 (1993): 210–19.

Arendt, Hannah. "'The Rights of Man' What Are They?" *Modern Review* 3, no. 1 (1949): 24–37.

———. "The Stateless People." *Contemporary Jewish Record* 8, no. 2 (1945): 137–53.

———. "We Refugees." *Menorah Journal* 31, no. 1 (1943): 69–77.

Aron, Robert. *Histoire de l'épuration*. Paris: Fayard, 1967.

Assaraf, Robert. *Une certaine histoire des juifs du Maroc*. Paris: Gawsewitch, 2005.

———. *Mohammed V et les juifs du Maroc à l'époque de Vichy*. Paris: Plon, 1997.

Ayache, Albert. "Les communistes du Maroc et les marocains (1936–1939)." In R.

Gallissot, *Mouvement ouvrier, communisme et nationalismes dans le monde arabe*, 159–72. Paris: Eds. Ouvrières, 1978.

———. *Le mouvement syndical au Maroc* (Racines du present). Paris: L'Harmattan, 1982.

Azagury, Yaëlle. "Choosing Which Language to Live In," *Lilith* 41, no. 1 (2016): 36–39.

———. "A Jewish Moroccan Childhood." In *Women Writing Africa*, vol. 4, *The Northern Region*, edited by F. Sadiqi, 388–94. New York: Feminist Press at City University of New York, 2009.

Baïda, Jamaa. "Le communisme au Maroc pendant la période coloniale (1912–1956)." In *Rethinking Totalitarianism and Its Arab Readings*. Orient-Institut Studies 1 (2012): https://prae.perspectivia.net/publikationen/orient-institut-studies/1-2012/baida_communisme.

———. "The Emigration of Moroccan Jews, 1948–1956." In *Jewish Culture and Society in North Africa*, edited by E. Benichou Gottreich and D. J. Schroeter, 321–33. Bloomington: Indiana University Press, 2011.

———. "Les 'réfugiés' juifs européens au Maroc pendant la Seconde Guerre mondiale." In *La bienvenue et l'adieu: Migrants juifs et musulmans au Maghreb XVe–XXe siècles*, vol. 2, *Ruptures et recompositions: Actes du colloque d'Essaouira*, edited by Karima Dirèche, Rita Aouad, and Frédéric Abécassis, 57–66. Paris: Karthala, 2012.

———. "Sidi Mohamed V et les lois antijuives." *Zamane* (May 2013): 42–45.

Bar-Asher, Shalom. "Jewish Refugees from Nazi Europe in North Africa: A Document from the Archive of Cazes Ben-Attar" [in Hebrew]. *Pe'amim: Studies in Oriental Jewry* 114–115 (2008): 257–62.

Barthes, Roland. *Camera Lucida: Reflections on Photography*. Translated by Richard Howard. New York: Hill and Wang, 1981.

Bashkin, Orit. *Impossible Exodus: Iraqi Jews in Israel*. Stanford, CA: Stanford University Press, 2017.

Bauer, Yehuda. *American Jewry and the Holocaust: The American Jewish Joint Distribution Committee, 1939–1945*. Detroit: Wayne State University Press, 1981.

———. *Jews for Sale? Nazi-Jewish Negotiations, 1933–1945*. New Haven, CT: Yale University Press, 1994.

Benatar, Hélène Cazes. "North Africa." In *American Jewish Yearbook*. Philadelphia: Jewish Publication Society, 1953–1956.

Benatar, M. M. "Plan de réorganisation de la communauté israélite de Casablanca." Casablanca: Impriméries Réunies de *La Vigie Marocaine* et du *Petit Marocain*, 1939.

Bénédite, Daniel. *La filière marseillaise: Un chemin vers la liberté sous l'occupation.* Paris: Éditions Clancier Guénaud, 1984.

Benjamin, Walter. "The Storyteller: Reflections on the Works of Nicolai Leskov." In *Illuminations, edited and translated by* H. Zohn. Introduction by H. Arendt. New York: Harcourt Brace Jovanovich, 1968.

Bensimon-Donath, Doris. *Évolution du judaïsme marocain sous le Protectorat français, 1912–1956.* La Haye: Mouton, 1968.

Ben Ya'akov, Michal. "European Jewish Refugees in Morocco During World War II." *Avotaynu* 31, no. 2 (2015): 41–45.

———. "Hélène Cazes Benatar et ses activités en faveur des réfugiés juifs au Maroc, 1940–1943." In *Les juifs d'Afrique du Nord face à l'Allemagne nazie,* edited by Haim Saadoun and Dan Michman, 177–98. Paris: Perrin, 2018.

Bernadac, B., and P. Gallocher, *Histoire de la compagnie de navigation Paquet et des relations France-Maroc-Levant-Sénégal de 1863 à nos jours.* Marseille: Tacussel, 1991.

Bernard, Mathilde. "La communauté juive de Casablanca au temps du Protectorat." Mémoire de Maitrise, Université de Paris I (Panthéon-Sorbonne), 1998.

Berque, Jacques. *French North Africa: The Maghrib between Two World Wars.* New York: Praeger, 1967.

Bin-Nun, Yigal. "The Contribution of World Jewish Organizations to the Establishment of Rights for Jews in Morocco (1956–1961)." *Journal of Modern Jewish Studies* 9, no. 2 (July 2010): 251–74.

Blandin [*sic*]. "La population de Tanger en 1940." *Revue Africaine* 88 (1944): 88–115.

Blumenfeld, Erwin. *Eye to I: The Autobiography of a Photographer.* London: Thames and Hudson, 1999.

Boum, Aomar. "Eyewitness Djelfa: Daily Life in a Saharan Vichy Labor Camp." In *The Holocaust and North Africa,* edited by A. Boum and S. Stein, 149–67. Stanford, CA: Stanford University Press, 2018.

Boum, Aomar, and Sarah A. Stein, eds., *The Holocaust and North Africa.* Stanford, CA: Stanford University Press, 2018.

Borgwardt, Elizabeth. *A New Deal for the World: America's Vision for Human Rights.* Cambridge, MA: Harvard University Press, 2005.

Breitman, Richard, and Alan M. Kraut. *American Refugee Policy and European Jewry, 1933–1945.* Bloomington: Indiana University Press, 1987.

Browning, C. R. "Who Resisted the Nazis?" *New York Review of Books,* July 2, 2020, 24–25.

Calderwood, Eric. "Moroccan Jews and the Spanish Colonial Imaginary, 1903–1951." *Journal of North African Studies* 24, no. 1 (2019): 86–110.

Caron, Vicki. *Uneasy Asylum: France and the Jewish Refugee Crisis, 1933–1942.* Stanford, CA: Stanford University Press, 1999.

Childs, J. Rives. *Diplomatic and Literary Quests*. Richmond, VA: Whittet, Sheppard-son, 1963.

Chouraqui, André. *La condition juridique de l'israélite marocain*. Paris: Presses du Livre Français, 1950.

———. *Histoire des juifs en Afrique du Nord*. Paris: Hachette, 1985.

———. *Les juifs d'Afrique du Nord: Marche vers l'Occident*. Paris: PUF, 1952.

Cohen, Gerald Daniel. *In War's Wake: Europe's Displaced Persons in the Postwar Order*. New York: Oxford University Press, 2011.

———. "The Politics of Recognition: Jewish Refugees in Relief Policies and Human Rights Debates, 1945–1950." *Immigrants and Minorities* 24 (July 2006): 125–43.

Cohen, J.-L. "Henri Prost and Casablanca: The Art of Making Successful Cities (1912–1940)." *New City* 3 (1996): 106–21.

Cohen, J.-L., and M. Eleb. *Casablanca: Mythes et figures d'une aventure urbaine*. Paris: Hazan, 1998.

Cohen, J.-L., and M. Eleb. "The Whiteness of the Surf: Casablanca." *ANY: Architecture New York* 16 (January 1996): 16–19.

Cohen, Prosper. *Congrès juif mondial: Conférence extraordinaire de guerre, 26–30 novembre, 1944*. Casablanca: SIPEF, 1946.

———. *La grande aventure: Fragments autobiographiques*. Jerusalem: Graphit Press, 1993.

Cyrulnik, B. "Entretien avec Denis Peschanski." *Mémoire et traumatisme: L'individu et la fabrique des grands récits*. Bry-sur-Marne, France: Eds. INA, 2012.

Dahan, Jacques. *Regard d'un juif marocain sur l'histoire contemporaine de son pays: De l'avènement de sa majestè le Sultan Sidi Mohammed Ben Youssef, au dénouement du complot d'Oufkir (1927–1972)*. Paris: L'Harmattan, 1995.

D'Herama, Paul. *Tournant dangereux: Mémoires d'un déporté politique en Afrique du Nord (1940–1945)*. La Rochelle, France: Imp. Jean Foucher, 1957.

Dijour, Ilya. "The Refugee Problem." *American Jewish Yearbook* 46 (1944–1945): 302–11.

Dray-Bensousan, Renée. "Les filières d'émigration juive de 1940 à 1942." In *Varian Fry, Actes du colloques du 20 mars 1999*, 15–33. Aix-en-Provence, France: Actes-Sud, 2000.

———. *Les juifs à Marseille pendant la Seconde Guerre mondiale; août 1939-août 1944*. Paris: Les Belles Lettres, 2004.

Dwork, Deborah. "Rescuers." In *Oxford Handbook of Holocaust Studies*, edited by Peter Hayes and John K. Roth, 170–84. New York: Oxford University Press, 2010.

Edwards, Brian T. *Morocco Bound*. Durham, NC: Duke University Press, 2005.

Eisenbeth, M. *Les juifs de l'Afrique du Nord: Démographie & onomastique.* Algiers: Imprimerie du Lycée, 1936.

Eleb, Monique. "Apartment Buildings in Casablanca." *New City: "Modern Cities"* 3 (1996): 95–106.

Erbelding, Rebecca. *Rescue Board: The Untold Story of America's Efforts to Save the Jews of Europe.* New York: Doubleday, 2018.

E. W. [*sic*]. "The Last Phase of the War in Europe: A Personal Impression from Switzerland," *World Today* 1, no. 3 (September 1945).

Farge, Arlette. *The Allure of the Archives.* New Haven, CT: Yale University Press, 2013.

Ferrara, Antonio. "Eugene Kulischer, Joseph Schechtman and the Historiography of European Forced Migrations." *Journal of Contemporary History* 46, no. 4 (October 2011): 715–40.

Fiddian-Qasmiyeh, E., G. Loescher, K. Long, and N. Sigona. *The Oxford Handbook of Refugee and Forced Migration Studies.* Oxford: Oxford University Press, 2014.

Fink, Carole. *Defending the Rights of Others: The Great Powers, the Jews, and International Minority Protection, 1878–1938.* New York: Cambridge University Press, 2004.

Flamand, Pierre. *Diaspora en terre d'Islam: Les communautés israélites du sud marocain.* Casablanca: 1959?

Flanner, Janet. "Letter from Paris." *New Yorker,* June 1, 1946.

———. *Paris Was Yesterday, 1925–1939.* New York: Viking, 1972.

Freud, S. *Living in the Shadow of the Freud Family.* Edited by E. D. Freud. Westport, CT: Praeger Publishers, 2007.

Fry, Varian. "The Massacre of the Jews." *New Republic,* December 21, 1942, 816–19.

———. "Our Consuls at Work." *The Nation* 154, no. 18 (May 2, 1942): 507–9.

———. *Surrender on Demand.* New York: Random House, 1945.

Gaida, Peter. *Camps de travail sous Vichy: Les "groupes de travailleurs étrangers" (GTE) en France et en Afrique du Nord, 1940–1944.* Paris: ANRT, 2008.

Gallissot, René, Albert Ayache, and Georges Oved, eds. *Dictionnaire biographique du mouvement ouvrier: Maghreb.* Paris: Éditions de l'Atelier, 1998.

Gemie, Sharif, Fiona Reid, and Laure Humbert, with Louise Ingram. *Outcast Europe: Refugees and Relief Workers in an Era of Total War, 1936–48.* London: Continuum, 2012.

Gershon, Yitzhak. "L'aide aux réfugiés juifs du Maroc pendant la Seconde Guerre mondiale." Translated from Hebrew by Claire Drevon. *Revue d'Histoire de la Shoah* 2 (2016): 413–46.

Ginio, Ruth. "La propagande impériale de Vichy." In *L'empire colonial sous Vichy,* edited by Jacques Cantier and Eric T. Jennings, 117–27. Paris: O. Jacob, 2004.

Gottschalk, Max. "The Jewish Emigrant—1941." *The Contemporary Jewish Record* 4 (1941): 261–68.

Gouvernment Cherifien, Service Central des Statistiques. *Recensement général de la population en 1951–1952*. Vol. 4, *Population marocaine israélite*. Rabat, n.p., 1953.

Guernier, E., ed. *Encyclopédie colonial et maritime, Le Maroc*. 3rd ed. Paris: Encyclopédie Coloniale et Maritime, 1941.

Hammoudi, Abdellah. *Master and Disciple: The Cultural Foundations of Moroccan Authoritarianism*. Chicago: University of Chicago Press, 1997.

Hardy, André. *Sidi El Hakem: Mémoires d'un contrôleur civil au Maroc 1931–1956*. Rabat: Éditions La Porte, 2003.

Harmetz, Aljean. *Round Up the Usual Suspects; The Making of* Casablanca: *Bogart, Bergman, and World War II*. New York: Hyperion, 2002.

Heckman, Alma R. "Jewish Radicals of Morocco: A Case Study for a New Historiography." *Jewish Social Studies* 23, no. 3 (2018): 67–100.

———. "Multivariable Casablanca, Vichy Law, Jewish Diversity, and the Moroccan Communist Party." *Hespéris-Tamuda* 51, no. 3 (2016): 13–32.

———. *The Sultan's Communists: Moroccan Jews and the Politics of Belonging*. Stanford, CA: Stanford University Press, 2020.

Hindley, Meredith. *Destination Casablanca: Exile, Espionage, and the Battle for North Africa in World War II*. New York: Public Affairs, 2017.

Hoisington, William A. *The Casablanca Connection: French Colonial Policy, 1936–1943*. Chapel Hill: University of North Carolina Press, 1984.

Isenberg, Noah William. *We'll Always Have Casablanca: The Life, Legend, and Afterlife of Hollywood's Most Beloved Movie*. New York: W. W. Norton & Co., 2017.

Jackson, Julian. *De Gaulle*. Cambridge, MA: Harvard University Press, 2018.

———. *France: The Dark Years, 1940–1944*. New York: Oxford University Press, 2001.

Jalée, Pierre. *L'ancre dans l'avenir: Mémoires d'un militant heureux*. Paris: Karthala, 1981.

Jennings, Eric. "'The Best Avenue of Escape': The French Caribbean Route as Expulsion, Rescue, Trial, and Encounter." *French Politics, Culture & Society* 30, no. 2 (2012): 33–52.

———. "Last Exit from Vichy France: The Martinique Escape Route and the Ambiguities of Emigration." *Journal of Modern History* 74, no. 2 (June 2002): 289–324.

———. "La politique coloniale de Vichy." In *L'empire colonial sous Vichy*, edited by Jacques Cantier and Eric T. Jennings, 13–27. Paris: O. Jacob, 2004.

———. *Vichy in the Tropics: Pétain's National Revolution in Madagascar, Guadeloupe, and Indochina, 1940–1944*. Stanford, CA: Stanford University Press, 2001.

Julien, C. A. *Le Maroc face aux imperialismes, 1415–1956*. Paris: Ed. Jeune Afrique, 1987.

Kably, Mohammed, et al. *Histoire du Maroc: Réalisation et synthèse*. Rabat: RRHM, 2011.

Kaplan, Marion. *Hitler's Jewish Refugees; Hope and Anxiety in Portugal*. New Haven, CT: Yale University Press, 2020.

———. *Lisbon Is Sold Out! The Daily Lives of Jewish Refugees in Portugal during World War II*. New York: Tikvah Center for Law and Jewish Civilization, NYU School of Law, 2013. http://www.nyutikvah.org/publications.html.

Kaspi, A., et al., eds. *Histoire de l'Alliance Israélite Universelle de 1860 à nos jours*. Paris: Armand Colin, 2010.

Katan, Yvette. *Oujda: Une ville frontière du Maroc (1907–1956): Musulmans, juifs et chrètiens en milieu colonial*. Paris: L'Harmattan, 1990.

Kenbib, Mohamed. "Les années de guerre de Robert Montagne (1939–1944)." In *La sociologie musulmane de Robert Montagne; Actes du colloque EHESS et Collège de France—Paris, 5–7 juin 1997*, edited by François Pouillon and Daniel Rivet, 185–209. Paris: Maisonneuve & Larose, 2000.

———. "Les juifs du Maroc pendant la Deuxième Guerre mondiale: La phase 1939–1942." *Hespéris-Tamuda* 37 (1999): 199–205.

———. *Juifs et musulmans au Maroc, 1859–1948*. Rabat: Université Mohammed V, 1994.

———. "Juifs et musulmans au Maroc à l'époque du Front populaire, 1936–1938." *Hespéris-Tamuda* 24–25 (1987): 169–89.

———. "Moroccan Jews and the Vichy Regime." *Journal of North African Studies* 19, no. 4 (September 2014): 540–53.

Kenbib, M. "Samuel-Daniel Lévy." In *Encyclopedia of Jews in the Islamic World*. Leiden: Brill, 2010.

Kulischer, Eugene M. *The Displacement of Population in Europe*. Montreal: International Labour Office; London: P. S. King & Staples, 1943.

———. *Jewish Migrations: Past Experiences and Post-War Prospects*. New York: American Jewish Committee, 1943.

Laredo, Abraham Isaac. *Les noms des juifs du Maroc: Essai d'onomastique judéo-marocaine*. Consejo Superior de Investigaciones Científicas E3. Madrid: Instituto B. Arias Montano, 1978.

Laredo, Isaac. *Memorias de un viejo tangerino*. Madrid: C. Bermejo, 1935.

Laskier, Michael. *The Alliance Israélite Universelle and the Jewish Communities of Morocco, 1862–1962*. Albany: State University of New York Press, 1983.

———. "Between Vichy Antisemitism and German Harassment: The Jews of North Africa during the Early 1940s." *Modern Judaism* 11, no. 3 (1991): 343–60.

Le Crom, J.-P. "La Croix-Rouge française pendant la Seconde Guerre mondiale;

la neutralité en question." *Vingtième Siècle: Revue d'Histoire* 101, no. 1 (2009): 149–62.

Levisse-Touzé, Christine. *L'Afrique du Nord dans la guerre, 1939–1945.* Paris: A. Michel, 1998.

———. "Les camps d'internement d'Afrique du Nord ; politiques répressives et populations." In *L'empire colonial sous Vichy*, edited by E. Jennings and J. Cantier, 177–94. Paris: O. Jacob, 2004.

———. "La contribution du Maroc pendant la Seconde Guerre mondiale (1940–1945)." In *Maroc-Europe; Histoire, economies, sociétés, "La armée marocaine à travers l'histoire,"* 209–17. Rabat: Éditions La Porte, 1994.

———. "La préparation économique, industrielle et militaire de l'Afrique du Nord à la veille de la guerre." *Revue d'Histoire de la Deuxième Guerre mondiale et des Conflits Contemporains* 36, no. 142 (1986): 1–18.

Lévy, Simon. "La communauté juive dans le contexte de l'histoire du Maroc." In *Essais d'histoire et de civilisation judéo-marocaines,* 95–145. Rabat: Centre Tarik Ibn Zyad, 2001.

Litsky, Elliott B. "The Murphy-Weygand Agreement: The United States and French North Africa (1940–1942)." PhD diss., Fordham University, 1986.

Loeffler, James. *Rooted Cosmopolitans: Jews and Human Rights in the Twentieth Century.* New Haven, CT: Yale University Press, 2018.

Loeffler, James, and Moria Paz, eds. *The Law of Strangers: Jewish Lawyers and International Law in the Twentieth Century.* Cambridge: Cambridge University Press, 2019.

Marglin, Jessica M. *Across Legal Lines: Jews and Muslims in Modern Morocco.* New Haven, CT: Yale University Press, 2016.

———. "Modernizing Moroccan Jews: The AIU Alumni Association in Tangier, 1893–1913." *Jewish Quarterly Review* 101, no. 4 (Fall 2011): 574–603.

Marrus, Michael Robert. *The Nazi Holocaust. Part 8: Bystanders to the Holocaust.* Munich: De Gruyter Saur, 1989.

———. *The Unwanted: European Refugees in the Twentieth Century.* Philadelphia: Temple University Press, 2002.

Mazower, Mark. *Hitler's Empire: How the Nazis Ruled Europe.* New York: Penguin Press, 2008.

———. "Minorities and the League of Nations in Interwar Europe." *Daedalus* 126, no. 2 (1997): 47–63.

———. *No Enchanted Palace: The End of Empire and the Ideological Origins of the United Nations.* Princeton, NJ: Princeton University Press, 2008.

———. "Violence and the State in the Twentieth Century." *American Historical Review* 107, no. 4 (2202): 1158–78.

Meakin, Budgett. *The Moors: A Comprehensive Description*. London: S. Sonnen-
schein & Co., 1902.

Megargee, Geoffrey P., and Joseph R. White, eds. "Vichy Africa." In *The United
States Holocaust Memorial Museum Encyclopedia of Camps and Ghettos*, 240–300.
Bloomington: Indiana University Press, 2018.

Metzger, Chantal. "L'empire colonial français dans la stratégie du troisième Reich
(1936–1945)." *Relations Internationales* 101 (Spring 2000): 41–55.

Michman, Dan. "Le sort des juifs d'Afrique du Nord pendant la Seconde Guerre
mondiale: Fait-il partie de la Shoah?" In *Les juifs d'Afrique du Nord pendant la
Seconde Guerre mondiale*, edited by Haim Saadoun et Dan Michman. Paris: Ben
Zvi Institute and Yad Vashem, 2016.

Middleton, Drew. "The Battle for North Africa." *New York Times*, November 7, 1982.

———. "Disbelief in Allies Found in Morocco." *New York Times*, January 28, 1943.

———. *Our Share of Night, a Personal Narrative of the War Years*. New York: Viking,
1946.

———. "Together We Can Lick the World." *New York Times*, December 27, 1942.

Miège, J.-L. "Chronique de Tanger." *Revue Maroc Europe* 1 (1991): 15–38.

———. *Chronique de Tanger, 1820–1830, Journal de Bendelac*. Rabat: La Porte, 1995.

———. *Le Maroc et l'Europe*. 4 vols. Rabat: La Porte, 1989.

Miller, Susan Gilson. "*Dhimma* Reconsidered: Jews, Taxes, and Royal Authority in
Nineteenth Century Tangier." In *In the Shadow of the Sultan: Culture, Power and
Politics in Morocco*, edited by R. Bourqia and S. G. Miller, 103–26. Harvard Mid-
dle Eastern Monographs 31. Cambridge, MA: Harvard University Press, 1999.

———. "Filling a Historical Parenthesis: An Introduction to 'Morocco from World
War II to Independence.'" *Journal of North African Studies* 19, no. 4 (2014):
461–74.

———. *A History of Modern Morocco*. Cambridge: Cambridge University Press,
2013.

———. "Kippur on the Amazon: Jewish Emigration from Northern Morocco in the
Late Nineteenth Century." In *Sephardi and Middle Eastern Jewries: History and
Culture in the Modern Era*, edited by Harvey Goldberg, 190–209. Bloomington:
Indiana University Press, 1996.

Moine, André. *La déportation et la résistance en Afrique du Nord (1939–1944)*. Paris:
Éditions Sociales, 1972.

Moreno, Aviad. "Moroccan Jewish Emigration to Latin America: The State of Research and New Directions." *Hespéris-Tamuda* 51, no. 2 (2016): 123–40.

Morgan, P. *Hitler's Collaborators: Choosing between Bad and Worse in Nazi-Occupied
Western Europe*. Oxford: Oxford University Press, 2018.

Moyn, Samuel. "Imperialism, Self-Determination, and the Rise of Human Rights." In

The Human Rights Revolution: An International History, edited by Akira Iriye, Petra Goedde, and William I. Hitchcock. New York: Oxford University Press, 2012.

———. "Two Regimes of Memory." *American Historical Review* 103, no. 4 (October 1998): 1182–86.

Murphy, Robert D. *Diplomat among Warriors*. Garden City, NY: Doubleday, 1964.

Nesry, Carlos de. *Les israélites marocains à l'heure du choix*. Tanger: Éditions Internationales, 1958.

———. *Le juif de Tanger et le Maroc*. Tanger: Éditions Internationales, 1956.

———. "Les juifs du Maroc nouveau." *Information juive (Algiers): Organe du comité juif algérien d'études sociales* (July–September 1957): 89–90.

Nora, Pierre. "Between Memory and History: Les Lieux de Mémoire." *Representations* 26 (1989): 7–24.

Novick, Peter. *The Resistance versus Vichy: The Purge of Collaborators in Liberated France*. London: Chatto & Windus, 1968.

Oliel, Jacob. "Les camps de Vichy en Afrique du Nord (1940–1944)." *Revue d'histoire de la Shoah* 198 (2013): 227–44.

———. *Les camps du Vichy; Maghreb-Sahara, 1939–1944*. Montreal: Éditions du Lys, 2005.

Ouaknine-Yekutieli, Orit. "Corporatism as a Contested Sphere: Trade Organization in Morocco under the Vichy Regime." *Journal of the Economic and Social History of the Orient* 58, no. 4 (2015): 453–89.

Palmier, Jean-Michel, and David Fernbach. *Weimar in Exile: The Antifascist Emigration in Europe and America*. London: Verso, 2006.

Paloma, V. "Judeo-Spanish in Morocco: Language, Identity, Separation, or Integration?" In *La bienvenue et l'adieu: Migrants juifs et musulmans au Maghreb (XVe–XXe siècle), Actes du colloque d'Essaouira*, 3 vols., ed. F. Abécassis and K. Dirèche, 1:103–12. Casablanca: La Croisé des Chemins, 2012.

Patt, Avinoam, and K. Crago-Schneider. "Years of Survival: The JDC in Postwar Germany, 1945–1957." In *The JDC at 100: A Century of Humanitarianism*, edited by A. Patt, A. Grossmann, L. Levi, and M. Mandel, 361–420. Detroit: Wayne State University Press, 2019.

Paxton, Robert. *Parades and Politics at Vichy: The French Officer Corps under Marshal Pétain*. Princeton, NJ: Princeton University Press, 1966.

———. "The Truth about the Resistance." *New York Review of Books*, February 25, 2016.

———. *Vichy France: Old Guard and New Order, 1940–1944*. New York: Knopf, 1972.

Penkower, Monte N. "The World Jewish Congress Confronts the International Red Cross during the Holocaust." *Jewish Social Studies* 41, nos. 3–4 (1979): 229–56.

Peschanski. Denis. "1939–1945, les camps français d'internement." *Hommes & Migrations* 1175 (1994): 11–19.

———. "Communistes, juifs, collabos, la France des camps." *L'Histoire* 264 (April 2002): 73–81.

———. *Des étrangers dans la Résistance.* Paris: Atelier, 2002.

Pol, Heinz. "Vichy's Slave Battalions." *The Nation* 152, no. 18 (May 1941): 527–29.

Poznanski, Renée. "Rescue of the Jews and The Resistance in France: From History to Historiography." In *French Politics, Culture & Society* 30, no. 2 (Summer 2012): 8–32.

Le procès du Général Noguès devant la Haute Cour de Justice. Ministère Public. Paris: René Bluet, 1947.

Prost, Antoine, and J. M. Winter. *René Cassin and Human Rights: From the Great War to the Universal Declaration.* Cambridge: Cambridge University Press, 2013.

Prost, Henri. "Le plan de Casablanca." *France-Maroc* 1, no. 8 (August 1917): 7–12.

Rabinow, Paul. *French Modern: Norms and Forms of the Social Environment.* Chicago: University of Chicago Press, 1995.

Reinisch, Jessica. "Internationalism in Relief: The Birth (and Death) of UNRRA." *Past & Present* 210, suppl. 6 (2011): 258–89.

———. "'We Shall Rebuild Anew a Powerful Nation': UNRRA, Internationalism and National Reconstruction in Poland." *Journal of Contemporary History* 43, no. 3 (2008): 451–76.

Resolutions: War Emergency Conference of the World Jewish Congress, Atlantic City, New Jersey, November 26–30, 1944. New York: World Jewish Congress, 1944.

Rivet, Daniel. "Hygiénisme colonial et médicalisation de la société marocaine." In *Santé, médicine et société dans le monde arabe,* edited by E. Longuenesse, 105–28. Paris: L'Harmattan, 1995.

———. *Lyautey et l'institution du Protectorat français au Maroc (1912–1925).* 3 vols. Paris: L'Harmattan, 1988.

———. *Le Maghreb à l'épreuve de la colonisation.* Paris: Hachette Littératures, 2002.

———. "La récrudescence des épidémies au Maroc durant la Deuxième Guerre mondiale: Essai de mesure et d'interpretation." *Hespéris-Tamuda* 30, no. 1 (1992): 93–11.

———. "Des reformes portées par des réformistes? La parenthèse de 1944–1947 dans le Protectorat français au Maroc." *Hespéris-Tamuda* 39, no. 2 (2001): 195–213.

Roberts, Sophie. *Citizenship and Antisemitism in French Colonial Algeria, 1870–1962.* Cambridge: Cambridge University Press, 2017.

Rodrigue, Aron. *French Jews, Turkish Jews: The Alliance Israélite Universelle and the*

Politics of Jewish Schooling in Turkey, 1860–1925. Bloomington: Indiana University Press, 1990.

Roosevelt, Elliott. *As He Saw It*. New York: Duell, Sloan and Pearce, 1946.

Rosen, Lawrence. *Two Arabs, a Berber, and a Jew: Entangled Lives in Morocco*. Chicago: University of Chicago Press, 2016.

Rousso, Henry. "L'épuration en France: Une histoire inachevée." *Vingtième Siècle* 33 (1992): 78–105.

———. *The Vichy Syndrome: History and Memory in France since 1944*. Cambridge, MA: Harvard University Press, 1991.

Rozen, M. "Jews and Greeks Remember Their Past: The Political Career of Tzevi Koretz." *Jewish Social Studies* 12, no. 1 (Fall 2005): 111–66.

Satloff, Robert. *Among the Righteous: Lost Stories from the Holocaust's Long Reach into Arab Lands*. New York: Public Affairs, 2007.

Schine, Catherine. "It Had To Be Her." *New York Review of Books*, January 16, 2020.

Schroeter, Daniel J. "From Dhimmis to Colonized Subjects: Moroccan Jews and the Sharifian and French Colonial State." In *Studies in Contemporary Jewry*, vol. 19, *Jews and the State: Dangerous Alliances and the Perils of Privilege*, edited by Ezra Mendelsohn, 104–23. Oxford: Oxford University Press, 2004.

———. "The Shifting Boundaries of Moroccan Jewish Identities." *Jewish Social Studies* 15, no. 1 (Fall 2008): 145–64.

———. "Vichy in Morocco: The Residency, Mohammed V, and His Indigenous Jewish Subjects." In *Colonialism and the Jew*, edited by Lisa Moses Leff, Ethan B. Katz, and Maud S. Mandel, 215–50. Bloomington: Indiana University Press, 2017.

Schroeter, Daniel J., and Joseph Chetrit. "Emancipation and Its Discontents: Jews at the Formative Period of Colonial Rule in Morocco." *Jewish Social Studies* 13, no. 1 (2006): 170–206.

Seghers, Anna. *Transit*. Edited by Margot Bettauer Dembo. New York: New York Review of Books, 2013.

Selke, Rudolf. "Trans-Saharan Inferno." *Free World*, February 1942.

Shephard, Ben. *The Long Road Home: The Aftermath of the Second World War*. New York: Anchor, 2012.

Siegelberg, Mira L. *Statelessness: A Modern History*. Cambridge, MA: Harvard University Press, 2020.

Simon, Reeva. *The Jews of the Middle East and North Africa: The Impact of World War II*. Abingdon, UK: Routledge, 2020.

Stenner, David. *Globalizing Morocco: Transnational Activism and the Postcolonial State*. Stanford, CA: Stanford University Press, 2019.

Stonebridge, Lyndsey. *The Judicial Imagination: Writing after Nuremberg*. Edinburgh, UK: Edinburgh University Press, 2011.

Stuart, Graham. "The Future of Tangier." *Foreign Affairs* 23, no. 4 (July 1945): 675–79.

Szajkowski, Zosa. *Jews and the French Foreign Legion*. New York: Ktav, 1975.

———. "The Soldiers That France Forgot," *Contemporary Jewish Record* 5 (1942): 589–96.

Tartakower, Aryeh, and Kurt R. Grossmann. *The Jewish Refugee*. New York: Institute of Jewish Affairs of the American Jewish Congress and World Jewish Congress, 1944.

Thabault, Roger. "Le Maroc à l'heure du Vichyisme." *Les Nouveaux Cahiers* 1975, no. 3 (1975): 16–20.

Théolleyre, Jean-Marc. *Ces procès qui ébranlèrent la France*. Paris: Ed. Bernard Grasset, 1966.

Thomas, Benjamin. "The Railways of French North Africa." *Economic Geography* 29, no. 2 (April 1953): 95–106.

Torricelli, Robert G., and Andrew Carroll, eds. *In Our Own Words: Extraordinary Speeches of the American Century*. New York: Kodansha International, 1999.

Tsur, Yaron. "L'AIU et le judaïsme marocain en 1949: L'émergence d'une nouvelle démarche politique." *Archives Juives* 34, no. 1 (2001): 54–73.

———. "The Brief Career of Prosper Cohen: A Sectorial Analysis of the North African Jewish Leadership in the Early Years of Israeli Statehood." In *Sephardic Jewry and Mizrahi Jews*, edited by Peter Y. Medding, 66–99. Oxford: Oxford University Press, 2007.

———. *Kehilah keru'ah: Yehude Maroko veha-le'umiyut 1943–1954* [A torn community: The Jews of Morocco and nationalism, 1943–1954]. Tel Aviv: Am Oved, 2001.

Twain, Mark. *The Innocents Abroad; or, The New Pilgrims' Progress; Being Some Account of the Steamship Quaker City's Pleasure Excursion to Europe and the Holy Land; with Descriptions of Countries, Nations, Incidents and Adventures, as They Appeared to the Author*. New York: Random House, 2003.

Van Hecke, A. S. *Les chantiers de la jeunesse au secours de la France (Souvenirs d'un soldat)*. Paris: Nouvelle Éditions Latines, 1970.

Vanikoff (Vanino), Maurice. *Le temps de la honte: De Rethondes à l'isle de Yeu*. Paris: Creator, 1952.

Wachsmann, Nikolaus. *KL: A History of the Nazi Concentration Camps*. New York: Farrar, Straus & Giroux, 2015.

Wagenhofer, Sophie. "Contested Narratives: Contemporary Debates on Mohammed V and the Moroccan Jews under the Vichy Regime." *Quest: Issues in Contemporary Jewish History, Journal of Fondazione CDEC* 4 (November 2012).

Waterbury, John. *The Commander of the Faithful: The Moroccan Political Elite, a Study in Segmented Politics*. New York: Columbia University Press, 1970.

Watson, Robert. "Between Liberation(s) and Occupation(s): Reconsidering the Emergence of Maghrebi Jewish Communism, 1942–1945." *Journal of Modern Jewish Studies* 13, no. 3 (2014): 381–98.

Wieviorka, Olivier. *Divided Memory: French Recollections of World War II from the Liberation to the Present*. Stanford, CA: Stanford University Press, 2012.

———. *The French Resistance*. Translated by J. M. Todd. Cambridge, MA: Harvard University Press, 2016.

Woolf, Virginia. *A Room of One's Own*. 1929. New York: Harcourt, Brace, Jovanovich, 1981.

Wriggins, W. Howard. *Picking up the Pieces from Portugal to Palestine: Quaker Refugee Relief in World War II: A Memoir*. Lanham, MD: University Press of America, 2004.

Wright, Gwendolyn. *The Politics of Design in French Colonial Urbanism*. Chicago: University of Chicago Press, 1991.

Yehuda, Zvi. "The Place of Aliyah in Moroccan Jewry's Conception of Zionism." *Studies in Zionism* 6, no. 2 (1983): 199–210.

Zytnicki, Collette. "La politique antisémite du régime de Vichy dans les colonies." In *L'empire colonial sous Vichy*, edited by Jacques Cantier and Eric T. Jennings, 153–76. Paris: O. Jacob, 2004.

Index

Page numbers in italics refer to figures and photographs.

❋ WORLDING THE MIDDLE EAST

Emily Gottreich and Daniel Zoughbie, editors
Center for Middle East Studies, University of California, Berkeley

This series investigates the "worlding" of the Middle East and the ever-changing, ever-becoming dynamism of the region. It seeks to capture the ways in which the region is reimagined and unmade through flows of world capital, power, and ideas. Spanning the modern period to the present, Worlding the Middle East showcases critical and innovative books that develop new ways of thinking about the region and the wider world.

———————

Amélie Le Renard, *Western Privilege: Work, Intimacy, and Postcolonial Hierarchies in Dubai*
2021